playing to wiin

NINTENDO
AND THE
VIDEO GAME INDUSTRY'S
GREATEST COMEBACK

playing to wiin

NINTENDO
AND THE
VIDEO GAME INDUSTRY'S
GREATEST COMEBACK

DANIEL SLOAN

WILEY

John Wiley & Sons (Asia) Pte. Ltd.

Copyright © 2011 John Wiley & Sons (Asia) Pte. Ltd.
Published in 2011 by John Wiley & Sons (Asia) Pte. Ltd.
2 Clementi Loop, #02-01, Singapore 129809

Other Wiley Editorial Offices
John Wiley & Sons, 111 River Street, Hoboken, NJ 07030, USA
John Wiley & Sons, The Atrium, Southern Gate, Chichester, West Sussex, P019 8SQ, United Kingdom
John Wiley & Sons (Canada) Ltd., 5353 Dundas Street West, Suite 400, Toronto, Ontario, M9B 6HB, Canada
John Wiley & Sons Australia Ltd., 42 McDougall Street, Milton, Queensland 4064, Australia
Wiley-VCH, Boschstrasse 12, D-69469 Weinheim, Germany

Library of Congress Cataloging-in-Publication Data
ISBN 978-0-470-82512-9 (Hardcover)
ISBN 978-0-470-82891-5 (ePDF)
ISBN 978-0-470-82691-1 (Mobi)
ISBN 978-0-470-82693-5 (ePub)

Typeset in 11/15 Minion Pro by MPS Limited, a Macmillan Company, Chennai, India
Printed in Singapore by Saik Wah Press Pte. Ltd.
10 9 8 7 6 5 4 3 2 1

For Hiroyuki Muramoto, who by example made others better colleagues and people.

CONTENTS

ACKNOWLEDGMENTS

I F THERE WAS A VIDEO GAME IN WHICH THE MAIN TASK WAS TO write a book and the players could choose avatars based on professional and personal history related to the subject, I know whom I'd select. I'd be a Kyoto taxi driver—the one I met in late 2009, who detailed Nintendo's travails over the last half-century, as well as its leaders Hiroshi Yamauchi and Satoru Iwata, as they pushed the firm and its wares beyond the former capital city to the farthest corners of the world.

When explaining the timing of Nintendo's move to its current headquarters south of Kyoto station, the local cabbie put it in the plainest of terms for an outsider: "It was when the Seattle Mariners acquired Ichiro."

Thankfully, he and many others—particularly journalists covering the industry—have shared directly or indirectly their passion for this company and its story. This work's aim is to distill all into the last decade of change for the company and its main competitors, when it faced an existential crisis in leadership and product and—as befitting a card company—came up aces.

In particular, two books have been instrumental in showing how such a task should be undertaken and respected: *Game Over: How Nintendo Conquered the World,* by David Sheff, and *The Ultimate History of Video Games,* by Steven L. Kent. The numerous other articles and authors I consulted are listed in the notes for each chapter.

Playing to Wiin looks to portray changes faced by Nintendo and its industry. It focuses on the way unorthodox business decisions—by Hiroshi Yamauchi in choosing his successor, and by Satoru Iwata and others in charting 21st-century direction—returned to Nintendo, at least for a time, the mantle of the world's greatest video game company.

The book is indebted to many who have covered and analyzed the industry, as well as to Nintendo itself through its "Iwata Asks" Web segments and appearances by Satoru Iwata and Shigeru Miyamoto at the Foreign Correspondents' Club of Japan and other corporate events. Nintendo in no way facilitated my undertaking, which may reflect its past experiences or the still large shadow of Hiroshi Yamauchi and his penchant for corporate aloofness, for which Kyoto itself is also famous.

My deepest thanks to those at John Wiley & Sons who launched the book and led it to fruition—C.J. Hwu and Nick Wallwork, and to my friend Ken Belson, my mother Nancy Sloan, and the countless others who read early versions of the book, colleagues at Reuters who gave encouragement, and my family—Kanae, Theo, and Sera—who offered space and time to complete the job.

INTRODUCTION

B Y LATE IN THE 20TH CENTURY, NINTENDO HAD BECOME A multibillion-dollar company. Since its formation as a boutique house for Kyoto artisans making playing cards, it had grown into a colossus producing the world's most popular video games—always under the control of the Yamauchi family and nearly always linked to reasonably priced entertainment. In an industry known for volatility and brief attention spans, Nintendo was synonymous with gaming itself. It boasted a loyal following of consumers and investors alike for Mario, Zelda, and other iconic characters, including ones in its Pokemon franchise, as well as for its hardware—revolutionary handheld and monitor-linked consoles that included the Game Boy, Nintendo Entertainment System, and Super Nintendo Entertainment System.

The company, which began with the master brushstrokes and entrepreneurial genius of its 19th-century founder, Fusajiro Yamauchi, featured a stable of already legendary designers including Shigeru Miyamoto, who had pushed video games toward multidimensions and myriad purposes. Some even credited Nintendo with saving the industry on the back of its hit games in the 1980s.

However, not all was well in the "House of Mario" as its long-serving president, Hiroshi Yamauchi, neared retirement after five decades of often imperial rule without a clear successor. A number of corporate bridges had been burned as Nintendo rose to the top of the industry and other firms such as Atari withered or failed, and few would lament the Kyoto firm's humbling as its own hardware and software businesses began to struggle in the 1990s. By late in the decade, Nintendo ceded the global sales title to upstart Sony, which had found tremendous success with its PlayStation console, while new video game entrant Microsoft, insulated with billions of IT dollars, now aimed to become a player with its Xbox.

Some viewed Nintendo's troubles as a divine comeuppance for a company and president who had often been haughty and demanding while leading the industry. After former rival Sega abruptly decided to stop making consoles entirely after substantial losses, some corporate analysts looked at Nintendo's two latest hardware efforts, the Nintendo 64 and GameCube consoles, and encouraged the Kyoto giant to consider the same course, safely prospering off its software and branding rights.

Neither Yamauchi nor his successor would entertain such a proposition, but the bottom line for Nintendo was that the gaming population and sales had stopped growing, while in Japan a "gamer drift" phenomenon had started. Building consoles that doubled processing power every four or five years had become untenable—yielding only minimal changes to business performance along with substantial risk and cost. Yamauchi said Nintendo would no longer play by such rules or expectations, and the company that once touted the Nintendo "difference" badly needed more adults to play as well as pay for video games. Without that, it faced a further fall to the industry's bottom rung.

For Yamauchi, going against the business grain had been a recurring theme of his career ever since he took the helm of the family playing card firm from his grandfather at the age of 21. He purged the company of potential challengers, led its then provincial business toward international ties, including with Disney, and later tried a raft of unsuccessful ventures before migrating to the technology and potential of video games in the early 1970s. His business acumen was exceeded only by his disdain for established hierarchies, either societal or professional, and until late in his life, he eschewed recognition of the power of industry associations or of the feats that his own company had achieved as a waste of time and resources.

Many expected Yamauchi to tap son-in-law, Minoru Arakawa, to follow him, becoming only the fourth president in Nintendo's history. However, despite launching and leading its North American operations to unprecedented returns, Arakawa was not on the same page in terms of life and corporate returns as Yamauchi. He retired with his wife, Yoko, to Hawaii—with golf, an ocean view, and few regrets—as Nintendo began to take a very unconventional comeback path.

The 74-year-old patriarch selected a relative newcomer to lead the $4 billion company: Satoru Iwata, a software maven with a Dutch-boy haircut, neither family, Kyoto born, nor Nintendo bred. The decision defied corporate tradition and sparked some financial market disappointment, as reflected in the company's share performance, which continued to be a corporate barometer over the decade.

Iwata had been chief executive at a small start-up software maker, HAL Laboratory, which had gone from the brink of bankruptcy to become a profitable Nintendo stable firm. He joined the Kyoto company shortly before the new millennium, eventually becoming its president at 42. The age was exceptionally young for a Japanese boardroom and seen as either a reflection of his immense potential to lead or an indication of how desperate times had become.

He inherited a raft of problems beyond just trailing in the sales column: Nintendo saw its first loss in years; the GameCube was shaping up as its worst-performing hardware ever, and corporate critics claimed that Nintendo's games were immature and would never expand substantially beyond a pre-teen market. Some analysts questioned how much freedom Yamauchi would allow the new boss to make his own difference, tagging Iwata a puppet for the older man to continue his reign from the shadows, during an apparent Kyoto semi-retirement.

However, what Yamauchi saw in Iwata proved well-rewarded, while one handover the younger man would come to relish was the next-generation handheld console, a two-screen dynamo that wound up rewriting nearly every Nintendo sales record. The success of the Nintendo DS from its launch in 2004 relied heavily on the genius of Shigeru Miyamoto and a 21st-century team of game artisans, along with renewed third-party developer ties. The games would prove among the company's most popular ever, helping to alter the industry with Iwata's "Blue Ocean" strategy, which involved laying nets in consumer markets where others had yet to sail.

Iwata, from the rural north of Japan, became in an unassuming way Yamauchi's opposite, a president schooled in issues central to gamers and those developing their software and hardware for profit, while also refreshingly adept at managing others to greater achievement and corporate self-respect without relying on inspiring fear of his wrath. Moreover, he exuded public confidence but could laugh at himself, while Miyamoto and others such as new Nintendo of America boss Reggie Fils-Aime underscored that gaming was first and foremost about fun.

Nintendo's comeback did not occur in a vacuum, and the DS handheld thrived against a new portable console from Sony, while its self-training software irrevocably widened the definition and demographics of gaming. The company redesigned the DS with different sizes and added functions while still early in the console's business cycle. The new approach kept demand strong, as Nintendo looked to make the lifestyle product ubiquitous, resembling a smartphone in everything but the ability to make phone calls.

However, Nintendo's bombshell in the wings helped reclaim the overall crown from Sony and the slowly charging Microsoft. The Wii and its cordless remote untethered gaming from a sedentary experience. Indeed, some games actually linked an entertainment long known for its couch-potato ways with health, or at least a greater cognizance of well-being. The "Wii Sports" and "Wii Fit" franchises debuted in an era when yoga, Pilates, and fending off "metabolic syndrome" had become widespread, while families looked for activities they could do together regardless of age or game skill sets. The slim console would go on from late 2006 to trounce Sony's PlayStation 3 and Microsoft's Xbox 360, as each company faced its own set of development issues and corporate intrigue, while trying to sell more expensive hardware models as a global financial crisis loomed.

Sony's troubles escalated during the decade, forcing a change in leadership that would bring the company its first foreign CEO, while also ushering out the "Father of the PlayStation," Ken Kutaragi. Microsoft, meanwhile, spent billions of dollars before finding a profitable niche in the industry with its online retail services, but would have to scale back its own expectations from becoming No. 1 to finding a comfortable market share, before ultimately seeing its own changing of the guard.

Playing to Wiin: Nintendo and the Video Game Industry's Greatest Comeback is the story of a company in an existential crisis that not only found its way but regained the mantle of industry leader. With new hit products and games, as well as a new definition and demographics for the entertainment field, the Kyoto giant reached heights and wealth that all three generations of its past leadership could only have dreamed of.

CHAPTER 1

Leave Luck to Heaven

A FTER MORE THAN A HALF A CENTURY AS NINTENDO'S president and with hundreds of billions of yen to show for it, Hiroshi Yamauchi approached retirement and the new millennium financially secure. Yet even though prosperous and a legend in his own industry after more than a half century in charge, he was in dire need of a hit product and a worthy successor to manage it.

Yamauchi had led Nintendo to a corporate pinnacle in the 1990s, yet despite the fire still raging in his words and deeds, the hour for transfer of the corporate baton was at last nearing. The imperious 74-year-old Yamauchi, only the third boss in Nintendo's 113-year history, would—as he did with most company issues—decide when and how he would leave the headquarters of the Kyoto entertainment giant.

Yamauchi, a man who had known only one company in his entire career (and only one title—boss), had floated the idea of departure before. But he'd always stepped back from it, returning to the exacting management style that had established one of the world's great companies and made him both loved and loathed. Nintendo had become synonymous with the game industry's tremendous growth—from dark arcades and bars to living rooms across the world—a global business estimated around the year 2000 to be worth more than $20 billion.

As a soon-to-be-retiree, the dapper Yamauchi remained a handsome gentleman with slicked-back gray hair, tinted glasses, and a fondness for

1

purple suits and ties. His astute leadership and blunt style included occasional outbursts at game industry competitors and suppliers, as well as at reporters covering the industry. This overt indifference to traditional Japanese business operations—and appearance—had included refusal to pick a successor at any point in his long tenure.

This time, though, Yamauchi's retirement appeared a done—if not immediate—deal, although it would come at a very critical juncture for the former industry No. 1. After its high-tech, TV-linked entertainment console had flopped badly in the late 1990s, Nintendo was now badly trailing Sony and its PlayStation video game franchise.

The handheld console business was still sturdy and plans for next-generation game machines were under way. Nonetheless, Yamauchi intended to keep everyone guessing as to what was in store for his family heirloom, saying only, "I've been thinking about it for more than two years now, but I want to retire before this summer. Nintendo isn't going to work under one person anymore, though it will be run under a group-leadership system."[1]

However, the real nagging question for Yamauchi, Nintendo's over 3,000 employees, and investors in the global firm was whether any new boss—or even bosses—would be able to run the greatly expanded business, which some gamers and company analysts said had lost its way since dominating the industry only 10 years earlier.

ORIGINS

Fusajiro Yamauchi, Hiroshi's great-grandfather, launched "Nintendo Koppai" in September 1889 as a *hanafuda* card business. Fusajiro saw Kyoto's gamblers as well as its landed elite, students, and laborers as yearning for the turn of a friendly, well-made card. The city had been home to Japan's emperors from the 8th century into the 19th, but like the entire nation it had endured a ban on card gambling for about 250 years.

The new Meiji Era government, as a sign of its progressive agenda, decided to allow card games using pictures instead of numbers—one of many changes under a new Constitution that included weightier moves such as national elections and the end of serfdom. With the end of the card-playing prohibition, Fusajiro had a ready market for his "flower cards," which stunned players with their beauty. They presented 48 paintings in 12 suits based on the months of the year.

His product soon outsold rivals because of the brilliant artwork on the mulberry-bark cards, which soon became available at shops in Kyoto and Osaka. Gambling with the sturdy cards became popular, particularly among Japanese *yakuza*, gangsters who wanted a new deck for each game. Eventually, demand exceeded manufacturing capabilities of the hand-painting shop, so the firm hired staff to begin mass production, adding space as the fledgling industry gradually expanded.

Fusajiro retired in 1929, passing the company to son-in-law Sekiryo, who had taken the last name Yamauchi as the clan had no male heirs. Sekiryo moved the company's headquarters to a building next door in 1933.

Today, the small two-story launch site is relatively empty and anonymous, except for a "Nintendo Karuta" plaque that hints at what the Kyoto workspace eventually became. In its long history, the firm would continue to make cards, or *hwatu,* as the flowery decks still are known in Korea, intent on retaining its roots but incapable of surviving only on them.

A NEW GAME

Hiroshi Yamauchi became president in 1949, as Japan with post–World War II recovery. However, the actions of his parents, Kimi Yamauchi (the granddaughter of founder Fusajiro) and Shikanojo Inaba (a Kyoto craftsman who had married into the family with the intention of becoming Nintendo's third president), had forced the young man to grow up quickly.[2]

Hiroshi's father ran off when he was six, and his mother asked her parents to raise the young boy, leaving him without great sentimentality or deep family connection. Shortly before his death from stroke, Hiroshi's grandfather tapped the young man—then still a Waseda University law student—to become his successor, hoping the brash upstart could put a modern varnish on the now six-decade-old enterprise of making and selling domestic playing cards.

Before agreeing to drop out of school and take the job, Hiroshi demanded that his grandfather dismiss other family members to leave no doubt as to who would steer the company leadership. On taking the helm, Hiroshi quickly grew unpopular, if not feared, as a result of his age and manners—a relatively obnoxious management style he brandished often over ensuing decades. He gradually replaced every manager and long-time employee in a further purge of potential opposition or divided loyalty. Meanwhile, Hiroshi began the hunt for a new business niche that would lead beyond Kyoto and even Japan.

That growth, however, was starting from a very low base for the company and all of Japan. In fact, one of the later things he had to do was stave off corporate bankruptcy, after a slate of side ventures ranging from instant rice to "love hotels" failed to take off.

At the time, Japan's Ministry of International Trade and Industry had just been created, a fixed foreign exchange rate of 360 yen to the dollar was set, and stock exchanges were opened in Tokyo, Osaka, and Nagoya. Total exports from the country stood at ¥298 billion as of 1950—a level that rose to ¥51 trillion by the end of the century, or a jump from about $828 million in the postwar nation to about $500 billion.[3]

The newly minted executive changed the company name in 1951 to Nintendo Karuta (Nintendo Playing Card Company), aiming to promote its main source of income as well as secure deals with American firms, then the industry's titans. Later in the decade, he signed a crucial contract with Disney for rights to put its iconic animated characters on his playing cards (now coated with plastic), a template for future business maneuvers that would broadly open Nintendo's doors to children and the world.

Launching his own family, Hiroshi wed Michiko Inaba in an arranged marriage, as is often customary in Japan. The new family yoked two artisan clans of Kyoto and produced two daughters and a son. His family, though, rarely saw the busy company president, who concentrated on work and great expectations.

Outward Bound

The Disney deal proved incredibly lucrative, as sales reached over 600,000 card decks a year. However, Hiroshi soon learned that the card business in the United States was a fading star, unlikely to be a profit center of the second half of the century. With more ambitious hopes of expansion, Yamauchi took the company public in 1962 to raise cash for new ventures, and soon afterward shortened the company name to one word, Nintendo. He began a push toward worldwide expansion, although he kept the country's ancient capital as his headquarters. Nonetheless, he decided early on that the ports of Japan would not be the end-destination for Nintendo's products, while also encouraging a migration from cards to toys and electronic entertainment in the 1970s that proved the company's saving grace.

Along with Kyoto corporate giants such as Kyocera, Omron, and Ricoh, Nintendo found that the road to success involved trial-and-error and missteps, and the nonstarters also included baseball batting machines, a taxi business, and even bowling alleys, all in a search for an avenue that would ensure demand at home and eventually across the globe.[4]

The marketing channels Nintendo had plowed in Japan with its playing cards, though, had become a clear advantage, if the firm could find another winner besides cards to market. To achieve this, Yamauchi created a new research and development department called "Games," tasking a young engineer named Gunpei Yokoi to make a must-have.

One of Nintendo's first hit products was Yokoi's 1966 "Ultra Hand," a scissor-like plastic gripper that extended children's reach—and the company's—into parents' pockets. It sold more than 1.2 million units in its first holiday season. The 1970s saw greater movement toward technology, with Yokoi's "Love Tester" game and a laser shooting gallery, first located in Nintendo's old bowling alley sites and later co-developed for home play.

Nintendo's "Beam Gun" series employed opto-electronics that fired at virtual clay pigeons, while advances in the nascent U.S. gaming industry helped bring the arcade experience to home televisions. At the same time, Yamauchi tied up with Magnavox to sell the games in Japan. With Mitsubishi Electric, Nintendo developed home video game systems from 1977, called not so creatively "TV Game 15" and "TV Game 6," using an electronic video recording player.

Hardware

Nintendo increasingly committed resources to gaming, resulting in Yokoi's early brainchild, Game & Watch, which from 1980 became an alternative to plugging coins into machine arcades, as players could take the portable unit with them, enjoying the small unit until its battery ran down. The handheld G&W raised the bar for the mobility and utility of consoles, while its creation cemented a young software and hardware development team that was about to create something extraordinary.

To meet growing demand, the company built a factory in the city of Uji in Kyoto Prefecture. This move both increased capacity and gave Nintendo greater control of its own destiny. The implosion of former giant Atari taught Yamauchi the importance of software control and the need to sell proprietary cartridges made at his own plants or through loyal sub-contractors with exacting oversight on quality and supply.

Nintendo moved increasingly into game and console production, and negotiations with parts suppliers and software makers usually came with advantageous terms for the growing Kyoto firm. Much of the profit from out-sourced hits became Nintendo's, while the risk and onus of development often sat with software makers, ultimately weighing on their future allegiance.

Nintendo's U.S. beachhead was made by Yamauchi's son-in-law Minoru Arakawa in the early 1980s, initially in New York and then in the Seattle suburb of Redmond, Washington, a move that helped write the history of video gaming. Essential to expansion was the creation of "Donkey Kong," the brainchild of then novice game designer Shigeru Miyamoto, who (along with his Jumpman character, later to be known as Mario) helped make the Nintendo name eponymous with the industry, while creating essential branded content that made it easier to sell low-priced hardware.

Yamauchi had insisted on the unusual name for the gorilla arcade game, which became a key title for Masayuki Uemura's watershed Family Computer, or "*Famicom*" in Japan, introduced in 1983. The machine was a marvel of simplicity and pricing. After becoming a domestic mega-hit, Yamauchi pushed it heavily to go global. That console, called the Nintendo Entertainment System (NES), landed when many world retailers had given up on gaming as a viable home business, after the industry's early implosion.

By 1987, the NES was the No. 1 toy in the United States, while Miyamoto's software game, "The Legend of Zelda," joined Mario in a new pantheon of software immortals, becoming the first home video game to sell one million units. An array of games and branded content—with the plumber Mario, his brother Luigi, or other set characters, and a plethora of "Mushroom Kingdom" or other multidimensional settings, along with professions ranging from doctor to race car driver—would go on to dominate global sales for more than a quarter-century, while hundreds of millions of young and old would eventually trace their introduction to video gaming to Miyamoto's work.

On the handheld front, Gunpei Yokoi's portable Game Boy debuted in Nintendo's centennial year of 1989, helping redefine the industry and putting the firm on even more annual holiday shopping lists. By its 100th anniversary, which at Yamauchi's behest the company did not commemorate, Nintendo had become the most dominant firm in the global entertainment industry, and it had also become Japan's most profitable.

As with many Japanese manufacturers, video game software and hardware production soared from the early 1980s. The United States was the key export market for games as well as other products, the destination for over 50 percent of the nation's output, according to the Japan External Trade Organization.[5]

Nintendo was at the forefront of this expansion, while its stable of game favorites, later including Pikachu of "Pokemon" fame, with all appearing in branded films and TV, on trading cards, and on countless items of two- and three-dimensional merchandise. All of this made

Yamauchi a very wealthy man, as well as an even tougher businessman, someone who demanded much and apologized rarely.

Pokemon alone saw licensing deals ranging from All Nippon Airways and automaker Chrysler to meat giant Oscar Mayer and fast-food chain Burger King, while Nintendo opened domestic and overseas stores, including in New York and London, to sell Pokemon goods.

"This is one of the many measures that I have in mind to help Nintendo stay successful even after I leave the company," Yamauchi said in late 2000.[6]

Console Wars

Yamauchi's Nintendo of America subsidiary had long contended that the company had saved the video game industry from collapse with its Mario and Game Boy onslaught in the 1980s, only later to be slapped by U.S. trade regulators for playing hardball with retailers on which games they sold and where they were located in stores. Regardless, the multibillion-dollar entertainment juggernaut had navigated the wreckage of three decades of boom and bust cycles better than nearly every firm, winning the hearts and wallets of a virtual planet of young gamers.

Nintendo's Game Boy console had been around for more than 12 years in various editions, selling more than 110 million units and making the company the unquestioned handheld leader with a fertile line of software titles to play. However, its new 128-bit GameCube console, the follow-up to the unsuccessful Nintendo 64 home video machine, was finding early consumer response tepid in the shadows of Sony's PlayStation 2. Coming on the heels of the N64, which had many cutting-edge attractions (such as 3D graphics and revved up CPU processing power but was cartridge-based and late to market with only a limited number of more expensive games), the GameCube was an attempt not to repeat the same mistakes.

However, Nintendo had again been late with its latest next-generation console, trailing Sony and Sega to store shelves, and now was paying the price in the financial markets and with consumers at the cash register. The GameCube had debuted in August 2000 at Spaceworld, Nintendo's

Shoshinkai show in Japan, which featured over 100 bobbing Marios in an attempt to highlight the console's now double hard-drive firepower.

In a telling sign of the times and GameCube's future, though, Nintendo shares fell sharply the next day due to an admission that the console's release would be delayed further, as early delivery to stores increasingly dictated retail shelf space and a marketing advantage over rivals. At the event, Yamauchi did not introduce the new machine, code-named "Dolphin," which sparked industry rumors that the console's name had been changed from "StarCube" at the last minute without his approval, while his silence was seen as an ominous expression of disapproval for what would prove Nintendo's most sales-challenged console ever.

Whether dubbed "Dolphin," "Star" or "Game," the dice-like cube was quickly viewed as a console for kids rather than adults. When 500,000 of the boxes finally arrived at stores—in September 2001, when the world was reeling from the 9/11 attacks on the United States and global sales had slowed—the console's carrying handle quickly helped to earn the near $200 console the sobriquet of "lunch box." This unfortunate nickname foreshadowed that the high-tech wonder would be perceived more as a school kid's property than a TV-linked video game dynamo, and ultimately, Nintendo would have a difficult time convincing "core" gamers, or most consumers, that the machine was worth the price.

Squaring the Cube

The GameCube's sales debut coincided with the launch of Microsoft's $300 Xbox, as both firms tried to scratch away some of No.1 Sony's near 70 percent market share. Nintendo, which traditionally kept console prices close to break-even levels in hopes of making returns on software, tried the same with GameCube, with Yamauchi pressuring the retail business.

"The price should be as cheap as possible," he said. "People do not play with the game machine itself. They play with the software and are forced to purchase the machine."[7]

In GameCube's case, that compulsion appeared to be exceptionally weak.

Nintendo tried to sound enthusiastic about its year-end 2001 sales performance, but returns on increasingly more sophisticated and expensive technology had become more finite, while internally staff had sounded warnings since the N64 console that this strategy was misfiring. CPU processing power had doubled in less than five years with a slew of new technological options, but commensurate expansion in demand had not followed, and speculation began to grow about whether Nintendo intended to push the gigabyte envelope any farther, or possibly was even reconsidering a commitment to hardware manufacturing entirely.

Despite the GameCube's inauspicious sales start and with such existential questions swirling, Yamauchi had declared 2002 to be his last year as president. He would stay on, he said, to oversee the console's rollout. However, the eponymous box and limited game titles quickly proved not to be the Gibraltar on which to begin a relaxing retirement.

Initial game offerings for the optical disc-based console, which included a built-in hard drive and Internet connections, were thin. Nintendo had already delayed the launch to ensure that even this limited supply of kit and games could be delivered close to on time, albeit later than some rivals. The company had hoped the GameCube would be a counterpunch to Sony's PS2, which had already sold 15 million consoles, while potentially stiff-arming Microsoft's fledgling—but heavily promoted—Xbox console.

Yamauchi, with his usual bravado, said he lost no sleep over the entry of the U.S. giant into the gaming *dohyo*.

"We do not consider Microsoft to be our competitor," he said. "Microsoft is going after performance only and does not understand that the game is played with software. A Nintendo . . . is the most advanced machine for playing games, and it is totally different. It's like comparing a sumo wrestler and a pro wrestler."[8]

Nintendo may have been the experienced *yokozuna* of the not-so-ancient sport of video games, but the masked avenger in trunks—Microsoft—had budgeted an eye-popping $500 million to unveil and promote its new console wonder. Co-founder and boss Bill Gates had no track record of blithely accepting financial losses just to build brand, while industry leader Sony had cut its PS2 console's price in June to $300 in a preemptive strike.

Nintendo's storied history and treasure chest of game characters alone were to some degree keeping GameCube's place on store shelves. However, the overall move away from video gaming as a pastime had already become a trend in Japan, despite the promise of a fourth generation of new consoles. U.S. sales for the industry had grown by about 15 percent annually since 1997, becoming as large a business as the domestic film industry and bolstering revenue hopes, but Japan was often used as a template for how gaming consumers would eventually respond in other countries, and the graph direction was heading south and in deep need of an industry savior to reverse course.

GAMER DRIFT

The Computer Entertainment Supplier's Association said Japanese consumer software sales had fallen from an annual peak of ¥389 billion to ¥293 billion by the year 2000, even with Sony's emergence and broad expansion of software development. This was an approximate drop of about $1 billion, depending on exchange rates.

Nintendo, in one of many signs of its haughtiness under Yamauchi, had never joined CESA as a full member, unlike rivals Sony Computer Entertainment (SCE) and Microsoft, as well as nearly every Japanese software supplier with whom it now shared the same sales pain. Meanwhile, Nintendo's earnings by the end of the decade had slowed considerably, which Yamauchi blamed on the yen's appreciation against the U.S. dollar rather than on internal missteps.

Within two years, though, Nintendo would see its first loss since publicly listing its shares in 1962, something the company could no longer attribute mainly to foreign exchange travails. Even with aggressive pricing and a raft of games planned amid the intense competition, consumer interest—or at least sales—had not resulted in greater expenditure, supporting claims by Yamauchi of a possible industry disaster ahead.

"The recent TV game market is losing momentum. Naturally, it's because of too many boring or too complicated software that ordinary users can't enjoy playing," he said in one of the many predictions of potential doom that laced his last years at Nintendo's helm. "We can't have a bright future prospect for TV video games right now."[9]

No one was particularly crying for the Kyoto septuagenarian or for Nintendo, as the master of the "Mushroom Kingdom" had been arrogant and dismissive of competitors over the years. Some who recalled his tough treatment of Sega, software suppliers, and then Sony, found it divine justice when his company was forced to ride the comeback trail, and even more humbling, to have to rebuild what had been more than a few burnt corporate bridges.

As late as 1997, Yamauchi had called the challenge to his firm's top position an attempt that would "amount to nothing." He blasted the volume and quality of games played on Sony's 32-bit PlayStation, which would go on to sell over 100 million consoles before passing the torch to the next-generation PS2. That hardware would also blitz Nintendo and other competitors, without leading to more circumspect pronouncements from Yamauchi.

Some Sony games were now supplied by Namco, whose president, Masaya Nakamura, had earlier fallen out with Yamauchi, while others such as Square, a supplier of Nintendo software since the NES, had abandoned ties with the Kyoto firm in 1996 to supply its Japanese rival with its tremendously popular "Final Fantasy" series. Yamauchi had responded in 1999 that those who enjoyed the role-playing gaming (RPG) of "Final Fantasy" were "depressed gamers who like to sit alone in their dark rooms and play slow games."[10]

Some thought the comments refreshingly candid, but for an industry under sales siege, potentially insulting those who were still buying its games did not translate into the next key marketing vision. However, despite acerbic and often entertaining vows from Yamauchi never to let the departed companies back into his supplier stable, Nintendo eventually accepted rapprochement based on its changing fortunes. The N64 console had packed twice the technological muscle of Sony's PS but failed to catch on with an overwhelmed audience, and it now appeared that the GameCube was in danger of the same fate as the popularity of the new PS2 surged further.

The No. 1

Indeed, confounding Yamauchi's predictions of industry disaster, Sony's games division had quickly made $5.5 billion in revenues by fiscal 1998, riding the success of the PS, as well as a blitz of aggressive software tie-ups and marketing deals that ultimately provided more than 10 percent of the electronics conglomerate's revenues. Yamauchi's counterpart at Sony, then the operatic maestro Norio Ohga, could not control his glee at the near $900 million in profit that gaming alone had generated

"We've never had a business like this," he said.[11]

The strategies Sony intended with its next high-end PS console portended even greater injury—as well as insult—for Nintendo if successful. Its computer entertainment division, led by "Father of the PlayStation" Ken Kutaragi, was growing its gaming pie with the second-generation PS2, equipped with a DVD player that began to tie into the firm's broad content-delivery possibilities. Sony ultimately aimed to sell multimedia home entertainment centers that would link the conglomerate's many consumer electronic products and growing library of movies and music. Executives such as new Sony boss Nobuyuki Idei had paid hundreds of millions of dollars to amass such content, which now looked to have an outlet beyond the local Blockbuster store.

Meanwhile, Microsoft's Gates, who had sanctioned the giant's entry into gaming in 1999, wanted his new Xbox to become a platform to highlight the firm's software dominance and budding online presence, along with its own media content relationships. He committed billions of IT dollars for marketing as well as research and development.

Yamauchi was never a game player, but like his ancestors he was a consummate peddler and strategist. He seemed to sense the uncomfortable crossroads ahead for Nintendo in trying to compete simultaneously with the information technology, entertainment, and video game industries—all of whose audiences were notoriously demanding while known for short attention spans.

Since the late 1990s, Yamauchi had stressed how Nintendo ran a different business, contending that PCs and the Internet, as well as movies and music, did not matter to gamers. Following the mantra of some of his most gifted game and console designers, he became a chief priest of gaming "fun."

"Our focus will still be strictly on games, different from those of Sony and Microsoft," he said. "Sophisticated features such as beautiful pictures and heart-stopping sounds are not what gamers are really looking for—they just want to have fun."[12]

What *fun* was or would be remained open for debate, but clearly the Internet era, the expansion of cable television, and the prevalence of easily accessible multimedia content gave consumers an overwhelming array of choices that video game designers would now have to reckon with and compete against. Coupled with even shorter attention spans and a penchant for more active lifestyles, new games and consoles would not have to please everyone, just more people than up until that moment, if the company was to grow. Indeed, it would take more than technological precision for Nintendo to stage a comeback over the next few years—a difficult but not hopeless matter, as in the company's long history a eureka moment often happened when least expected.

The industry, though, appeared headed for "bells and whistles" whether Yamauchi sanctioned the advances or not, making adaptation or innovation essential to survival. Once-popular game arcades now increasingly struggled with growing home console ownership, while some titans of the gaming sector had merged, vanished, or now found themselves consigned to trivia questions and commoditized software reissue.

Home gaming penetration, as reflected in Japanese data, was substantial but relatively stagnant, awaiting a moderate-priced innovation that would move the entertainment to new pastures while simultaneously broadening its audience.

Yamauchi, a highly ranked Japanese *Go* player, had seen a possible endgame coming unless the terms of the contest changed, as spending for a relatively limited audience of young men was resulting in increasingly lower returns and—for a growing number of industry players—losses or failure. One such company, which had revolutionized video gaming in the early 1990s with its new characters and technology, was now mothballing its next-generation console and its hardware aspirations.

Sega's Exit

Sega, which entered the home video game market in 1986 and launched its first Genesis console three years later, pulled the plug on production of its Dreamcast in January 2001. Dreamcast sales had missed internal targets by more than a million units, effectively shutting down a hardware business that had been an industry pillar.

Sega's state-of-the-art 128-bit Dreamcast had debuted in 1999 with a Power/VR graphics card capable of high-resolution online gaming via an Ethernet port, as well as a small LCD screen. However, one of the biggest U.S. retailers, Kmart, dropped Dreamcast from its store shelves in August 2000, presaging a fourth consecutive annual loss and leading an already shell-shocked management to hit the "game over" button and focus solely on software.

Sega's hardware exit prompted Nintendo and Yamauchi to patch up the two companies' long breach, although Nintendo still had to deny rumors that it would buy its beleaguered former rival. (These rumors had briefly sent shares for the maker of Sonic the Hedgehog rocketing higher.) Sega's bowing out of the high-stakes industry poker game put Nintendo's plans under a more intense microscope, but the always-confident Yamauchi maintained, "A number of companies will be eliminated, but Nintendo will survive."[13]

Not all were convinced.

Nintendo's TV-linked hardware position continued to erode to the point where it flirted with becoming the industry's No. 3 upon the entry of Microsoft. Some observers and institutional investors opined that Nintendo was not certain to avoid the path of Atari, Coleco, or even

Sega—those once-mighty gaming masters that bet the ranch on eternal consumer respect or industry Edsels.

Nintendo stock slumped. This benchmark of investor confidence, while not always a sign of actual business performance, continued to reflect its perceived direction during the decade. Yamauchi remained the top shareholder in the now "public" family business, still commanding a multibillion-dollar war chest and paying less attention to Nintendo's paper roller coaster ride than its road ahead.

Nonetheless, in April 2001, Nintendo announced a share buyback of about one-tenth of outstanding company equity, which aimed to offset the plunge of more than 40 percent in operating profit that had sent its stock tumbling.

"We have more than 800 billion yen in cash and deposits, which is just too much. We aim to boost our return on equity," said Yamauchi, adding, "A company must defend itself in the face of consolidation. We decided to take this when we could afford to do so."[14]

More than defending its share price, Yamauchi—as the man who signed off on nearly every Nintendo product coming to market—was also sending a signal that his departure as the new console arrived was not a cut-and-run. He could claim substantial credit for the past three decades of success, but also could not deny responsibility for the clunkers, a club the moribund GameCube now risked joining.

The industry now seemed less focused on the creation of compelling new games and more on franchise updates with new Roman numerals that could be counted on to garner at least the interest of current players, although infusing little new blood into the consumer base. Yamauchi had long cried that it was software that needed to be better tended, but whether it was software or hardware that led consumers more was an open question.

His successor, therefore, would need experience with game and console design, marketing new products, as well as a fresh business perspective, as software development needed to take on even greater importance to expand the consumer pool. It was an exceptionally tall order, and—with Yamauchi likely to breathe heavily on his successor's neck—a job that would need thick skin to survive all the potential second-guessing.

Who would be willing—or naive enough—to try to step into Yamauchi's shoes remained uncertain. Meanwhile, the soon-to-retire emperor offered few clues, only that the transfer was coming soon. Some doubted that after so many decades—and so many unfulfilled promises to go—Yamauchi could actually leave Nintendo on his feet, rather than on a stretcher or a slab. However, the fate of the fourth-generation family heirloom currently appeared dangerously dependent on a high-tech box with a handle.

Yamauchi, though, was indeed intent on keeping his word to step down, regardless of GameCube's performance. What he was not convinced about was Nintendo's future as a family-run company, and he was considering all options in deciding who would become its next generation of leadership, including one of the rarest traits in any Japanese boardroom—youth.

NOTES

1. *Mainichi Shimbun,* January 17, 2002; available online: www.gamecubicle.com/news-archive-jan02.htm; access date: August 27, 2010.
2. David Sheff, *Game Over: How Nintendo Conquered the World* (New York: Vintage Books, 1994).
3. Ministry of Finance, "Trade Statistics of Japan," n.d.; available online: www.customs.go.jp/toukei/suii/html/nenbet_e.htm; access date: August 16, 2010.
4. David Sheff, *Game Over: How Nintendo Conquered the World* (New York: Vintage Books, 1994).
5. Japan External Trade Organization, "Japanese Video Game Industry: Japanese Economy Division," 2007; available online: www.jetro.go.jp/australia/market/index.html/japanesevideo.pdf; access date: August 16, 2010.
6. "Nintendo to Open New Pokemon Outlets Overseas," Reuters, September 8, 2000.
7. *Nihon Keizai Shimbun,* May 23, 2001; n.d. available online: www.nintendoworldreport.com/news/5995; access date: August 27, 2010.
8. Ibid.
9. Hiroshi Yamauchi, "The Prospects of the Entertainment Market," GameSpot, November 2, 1997; available online: www.gamespot.com/news/2467470.html; access date: August 18, 2010.

10. James Brightman, "Video Game Executives Say the Craziest Things"; n.d. available online: www.industrygamers.com/galleries/video-game-executives-say-the-craziest-things/13/; access date: August 28, 2010.
11. Irene Kunii and Steven V. Brull, "The Games Sony Plays," *Business Week,* June 15, 1998. Available online: www.businessweek.com/archives/1998/b3582040.arc.htm; access date: August 25, 2010.
12. Yuka Obayashi, "Nintendo to Unveil New Game Boy, Sparking a Battle," Reuters, March 21, 2001.
13. Irene Kunii, "Nintendo: Let's Play Survivor," *Business Week,* March 26, 2001; available online: www.businessweek.com/magazine/content/01_13/b3725166.htm; access date: August 27, 2010.
14. Yuka Obayashi, "Nintendo Stages Strong Rebound on Buyback News," Reuters, April 18, 2001.

CHAPTER **2**

The Kid

$4 BILLION COMPANY ENTERING ITS THIRD CENTURY OF business, with a history of three leaders all named Yamauchi, appeared rather unlikely to become a meritocracy open to outsiders. However, facing tremendous competition in the more than $20 billion industry, a graying senior management, and an increasingly gloomy product outlook as the industry's No. 2 or possibly even its cellar dweller, 70-something Hiroshi Yamauchi decided to break with the past at Nintendo.

Yamauchi, who took the helm himself directly from university and remained in the post for over a half century, had come to value traits rare in most Japanese boardrooms—youth or relative youth, game design experience, and actual management flair.

The idea of selecting for required skill sets and dispensing with the need for long years of labor appeared at odds with Japan's traditional corporate hierarchy, in which decades of accomplishment and gradually climbing up the pyramid ultimately dictated the reward of executive office. Meanwhile, the country's characteristic adage—"The nail that stands out gets hammered down"—also left little latitude that a home-grown wave of mavericks such as Apple's Steve Jobs or Microsoft's Gates would emerge.

Yet Yamauchi himself had been an iconoclast after inheriting the leadership role at a very young age and eliminating potential dissent, and a growing tolerance for unconventional thinking was beginning to blossom at Nintendo—and to some degree in the nation itself. Japan now saw its own new breed of CEOs—some born in the country, such as Masayoshi Son of Internet giant Softbank, and some outsiders installed as a result of domestic corporate woes, such as Nissan Motor's Carlos Ghosn. These executives, nearly always men in Japan, were leading their own companies or trying to work minor miracles in revitalizing the gray, middle-aged monoliths they inherited.

At Nintendo, the keys to leadership had historically been family ties and Kyoto residence, and most company-watchers assumed they'd be pre-requisites for its next boss as well. Hiroshi's great-grandfather, founder Fusajiro, did not have a son to take over the family business when he retired in 1923, but son-in-law Sekiryo had taken on the family's surname and held the top seat at the domestic playing card company through World War II. In a recurring pattern, Sekiryo—also without a male heir—prepared to tap his son-in-law to follow him, but a not-so-funny thing happened on the way to that succession.

The *shacho,* or company president-to-be, Shikanojo Inaba, decided to flee the Yamauchi household in 1933, abandoning his wife and child, a deed his son would never forgive or forget in his father's lifetime, leading to a blunt and unsentimental manner that dominated his later business affairs. As discussed in Chapter 1, the young Yamauchi came into the company in 1949, cleaning house of family and potential foes but becoming clearly the man responsible if business fortunes soured. As the years passed and Hiroshi neared what would normally be considered retirement age, he avoided declaration of a clear cultivated successor, or successors, as well as a hard deadline for his departure.[1]

At times over that reign, Nintendo would not have been much of a company to inherit, but with the tremendous success of its North American operations, its business had improved greatly and the next Yamauchi to head the company appeared a lock, or so it would seem.

ALL IN THE FAMILY

Hiroshi's son-in-law, Kyoto native Minoru Arakawa, led Nintendo of America (NoA) from its origins in New York through its relocation for shipping purposes to Redmond, Washington, helping to take the parent firm to horizons unforeseen by even the most optimistic company cheerleader.

A Massachusetts Institute of Technology graduate who repeatedly shunned the Yamauchi family business while remaining with his trading company in North America, Arakawa eventually agreed to try to launch Nintendo's presence on the continent. Along with Howard Lincoln, who had joined as legal counsel and held the post of NoA chairman from 1994, Arakawa drove expansion and navigation of the treacherous gaming landscape from the boom-and-bust 1980s onward, while still taking marching orders from Yamauchi in Kyoto.

Expanding on what initially was just an arcade business, Arakawa, known as a shy consensus builder, convinced Yamauchi to export Nintendo consoles even as giants Atari and Coleco fumbled in the industry. He ultimately helped to revive a market that many consumers and retailers had begun to give up on. If not for developer Shigeru Miyamoto's "Donkey Kong," though, these efforts might also have been consigned to a legacy of lost quarters, as Miyamoto's redesigned "Radarscope" game, which introduced the jumping plumber later to be known as Mario, became the fastest-selling arcade game of its time.

"When we started in the U.S., we definitely had a start-up atmosphere, with a few employees and even fewer products. In the very early days, I didn't know whether we would succeed in America, but after I saw someone play 'Donkey Kong' for the first time, I knew we were here to stay," Arakawa said.[2]

By 1989 and the launch of the Game Boy handheld console, Nintendo was taking heat from the Federal Trade Commission (FTC) for a 90 percent market share, proprietary chip and marketing strategies, as well as rising prices. The unapologetic NoA, though, said without its presence the gaming industry would have been an afterthought.

"We haven't done anything wrong here. What we've done in the last three and a half years is to single-handedly recreate a dead industry. We have resurrected the home video game business," Lincoln said, before ultimately coming to an accommodation with the FTC.

The run of hit consoles and software continued through the 1990s, making the parent company a global success and lifting Arakawa's star—and creating expectations that he was on his way back to Kyoto. Japan had continued to supply the technological innovations and NoA the key consumer market and promotional savvy in a two-tier front in which Yamauchi at the "master brain" headquarters remained the charismatic boss vetting new software and consoles, while the U.S. operations drove marketing and sales growth.

The U.S. pair became field generals for one of the greatest industry grabs ever, but competition was again heating up, this time with Sega. In an early sign that Yamauchi would not be bound by family ties alone, he promoted Lincoln over Arakawa as NoA chairman, publicly blasting his son-in-law for allowing the gaming rival and its cutting-edge consoles to gain ground at Nintendo's expense.

Ultimately, Lincoln chose baseball over video games, resigning his NoA position to head the company's *de facto* sports franchise and philanthropy, major league baseball's Seattle Mariners. His short but sweet farewell seemed to indicate how grueling life had been at Nintendo over the past 15 years:

"I am sure I will remain involved at Nintendo, but I'd kind of like to do more fishing," he said. "I think I'm going out at the right time."[3]

Arakawa took on double duty as NoA president and chairman in 1999, and with his friend and colleague Lincoln seemingly out of the boardroom picture, his succession now appeared a certainty. Game designer Miyamoto said in an interview with *Next Generation Magazine* that he expected Arakawa to get the post. "Common sense is it should be Mr. Arakawa. . . . We all know that Mr. Arakawa is the person who has built Nintendo of America to its current position."[4]

But Yamauchi, who had driven Arakawa to try to become as tough a businessman as himself, appeared to have pushed his son-in-law beyond his comfort zone, with disagreement about company direction also emerging. For better or worse, Hiroshi Yamauchi was indeed one of a kind.

Outside the Box

A Nintendo directors' meeting in early 2000 foreshadowed Arakawa's eventual resignation from the parent board and his move to the company's sidelines. His father-in-law, with a Dickensian indifference, told the *Nihon Keizai Shimbun* newspaper that a new breed of leader was essential.

"A certain person who will not succeed me was not reelected to the Board," he said in May 2000, a move that officially was attributed to Arakawa's intent to focus on North American operations. "The software business is really tough, and the requirements of management are different from other industries."[5]

Another version of the statement put the Board's decision in removing Arakawa directly at Yamauchi's door:

"I will not reappoint as a director someone who won't succeed me."[6]

Part of the family schism was attributed to company debt taken on by NoA, compared with the multibillion-dollar cash stockpile preferred by the fiscally conservative Yamauchi. However, the bottom line may have been the two men's divergent personalities and views of what life should be about. Arakawa apparently decided retirement in Hawaii would be a far more enjoyable fate than waging further console wars or waiting for his "retired" father-in-law's words of advice or rebuke.

Arakawa's retirement at 55 came in January 2002, five months ahead of Yamauchi's. (The latter finally stepped down at the age of 74.)

In 2004 and happily entrenched in a leisurely life in Hawaii, Arakawa told the BBC he had no ill feelings toward the company or Hiroshi Yamauchi:

"The game business was a very tough, difficult business. I worked there more than 20 years and I was ready to retire," he said with wife Yoko at his side, during an interview at their home overlooking the Pacific Ocean.

"Mr. Yamauchi's life is all business," Arakawa said. "He will continue to think about Nintendo until he dies."

"We invited him many times to Hawaii. If it's business, he doesn't mind coming. But if it's not, he would say 'Why should I come?'"

Yoko Arakawa was more to the point:

"I got to know him after I got married. I like him as a person, but he is not the type of man I would marry."[7]

Arakawa had stood down some of the most daunting marketing and legal challenges in modern business, as well as on occasion Yamauchi himself. His corporate farewell statement had tried to put the best possible spin on his departure.

"The U.S. video game industry is extremely strong, and NoA's position within the industry has never been better."[8]

Considering that storied history, the contention was highly debatable, as the *Seattle Times* noted in its report on Arakawa's departure that new consoles from Nintendo and Microsoft had sold 1.2 million and 1.5 million units, respectively, since their November launches, meaning Nintendo was on the cusp of becoming No. 3 in the industry.

"The recent impressive marketplace successes of both Game Boy Advance, and GameCube, along with NoA's unparalleled financial and management resources, allow me the opportunity to pursue new endeavors," Arakawa added.[9]

With that, the man who helped to redefine the industry, or even save it, as Lincoln opined, was out the door.

His former colleague, now ensconced in Seattle Mariners' baseball, sang his praises, but few words about his contributions came from Kyoto, other than naming his NoA successor. Tatsumi Kimishima, a former banker who had only been with Nintendo for two years as chief financial officer of the Pokemon Co., took his spot, looking to replicate the tremendous success of the animated character line, which had been added to the company stable in the mid-1990s. Kimishima ultimately thrived in the position, becoming NoA chairman in 2006.

Yamauchi had never stated his plans, but the end of familial leadership may have been his intention all along, seeing the job of chief company custodian as needing more than just blood ties. His own son, Katsuhito, had worked briefly for Nintendo Canada, as well as in advertising and as a producer for its animated Pokemon films, but he was not in consideration for the Board and far off the radar as a possible company chief.

Still, Arakawa's somewhat abrupt departure had raised eyebrows as to how steady future North American operations would be, as the move combined with the resignation of 15-year veteran Peter Main, NoA's sales and marketing chief, and the larger, still unsettled issue of Yamauchi's successor. Nintendo addressed some of the jitters in December 2003 by hiring Reggie Fils-Aime, who had worked at and managed VH1, Pizza Hut, and Procter & Gamble. Fils-Aime was an energetic and outspoken leader who recognized the traditional role of NoA but added a new marketing savvy to the subsidiary's global profile and approach.

Share Woes

Nonetheless, news a Japanese company steeped in history would not follow a playbook with imminent succession issues at hand sent Nintendo shares down nearly 15 percent the following week. The decline had only just started, while rival Sony's shares had risen by the same margin since the start of the year on high hopes for continued brisk sales of its PlayStation 2 console.

From mid-1999 until early 2002, the stock traded in a range between ¥16,000 and ¥23,000, or about $132 to $172 based on wide exchange rate fluctuations, but it began to explore lows near the handover although Nintendo had released the GameCube and a new handheld console. Long a darling of foreign investors because of its minimal debt load and a history of innovation, the company had to deal with the succession question in the most public way, while the exact denouement was still anyone's guess. Among prognostications about leading candidates for Yamauchi's post were Atsushi Asada, 68, who had joined the company from Sharp Corporation in 1999, and Yoshihiro Mori, 56, a senior managing director who had been with Nintendo since 1969.

The company had created two jobs—chairman and vice president—to expand the board and potentially offer a new boss or bosses more insight and opinion. Yamauchi, who initially said he would not become chairman, eventually took the title, as concerns emerged about the company's identity and charisma without him; he remained in the role until mid-decade.

The Japanese firm was not alone among major global companies in seeing significant leadership changes at the time. Bill Gates stepped down as CEO of Microsoft in 2000, Jack Welch at General Electric in 2001, and Louis Gerstner at IBM in 2002. However, in the 20th century, the number of global companies historically controlled by families had thinned, while the fraternity of exceptionally long-tenured executives of publicly traded firms had become even smaller.

Rival Sony had seen its own management changes with Nobuyuki Idei succeeding Norio Ohga in the 1990s, but Ohga's shadow never seemed far from company decisions, including the advancement of Ken Kutaragi, the creator of its hugely successful PlayStation console franchise.

Few—if any—corporate leaders had the near absolute control of Yamauchi, and speculation about Nintendo's next president and how much change he—or they—would be allowed remained rife. One of the first correct media calls on the next Nintendo boss appeared in a report by Irene Kunii for *Business Week* in March 2001, mentioning a young "much admired game creator" named Satoru Iwata, who had joined the company and board the previous year and could follow Yamauchi.[10]

Indeed, the relatively short, bespectacled gentleman, with his Dutch-boy haircut, would become the next Lord of Kyoto, as well as the hope of every Nintendo vassal whose future rested on the continuation of its century-plus of relative success. Yamauchi, rarely known for compliments, said Iwata had special talents, widely seen as software design expertise and—even at a young age—possessed great management skills.

"Iwata is the right guy for the job because he is acquainted with both game software and game hardware," Yamauchi said. "Software should come first and hardware second, but some people seem to see it the other way around."[11]

A NEW BREED

The new chief, 32 years younger than Yamauchi, had served as director and general manager of Nintendo's corporate planning for two years. Nonetheless, many saw him as a potential puppet for his predecessor, who as chairman was likely to continue to pull the strings. Iwata had joined design wizard Miyamoto to promote Nintendo's latest hardware and games at international gaming events such as the Electronic Entertainment Expo (E3), but he was certainly not a household name. His selection as successor surprised many company-watchers, as he simply wasn't as well known as the Father of Mario; some media even got his name wrong, identifying Nintendo's next boss as "Satoro," or "Toru."

On first impression, Iwata could easily be mistaken for a chief financial officer or chief technical officer instead of a CEO. In some ways, though, he was all three, based on his earlier experience as a game software designer and start-up executive who had learned the books as well as research and development essentials, which Yamauchi recognized as a strength. From the beginning, Iwata tried to make clear who was calling the technical and development shots, and that Nintendo was competing more with its own creative abilities than its console rivals.

"No matter how many consoles Sony sells, and whatever Microsoft does, it is important for us to make our game software attractive enough to drive consumers to buy our hardware," he said on his debut as president.[12]

Without question, the company he now oversaw was not running at peak performance, and some even advised a restart of its traditional business lines. In that regard, "Iwacchi," as he was later dubbed, preached the antithesis of high-tech gaming, the bland but essential prerequisite of "simple fun." He publicly eschewed consoles with higher resolution, more digitally enhanced sound, and intricate design, instead calling for a product that would broaden the consumer base and ultimately sell more.

Nintendo had spent most of its first two decades promoting how gaming was a defining difference between young and old, but now it needed to recruit adults to play as well as pay. In this mantra, Iwata joined a chorus that included Miyamoto, the late Nintendo design genius Gunpei Yokoi, and even the non-gamer Yamauchi.

Indeed, a genuine affinity for gaming was one of the two most striking contrasts between the 42-year-old and his predecessor. The other was a characteristic Yamauchi seldom displayed nor likely valued—a sense of humor, nurtured by Iwata's early days in Japan's hinterland.

From Kirby to King

Born in 1959 in Sapporo, on Japan's northernmost island of Hokkaido, Iwata was not a Yamauchi either by blood or by marriage, not Kyoto-bred, and not even fully Nintendo-spawned, having cut his gaming and management teeth at a company that supplied games for the parent firm. He grew up in one of Japan's poorest prefectures, where his father had served as a prefectural official and later as mayor of Muroran, a struggling steel and shipbuilding village.

Yet through luck and innate interest, the young Iwata migrated from the analog world of a Japanese Loretta Lynn toward the early days of computers and the "New Economy." He attended high school in relatively urban Sapporo, becoming a class officer as well as an early game programmer.

"The first video game I ever played . . . was Pong—and I loved it. By the time I was in high school, I was the first person in my class to buy an early Hewlett Packard Pocket Calculator. I think I was one of the original 'early adopters,'" he told an industry crowd years later. "But while most people used their calculators for higher mathematics, I used mine to program video games. My first creation was a baseball game. I don't think anyone can say it had bad graphics because it had no graphics. . . . But when I saw my friends playing that game and having fun, it made me feel proud."[13]

Iwata later studied engineering and the early basics of computer science at Japan's Tokyo Institute of Technology from 1978. He worked as a part-time game programmer while in college before helping to establish the eventual Nintendo stable firm HAL Laboratory. The young student was more interested in his motorcycle and video games than his studies, but still earned a degree with distinction.

"After class, when my friends went back to their rooms to study, I took off on my motorcycle for one retail store in Tokyo. This was the first store to have a department entirely dedicated to personal computers. That was my hangout—and I was not alone," he said. "We became friends, formed a club, and soon rented an apartment in the Akihabara district of Tokyo, where we began designing our own games. We worked until midnight or later every night, and that group of friends is what became the company known as HAL."[14]

Iwata said he was the fifth full-time employee in the small start-up, which shared a name with the runaway computer system in Stanley Kubrick's *2001: A Space Odyssey*. HAL later moved to Yamanashi Prefecture at the foothills of Mt. Fuji, beginning with lofty ambitions, but—like Muroran—facing financial hardship.

Iwata was its first programmer, but joined the Board of Directors by the age of 24, when HAL began developing software for the Nintendo Entertainment System (NES). He later worked on its "Kirby" series with Masahiro Sakurai, just as Nintendo was starting to dominate the gaming industry, but said HAL's first ties to Nintendo were humbling.

"The biggest moment in the history of HAL came when we heard the rumor that Nintendo was developing a machine capable of incredible new graphics—'the *Famicom*,'" he said.

"We knew this machine was for us, so we used every contact we could to get a meeting with Nintendo, sure that one of our ideas would become an instant hit.

"Nintendo did hire us, but not to amaze the world with one of our projects. Instead, they told us to fix one of their projects . . . It was eventually released as 'NES Pinball.'

"That experience taught us that even artists must know the business side of game development."[15]

A Young Gun

By the age of 33, he had become president and earned the nickname "director of problem-solving." Iwata remained with the company until late in the 1990s, helping to return HAL to the black through the development of hit products such as "Super Smash Bros." Iwata joked that his father would not talk to him for six months after he joined HAL, thinking the young man had entered a religious cult, but its ties to Nintendo would prove crucial.

"The person in charge at Nintendo was our customer. Sometimes they were satisfied with our output, sometimes not," he said years later. "I didn't think I had talent in management at first. It's easy to think you're not made for it. However, in my case, there was nobody else up for it; it was like destiny that the position came to me."[16]

His youthful experiences helped him to develop a self-deprecating style that he employed with staff and the media from the start, often making jokes, while the more imperial Yamauchi seldom deigned to be amused, even in a company touting "fun." For Iwata, any topic was fair game, including his diet.

"As every game developer understands, the three basic food groups are Fritos, Cheetos, and Doritos," the cherubic CEO jokingly told an industry gathering a few years later.[17]

As a designer and developer from outside the parent, Iwata paid due respect to Nintendo's pantheon of heroes, saying he had been awed by Miyamoto and the myriad of games and consoles he had helped to launch. "From the early days of my game development at HAL Laboratory, I was always watching and learning from him—from outside of Nintendo, my eyes wide as saucers," he said.[18]

"I have learned a vast amount about making video games from Miyamoto-*san*. It might be better to say that I didn't learn from him, but rather stole from him."

As president, he had watched the parent firm aid its recovery by promoting HAL's games overseas, while frequently receiving tutorials in Management 101 from Yamauchi, to whom he also gave credit.

"I got a lot from Mr. Yamauchi—the ability to place priorities, the confidence to firmly decide what you will not do, and the resolve not to leave anything half-done."[19]

After Iwata joined the firm, Yamauchi continued to tutor him. The 74-year-old appeared to see the young leader as a catalyst rather than an avatar to implement policies and changes that he himself could not. Iwata later said his conversations leading up to Yamauchi's decision to tap him appeared to match Kyoto's Buddhist temple environment.

"Sometimes Mr. Yamauchi would come up to me and talk like we were in the middle of a Zen dialog. He'd say things like, 'You can't be it if you want to be it, but you can run away.'

"Though I was sometimes puzzled by the things he would say, Yamauchi's feelings toward Nintendo and his sense of urgency were two things that were communicated so loud and clear that my ears still hurt.

"I joked to myself that if I really did end up being offered the position, I ought to at least prepare myself to not run away in panic.

"The first time I actually heard was just before the official announcement. Of course, it was a shock."[20]

As the new sheriff, Iwata appeared to be Yamauchi's opposite—a manager without any likely guarantee that wrath or guilt would get the job done. Instead, he would proffer his design and product expertise, as well as marketing and people skills, potentially winning a staff buy-in and sustained loyalty on recognition that he was technologically appreciative of the amazing work of the rank and file. In some ways, the struggles of HAL had also prepared him for Nintendo's financial needs.

"I was appointed [HAL] president in order to help reconstruct it. At that time, I was completely unable to read financial statements. I was a game developer, so I was forced to study the financial aspects of running a company," Iwata said in a later interview.[21]

The core of that experience, though, was in rolling up his sleeves and designing software, and later figuring out what platform could make the results viable.

"Since I myself come from a development background, I think I understand the minds of developers better than most executives. When I am discussing things with the developers here, I am not just a bystander."[22]

Iwata later admitted after a few years at the helm that he would have had no chance of succeeding by imitating the older man, Yamauchi. Rather, he tried to make his relative youth, lack of company baggage, and candor assets for the firm, while elevating the profiles and self-esteem of those working for him, even if they were older or had more Nintendo experience, which was almost always the case.

The Board

Iwata initially reported to Vice President Atsushi Asada, while an executive committee assisting him included Miyamoto, Genyo Takeda, Yoshihiro Mori, and Shinji Hatano. His first job at Nintendo had been coordinating Miyamoto's software development group with Takeda's hardware division as head of the Corporate Planning Division, and now that brief had expanded and become essential to the company's revival plan. Takeda had led Nintendo's Research & Development 3 since 1980, and was responsible for its many technological advances, as well as shepherding the production of its last two TV-linked consoles, the GameCube and Nintendo 64.

A major creative voice within the company since its laser-shooting range era in the 1970s and its first video games, Takeda became a Nintendo director in 2000, but had spent recent years talking about *hansei,* or "reflective regret," for the sales failures of its hardware. As Nintendo prepared to bring his GameCube to market at nearly the same time as Microsoft's Xbox, plans were already under way for its next generation of consoles, as was standard development policy.

Iwata's background as a game creator was sound training to understand the environment facing the GameCube and the mind-set of software supplier firms, which had seen sales fall as the gaming population stagnated and had become increasingly gun-shy about resource commitment. The number of Japanese gamers had declined by about 20 percent, meaning outside software firms faced a tougher time recouping their substantial investment and thus had become more selective in their allegiance.

Without such advance development, a new console such as the GameCube would be short of games, creating a deadly spiral if its sales did not quickly merit third-party software production. Indeed, that worst-case scenario was starting to brew with the new console, and that designer flight would torpedo its sales potential. Still, as Iwata took the helm in June 2002, he boldly predicted total sales of 50 million GameCube consoles by 2005.

That vote of confidence for Nintendo's latest Cadillac, though, stretched the imagination, as the PS2 had only sold 30 million in its first two years, and Sony expected just another 20 million consoles in the third. However, in a way that Yamauchi could no longer impart convincingly, Iwata's new role also included championing and selling products, whether great or not, honing this skill as GameCube pitchman at the E3 game summit in Los Angeles in 2001.

Iwata continued to tout the "Nintendo difference" compared to rivals Sony and Microsoft, showing games, including "Luigi's Mansion," "Metroid Prime," and Miyamoto's latest "Pikmin" edition. Analysts, though, said the company would need to find software reinforcements by the Christmas holiday season or it would not be a happy new year, and that call proved correct.

However, there were also missteps. In the same role at the 2003 E3 event, Iwata touted a four-way version of retro favorite "Pac-Man," which some observers said was stupefying, as it underscored every preconception of Nintendo losing its way and grappling for old standards, while the rest of the now $27 billion industry focused on adults.

GAMECUBED

The numbers ultimately showed the difference was not registering at retailers, as the PS2 had already sold more than seven times as many consoles at the time of Iwata's selection as the GameCube and Xbox. Iwata and the collective leadership turned their attention to their challenged console, the child of Yamauchi and Takeda that was now everyone's to rear.

Shortly before Iwata's appointment, Nintendo, sensing tough times, had cut the GameCube's domestic price, but this did not boost its fortunes. By April the following year, Nintendo had to revise down its earnings, which fell by almost 40 percent year on year to about $550 million.

Of Iwata's 50 million GameCube forecast, or 12 million sales target for the 2002–2003 business year, Nintendo had sold only 5.6 million consoles, part of a pronounced slowdown across the board. Even Miyamoto's "Zelda" and "Mario" game series had not been selling with the usual fervor with the GameCube, while the more adult-themed "Grand Theft Auto" series for the PS2 dominated the video game market.

Separately, the Sci-Fi shooter game "Halo" had led some core gamers to the Xbox, further supporting a view that Nintendo's audience was preteens, with the new "Mario Sunshine" software eliciting criticism that the firm was not interested in—or capable of—serving adults, a characterization that Microsoft and Sony game executives reiterated.

Industry estimates now gave the PS2 a 75 percent market share, while GameCube and Xbox were neck and neck with meager 13 and 12 percent shares respectively. Yamauchi was characteristically dismissive.

"There are many people in the industry who know nothing about games. In particular, a large American company is trying to engulf software houses with money, but I don't believe that will go well," he said.[23]

Nonetheless, some industry-watchers, such as Strategy Analytics, called for Nintendo to abandon traditional console-exclusive software, shorthand for dumping the GameCube and non-handheld hardware manufacturing altogether.

At the same time, as feared, some software makers, such as THQ, cut their number of titles for the GameCube, adding with mild conviction that they would not give up on Nintendo. Sega and even Capcom, then considered the most pro-Nintendo Japanese software maker, froze their sports title output for GameCube or shifted to rival platforms.

Some desperate retailers even made independent GameCube price cuts, a potential prelude to pulling them from the shelves altogether. Iwata, rapidly expanding his financial expertise to retail returns, could read the year-end numbers and see a weaker global economy could not be blamed, as PS2 sales had jumped over 24 percent.

The company's stock, meanwhile, fell to its lowest level in four years, despite a huge Nintendo buyback during the preceding quarter. Brokerages such as BNP Paribas cut their equity ratings on the Japanese video game maker, cautioning that its tanking share price had gone too far after slipping under ¥10,000,or about $85.

YEAR ONE

With less than a year's experience, Iwata found his hot seat growing even hotter, as he already faced questions of whether Nintendo would follow Sega in ending console production—and possibly be known as the man who turned off the lights on the Kyoto giant's hardware business.

"We are developing a new home game console with a plan to release the new system around the same time as rival makers do," he said in an interview in January 2003.[24] "When we withdraw from the home game console, that's when we withdraw from the video game business," he added, a pronouncement that likely made Hiroshi Yamauchi smile, if that was possible.

Others suggested the Nintendo should use its cash stockpile and buy its way out of hardship. Iwata, looking at the wealth of his two main rivals, said that was not a winning strategy either.

"They have reserves so vast they make us look rather poor," he said. "We have to find a way to compete without making it a question of which company is richer."[25]

However, the corporate ship was listing badly. Without a major hit product to promote, Iwata rapidly started to focus on Nintendo's next consoles, envisioning their debut in the next few years but admitting that predicting what the market wanted was difficult.

"We can't be optimistic about the game market," he said. "No matter what great product you come up with, people get bored. I feel like a chef cooking for a king who's full."[26]

Miyamoto, whose characters and games had been undeniably successful without any courting of a "mature" market, said Nintendo must begin to attract an older demographic as well as rethink how and for whom consoles would be constructed. That argument was not about equipping the hardware with DVDs or computers with state-of-the-art sound and vision, as Nintendo had already determined that such a strategy would be loss-making and was the source of a current industry malaise.

Iwata concurred.

"Nintendo has to concentrate on something which is really unique to Nintendo,"[27] he said at the industry E3 show in 2003, in a subtle rebuke of his inherited console and its game supply. "Nintendo, or more specifically the GameCube, does need a great variety of different software, which must be put into the market at appropriate intervals."

"It is true there is some perception that Nintendo's main titles are for children. . . . We have never said that Nintendo is making our products for our children. It's rather the images created by the PR strategies of our competitors," admitting Nintendo needed to attract a different demographic.

Nowhere was that more evident than in Japan, as the video game market shrank to $4.5 billion in 2002 from over $5.5 billion the year before, according to the Computer Entertainment Supplier's Association. Online game sales, meanwhile, skyrocketed—but still were barely 1 percent of the overall market.

Iwata was not convinced that the online market would attract more consumers any time soon, saying start-up costs and monthly fees would discourage major purchases. He preferred to focus on Nintendo's existing software ties.

BURYING THE HATCHET

In light of the desperate times for its industry and its own business, Nintendo began to lower its loyalty charges for software producers, and to provide easier development tools. Yamauchi, who had always been able to obtain favorable terms and strict compliance from internal and external game designers—with exile for disloyalty, led the rapprochement before the handover to Iwata, reestablishing ties with some software makers in moves that startled many industry-watchers.

Iwata also worked with key overseas partners such as Electronic Arts, maker of "Madden Football" and other hit games, letting Miyamoto consult with independent developers on game design, while increasing Nintendo's own research and development staff to almost 900.

Nintendo allowed Square, later to become Square Enix, to resume making Nintendo games after a nearly six-year absence, while also inking a joint development deal with Namco to produce Game Boy Advance and GameCube titles, and adding the estranged Bandai, which was later to merge with Namco.

Square had abandoned Nintendo in 1996 to make its "Final Fantasy" series exclusively for PlayStation, and its then president had criticized Nintendo's management, starting a blood feud that Yamauchi reveled in.

President Nao Suzuki later told the *Nihon Keizai Shimbun* in October 2001 that the rift had been exacerbated by his company's comments about the Nintendo 64 and luring Enix to join the defection, while the reasoning behind the shift was a desire to make games for Sony's CD-ROM system. Many had seen the departures of Square and its role-playing games (RPG) for Sony's PS consoles as one of the major reasons that the Nintendo 64 failed to win consumers with a technically superior machine.

By March 2002, Square had sold over 30 million copies of the hot franchise, but the company faced its worst-ever loss after a $137-million animated movie version of the game, *Final Fantasy: The Spirits Within,* bombed at the box office in the summer of 2001.

What made the reunion with Nintendo even stranger was Sony's $116 million stake in Square, making it the No. 2 investor with a 19 percent share of the software company. Sony had agreed to allow Square to return to the Nintendo fold, provided it did not affect Square's PS2 game development.

The Square affiliate under Akitoshi Kawazu, one of the developers of "Final Fantasy," used the Nintendo deal to aid its return to profitability. Nintendo also rekindled ties with Sega, which now depended solely on software sales after exiting the console business. Nintendo farmed out its "F-Zero" franchise to its former hardware rival, producing what some saw as the best racing game for the GameCube and also an arcade version, the futuristic "GX/AX."

Sega's mascot, Sonic the Hedgehog, which was created by Yuji Naka and had been a Mario rival in the 1990s, had his own Game Boy Advance title, later joining Miyamoto's hero in a set of Olympics-related games. The moves came as some foreign game developers such as Rare, long key suppliers with promised titles for the GameCube, began to leave the Japanese giant for Microsoft, forcing Nintendo to take drastic action.

As noted earlier, Nintendo had never been a full member of Japanese game or software industry organizations, or even the Nippon Keidanren, the nation's business lobby, but the company was rapidly learning greater humility. It opened a software development center in Tokyo in 2002, and the "retiring" Yamauchi invested about $160 million in a start-up called Fund Q, aimed at supporting software development venture businesses, such as that with Square.

The fund offered companies trying to develop games for Game Boy Advance and GameCube collateral-free loans averaging ¥1 billion, or about $8.3 million, aiming to have software delivered within a year. Yamauchi said in January 2002 that Japan's entertainment industry was in a rut and needed pump priming.

"The Japanese game software market is in the same situation Japanese theme parks are in. If you're not Universal Studios or Tokyo Disneyland, then times are very tough right now," he said.

"The industry is hurting for something new that's not an RPG or fighting game, and developing talent to make new genres takes money.

"With the IT slump, venture capital firms aren't giving any money to game developers and the banks aren't lending either. That's why I created the fund."[28]

He had financed the fund by selling his 1.18 million Nintendo shares (nearly 11 percent of the company) in after-hours trading—and then buying the shares back to use the capital gains for funding. In addition, Yamauchi, never known for nonprofit motivation, told the *Nihon Keizai Shimbun* in August 2002 of his post-retirement plans, which included video game promotion and marketing:

"I hope to establish a special school that teaches how to use computer graphics. I want to make efforts to develop software with a higher level of originality by using the ideas of young people, without focusing on making profits.

"We can offer a prize for game creators; then, we can invite bids for games that win awards, enabling software makers to commercialize and sell their games."[29]

That plan, like his long-touted farewell, was slow to find traction, while his actual departure had not drawn major responses from the business world with the exception of the head of his own baseball team.

"He's going to remain on the Board. He's going to remain as a consultant; he'll remain principal owner of the [Seattle] Mariners," Howard Lincoln said.[30]

In his final message as boss, Yamauchi focused on the product:

"Coincidental to my leaving the company, I would like to make one request—that Nintendo give birth to wholly new ideas and create hardware which reflects that ideal, and make software that adheres to that same standard," he said. "I'd ask that the company continue to follow this goal as my final and only request to the new management staff. I can't say what these new types of software will be, but I'm sure they'll release it during my lifetime."[31]

Yamauchi would live to see the new developments, but the departure of "Mario's master" (who also had other, less appealing nicknames) briefly veiled the tough conditions awaiting Iwata. The young CEO had asked Nintendo staff to promote new games at shopping malls during the 2003 Christmas season, backing a "Super Mario" media blitz, as earlier support measures for the GameCube had fallen flat.

In the first half of business year 2003, his company recorded a loss of $26 million, its first net loss since going public in 1962.[32]

The 20th anniversary of the launch of the Nintendo Entertainment System was beginning very poorly, and a few years later, when he had the latitude of a plate of successes behind him, Iwata noted his first crisis in a way Hiroshi Yamauchi never would or could.

"In the end, the GameCube was an extension of its predecessors," he said. "Really, there is no such thing as a product that everyone is completely satisfied with."[33]

NOTES

1. David Sheff, *Game Over: How Nintendo Conquered the World* (New York: Vintage Books, 1994).
2. Mike Dolan, "Behind the Screens: An Insider's Oral History of the Videogame," *Wired 9.05* (2001); available online: www.wired.com/wired/archive/9.05/history.html?pg=3&topic=&topic_set=; access date: August 27, 2010.
3. Jim Carlton, "Howard Lincoln Decides to Leave Nintendo," *Wall Street Journal,* July 26, 1999.
4. Mike Revier, "The Next Yamauchi", October 22, 1999; available online: www.nintendoworldreport.com/news/5361; access date: August 30, 2010.
5. "Nintendo Hits Console on Performance Over Entertainment," mmWire7, no. 157 (August 16, 2000).
6. Shinichiro Unozawa, "Nintendo Sees Generational Change," *Nihon Keizai Shimbun,* June 10, 2002 (available on Factiva).
7. "Outrageous Fortunes: Nintendo," April 2004, BBC; available online: www.youtube.com/watch?v=0aFhW56c2Vg&feature=related; access date: August 28, 2010.
8. "NoA's Minoru Arakawa Retiring," GameCubicle.com, January 8, 2002; available online: www.gamecubicle.com/news-nintendo_minoru_arakawa_retire.htm; access date: August 30, 2010.
9. Nintendo, press release, January 7, 2002; available online: www.gamespot.com/news/2837292.html; access date: August 18, 2010.
10. Irene Kunii, "Nintendo: Let's Play Survivor," *Business Week,* March 26, 2001; available online: www.businessweek.com/magazine/content/01_13/b3725166.htm; access date: August 27, 2010.
11. Hiroshi Suzuki, "Nintendo's Iwata to Push Yamauchi's Management Legacy," Bloomberg, June 10, 2001; available online: www.gamecubicle.com/news-nintendo_leadership_iwata.htm; access date: August 27, 2010.
12. Ibid.
13. Matt Casamassina, "GDC 2005: Iwata Keynote Transcript," IGN Gamecube, March 10, 2005; available online: http://cube.ign.com/articles/595/595089p1.html; access date: August 16, 2010.
14. Ibid.
15. Ibid.
16. "People Try to Show Superiority (5)," *Hobo Nikkan Itoi Shimbun,* January 7, 2002; available online; www.1101.com/iwata/2007-09-06.html; access date: August 27, 2010.

17. Satoru Iwata, GDC Keynote Address, 2006; available online: www.ninten doworldreport.com/news/11223; access date: August 18, 2010.
18. "Iwata Asks: Special Edition Interview," n.d.; available online: http://us.wii .com/iwata_asks/special_edition_interview/; access date: August 18, 2010.
19. *Shukan Toyo Keizai,* July 15, 2006; available online in Japanese: www.gaforum .org/showthread.php?t=134234&page=6; access date: August 27, 2010.
20. Ibid.
21. Nigell Kendall, "How Nintendo's Boss Rewrote the Rules of the Game," June 9, 2009; available online: http://technology.timesonline.co.uk/tol/news/ tech_and_web/article6461767.ece; access date: August 30, 2010.
22. "Iwata Asks: Special Edition Interview," n.d.; available online: http://us.wii .com/iwata_asks/special_edition_interview/; access date: August 18, 2010.
23. Matt Casamassina, "Top 10 Tuesday: Wildest Statements Made by Industry Veterans," IGN, March 14, 2006; available online: http://ds.ign.com/articles/ 695/695790p1.html; access date: August 31, 2010.
24. Yuka Obayashi and Keiko Kanai, "INTERVIEW: Nintendo Eyes Next-Generation Console Launch," Reuters, January 23, 2003.
25. Geoff Keighley, "Is Nintendo Playing the Wrong Game," *Business 2.0 Magazine,* August 1, 2003; available online: http://money.cnn.com/ magazines/business2/business2_archive/2003/08/01/346319/index.htm; access date: August 13, 2010.
26. Andrew Gumbel, "Is the Game Up for Console Makers?" *Independent,* June 7, 2002; available online: www.independent.co.uk/news/business/analysis-and-features/is-the-game-up-for-console-makers-or-can-price-cuts-win-over-jaded-players-644639.html; access date: August 27, 2010.
27. *Mainichi Shimbun,* January 2002; available online: www.nintendojo.com/ archives/fullfocus/view_item.php?1079984352; access date: August 27, 2010.
28. Lisa Heyamoto, "President of Game Maker Nintendo Steps Down," *Seattle Times,* May 25, 2002; available online: www.accessmylibrary.com/coms2/ summary_0286-6833872_ITM; access date: May 27, 2010.
29. "Interview: Nintendo's Yamauchi Says Focus Still on Fun Games," *Nihon Keizai Shimbun,* August 21, 2002 (available on Factiva).
30. "Nintendo Reports First-Ever H1 Loss," TechSpot, October 6, 2003; available online: www.techspot.com/news/8101-nintendo-reports-firstever-h1-loss. html; access date: August 29, 2010.
31. "IGN: Hiroshi Yamauchi Biography," n.d. available online: http://stars.ign. com/objects/919/919303_biography.html; access date: August 31, 2010.
32. "Nintendo Creates New Game Plan," *Nikkei Weekly,* January 3, 2004.
33. "Iwata Asks: Special Edition Interview," n.d.; available online: http://us.wii .com/iwata_asks/special_edition_interview/; access date: August 18, 2010.

CHAPTER 3

Character Issues

NINTENDO BEGAN BY PEDDLING PLAYING CARDS in the late 1800s—often to Japanese gangsters for use in gambling—but its late 20th-century business stuck to the straight and narrow. It focused on renting or creating hit characters that became world-renowned icons on games, television programs, and films, as well as on every sort of marketable spin-off product.

Starting the push in the early 1950s and looking for a way to revive Nintendo's moribund *karuta* card business, Hiroshi Yamauchi struck a deal with Disney in 1959 to put the entertainment giant's characters on cards. The marketing link to Disney, renowned for its appeal to children, was a lucrative connection for Nintendo, coming as Japan began to discover and crave all things Western. Ultimately, the connection helped Nintendo realize a new business direction.

Later, after the industry found one of its first major hits with the computer-generated paddle and ball of "Pong," Nintendo gravitated toward the new entertainment. Yamauchi had long been eyeing the need for a different business line and identity that could leverage off his already established domestic sales network. The company tested gaming waters with laser guns and submarine warfare games, but from its early 1980s "Donkey Kong" mega-hit and subsequent Mario franchise, Nintendo mainly produced and promoted cheery icons that progressed through obstacle levels and offered game-play puzzles or role-playing, along with fantastic settings, compelling stories, and uniquely creative visions.

Just as Disney found massive returns from a young audience on the animated backs of Mickey Mouse and Donald Duck, Nintendo, from its entry into gaming, inculcated its brand with successive generations, who often passed the torch on to friends and eventually to their own children. Characters would appear in a variety of games, with characteristics and skills changing somewhat to complement a new console's technological advances or a particular software feature.

Franchise characters were usually a must-have at launches to generate immediate consumer interest, but curiously the GameCube became the first Nintendo console not to have an official Mario title at its sales debut. Instead, it featured Mario's brother in "Luigi's Mansion," which sold a third of all its software in its first week in Japan, but like the console itself, slowly slid off the radar.[1]

The GameCube's marketing campaign, under the catchphrases "Born to Play" and "Who are You," displayed the desire—if not the product—to expand Nintendo's gamer demographic, but the company was hard-pressed to shake its image as the vendor for pre-teen gamers. Nintendo, until then, had been more or less resigned to its fate, with the Game Boy providing a stable revenue stream and the company unwilling to risk a potential backlash with blaring guns or risqué stories that could damage the brand.

Since its Disney card days, Nintendo had the invaluable cachet of parental confidence in its content and quality, making games for children whose parents usually did their shopping. Like Disney, this ultimately created a virtuous circle of comfort and ultimately nostalgia that had started to beget second-generation buying. However, Satoru Iwata realized that it was the untapped generation of new players that would be essential to the company's revival.

SHIFTING GEARS

A shift to higher-performance consoles increasingly demanded changes in graphics, speed, and sound, and in turn new software that would exercise the machine's potential. Similarly, this often increased the incentive to create a more violent or action-oriented game to lure an older audience, and a line of first-person shooter (FPS) games became standard for most software and console manufacturers, including Nintendo.

The origins of FPS play are traced to the 1970s, but the genre took off with greater console sophistication in the 1990s, particularly 3D visuals, finding pay dirt with Bungie's "Halo" for the Xbox in the new millennium. Such software titles, including Retro Studios' "Metroid Prime" developed for the GameCube—which the company called a "first-person adventure" game—dominated the early sales charts of the decade and came after a period when the gaming industry had to regulate itself or face government intervention.

During the 1990s, when consoles went from 8-bit to 128-bit processing power, growing objections to the increasingly violent content found in some software and arcade games had led the U.S. Congress to discuss video game content with some corporate chiefs. Nintendo did not entirely eliminate action or gunplay from its own games or other firms' supplied software, but it contended its versions, such as Acclaim Entertainment's popular "Mortal Kombat," were less violent than those of others.

Ultimately, like the motion picture industry, game makers in the United States created their own rating code to avoid greater public scrutiny or government intervention. The Entertainment Software Rating Board (ESRB) was created in 1994 by what was then called the Interactive Digital Software Association to apply ratings that ran the gamut from E (Everyone) to AO (Adults Only) to over 18,000 titles from more than 350 publishers.[2]

Nintendo of America's chairman, Howard Lincoln, who had spoken with Congress on the matter and blasted Sega's "Night Trap" game as having "no place in our society," later said the ratings system had to imbue trust: "If video games are going to form a mass-market industry, all of us within it have a responsibility to focus on improving the ratings system. The games business is being closely scrutinized by the public. Still, I'm confident that we'll be able to come up with great games without violence."[3]

Nintendo, Sony, and Microsoft all prohibited release or sale of AO games for their consoles, while key criteria for ratings included violence, gore, sexual content or language, drugs, or gambling references. An EC (Early Childhood) rating encompassed educational and basic content for kids aged 2 through 10, while other letter monikers included E10+ (Everyone 10 and older), the T (Teen) rating given to the majority of output, and M (Mature 17+) on games for audiences 17 and older.

Like motion pictures facing the film industry's "X" rating, game content was often toned down to receive an "M." Nonetheless, retailers such as Target and Walmart still required parental presence to purchase "M" games, similar to the requirements of an "R"-rated movie.

MATURE CONTENT

The GameCube saw over 600 titles in its life span, with "Luigi's Mansion" an "E" and most games, such as "Metroid Prime," receiving a "T" rating. However, in a mild sign of change, Nintendo allowed production and development of some 40 "M" titles for the console, such as Silicon Knights' "Eternal Darkness: Sanity's Requiem," and Capcom's "Resident Evil 4," as sales trends clearly indicated that cute was losing shelf space to the fast and increasingly furious.

On occasion, ratings still had flaws, seen later in the decade when Rockstar North's "Grand Theft Auto: San Andreas" was found to have an incomplete sex-themed mini-game within the software that could be unlocked despite its receiving an "M." On discovery, the ESRB later changed the rating to "AO," but not before substantial sales and a subsequent reissue had taken place. Rockstar North later issued "Manhunt 2," which carried an "AO" before editing changes allowed it to receive an "M" for retailers.

As consoles became interactive, Nintendo launched a "friend code" aiming to ensure that gaming communication could be controlled, and that improper contact with juveniles, which had arisen in some online chat rooms, did not plague its consoles, e-communities, or consumers. As video game firms gradually became online retailers themselves, Nintendo, Sony, and Microsoft barred minors from downloads of "M" games, but the titles' popularity was undeniable.

In 2002, an estimated 80 percent of the most popular game titles were rated "E" or "T." However, the cognoscenti of the industry believed there was no way Nintendo could, or should, remain "immature." A *Wired* headline from January 2003 read: "Why Nintendo Won't Grow Up," and asked if the man who invented the modern video game, Shigeru Miyamoto, could "connect with his inner adult."

Miyamoto, then 50, was portrayed—both flatteringly and unflatteringly—as the Disney of game design, a man responsible for creating 6 of the 10 best-selling console games as of 2002, producing more than $7 billion in sales with the "Mario" franchise and $10 billion overall, and yet somehow was in danger of a flawed legacy as the industry stepped on the gas:

> His path to Olympus has been paved with games that appeal unabashedly, if not exclusively to children. His characters are simple, and their predicaments can be readily grasped and negotiated using a single button and control stick.
>
> The Miyamoto formula: Devise controls that are intuitively engaging, puzzles that make players feel as though they're discovering solutions rather than being led to them, and characters that are disarmingly cute. Walk to bank. Cash check. Refine. Repeat.
>
> The industry that sprang up in Miyamoto's wake is ready to move on.[4]

THE FATHER OF MARIO

Miyamoto's impact on the industry had never been constrained by his Mario, Zelda, StarFox, or other perceived "safe" characters or titles, but even he admitted a kind of expectation paralysis beginning to plague Nintendo and the industry, which increasingly produced games with Roman numerals rather than tilling new ground. Miyamoto said technological considerations had become paramount in game design, while the demand for franchise sequels had not enlarged Nintendo's gamer pool.

Not surprisingly, the man who preached the gospel of gaming "fun" wanted to create something innovative. Reflecting later, Miyamoto told industry-watcher *Famitsu* that the launch of the GameCube was a crossroads for himself and Nintendo—with creative identity at stake:

"Nintendo was going in the direction of doing the same thing as other companies," he said. "If Nintendo's games fail to stand out . . . then it shows the creative process is for nothing, which made me very sad. That was especially obvious during the GameCube era.

"What with all the issues I had to tinker with in terms of rendering and processing speed, it got to the point where I didn't know who was making the games any longer."[5]

That moment was perhaps a career low for the man credited with helping the video game industry heal from its post-Atari woes, when Miyamoto followed up his "Donkey Kong" in the early 1980s with a string of hits and design innovations that continued through the 21st century. As chief designer of Nintendo's software for its next-generation consoles, Miyamoto, along with Iwata, recognized that the current gamer demographic clearly was not large enough, championing the view that a simple "fun" factor could attract more adults (and especially more women) to gaming than the most realistic chainsaws and machine guns would bring in.

Buy-in from Nintendo staff and board was possible based on his sales success and track record in two decades of innovative storytelling and design, often compared to Walt Disney, or—as game creation increasingly was called an animated form of cinema—the movies of directors Steven Spielberg and Orson Welles.

Born on November 16, 1952, and raised in the town of Sonobe, Kyoto Prefecture, Miyamoto, a son of an English schoolteacher, had always been more liberal arts-oriented than technology-obsessed as a child. He was raised in a rural home, without the growing middle-class staple of television. As a youngster, he drew comic books, created flip-book *anime*, and put on puppet shows. In earlier centuries, he might have become a *Bunraku* puppet master or *ukiyo-e* artisan in the nearby former capital, famed for its cultural offerings.

Miyamoto enrolled at the Kanazawa Municipal College of Industrial Arts and Crafts, which was not to be confused with the elite schools of the ancient basin, such as Kyoto University, Doshisha, or Ritsumeikan. He took five years to graduate, spending hours sketching and playing music before eventually taking a degree in industrial design. That major would turn out to be exceptionally important for Nintendo, as his broad skill sets included problem solving, key to many of the game functions he would create as well as essential for adaptation as the company entered some of its toughest hours.

Through a family friend's introduction to Hiroshi Yamauchi in 1977, Miyamoto joined the near-century-old firm, which had embraced the gaming industry but was still trying to find its way in pursuit of a modern business. Nintendo was licensing other firms' characters, such as Popeye, but in a period when the gaming industry was taking off exponentially with the success of Atari and others, he said Yamauchi made his staff objectives very plain:

"Make games that sell more."[6]

Miyamoto had been hired as a staff artist but was soon told to remodel a failed arcade game, later tested in 1981 in Seattle bars amid very low expectations for success. To some degree, he received the project because Nintendo's top designers were focused on new games for the Japanese market, assuming the repurposing of game cabinets for an American audience to be a relative dead end.

In the process of crafting a future for Nintendo, he met the company's top developers and producers. The legendary designer Gunpei Yokoi taught him the importance of treating the craft as the work of an artisan, as that of its first card makers had been. He also emphasized the absolute necessity of the search for "fun," which Miyamoto passed on to many others over the decades.

Gaming Fun

Yet as he analyzed the meaning of satisfaction, Miyamoto asked himself why people continued to pour quarters, or in Japan 100-yen coins, into arcade machines after losing, a fate they would inevitably endure again and again.

"I concluded that this was born of players being mad at themselves. . . . It was when I was mulling over these issues that a more-senior colleague, Gunpei Yokoi, was good enough to explain a lot of things."

"We began to flesh out the idea for a game based on the concept we had come up with—a fun game should always be easy to understand—you should take one look at it and know what you have to do."[7]

This eureka moment led to the sale of some 67,000 arcade cabinets over the next two years. The resulting game, which paired an angry barrel-throwing ape with a plump but muscular carpenter and kidnapped girlfriend, became the first "Donkey Kong." Its bare-basics Jumpman, later known as the mustache-bearing, overall-wearing Mario, launched a long line of related and unrelated characters in over 70 games that Miyamoto eventually helped bring to virtual life.

"I called him 'Mr. Video.' My plan was to use the same character in every video game I made," he said. "I thought the way Hitchcock cropped up in all the films he directed was really cool. . . . Or take manga artists like Osamu Tezuka and Fujio Akatsuka, who have the same characters popping up."[8]

Modifications of the original low-resolution "Radar Scope" game included assorted color-specific character tweaks that helped make movement easier to see, along with the use of features such as a mustache and hat instead of a mouth and hair to conserve pixels. Making video games in that era was a mathematical exercise in resource management, which Miyamoto had not been particularly innovative, until then.

He used the word "donkey" because of its connotation of stubbornness, and somehow Hiroshi Yamauchi, as final video game editor, did not change a thing. The choice became gaming lore, and "Donkey Kong" became the fastest-selling arcade game in history. As its popularity soared, Universal Studios tried—without success—to sue Nintendo for copyright infringement on the ape's resemblance to King Kong, learning later that it did not own the character itself. For its home console sales rights, Coleco won the honor, but that was one of the last outplacements. Nintendo was launching its family computer, or "*Famicom*," which would later become known as the Nintendo Entertainment System (NES), and phasing out the practice of producing game titles for other hardware makers.

The Franchise

Miyamoto had helped animated game characters display perceived personalities and more human representation, as well as actions and mobility that pushed the industry toward higher expectations for content. Mario's profession changed over the years (plumber, painter, doctor, driver, or whatever dovetailed with game needs), but his basic characteristics and eventual three-dimensional pursuits were similar enough to breed fan devotion and for its creator a rock star's status.

Miyamoto said later that he deferred to Yamauchi on game selection, but both knew the Mario character was a cash cow:

"I was allowed a great deal of autonomy when it came to the next game we would make—except sometimes Mr. Yamauchi approached me and said: 'Isn't this the time when we need to have the next Mario game?' Mr. Yamauchi was the same age as my parents, so maybe he was looking at me as a son or grandson doing something for him.

"Out of everyone, Mr. Yamauchi seemed to have the most precise forecasts as to how much a certain piece of software could sell."[9]

The young man later joined with Yokoi and composer Hirokazu Tanaka to work on "Mario Bros."—followed by the 40KB "Super Mario Bros." with Takashi Tezuka, which was released in Japan in September 1985 and in the United States the following year. The title, known for its flying turtles and mushrooms, has been called the all-time most copied game, with some 40 million sales.

"Super Mario Bros." combined a scrolling background with platform action, a blue—not black—background, altitude control, and freedom from a single screen of play. Some observers called it Miyamoto's *magnum opus*.

"Super Mario Kart" gave the character his own racing franchise, while "Super Mario 64," designed for the Nintendo 64 console in the mid-1990s, used 3D visuals to create a defining moment for the industry in the vein of a *Fantasia* or *Citizen Kane*. Nintendo's cutting-edge console itself ultimately proved a failure due to limited and delayed software, but "Super Mario 64" highlighted what the kit and a brilliant designer could do, as Miyamoto reinvented the genre with a game camera and play perspectives commensurate with the greater processing power.

"Super Mario 64" was not the first 3D game, fending off rivals from Sony and Sega at the same time, but it kept the cartridge-dependent Nintendo 64 moving off the shelves and offered differentiation from a wave of cheaper software hitting the market. Miyamoto, a natural wit who was inventive with language as well as with visuals and gameplay, said his creations needed special translation attention when going overseas, although there was one subtitle everyone could read: Sales.

In simple dollars, the Mario franchise alone had grossed over $7 billion in software sales worldwide by 2002, with 160 million games sold. The character—with his multitudes of brothers, doppelgangers, friends, and foes—spread to television and film, toys, and anything Nintendo was willing to sell. The company that had paid Disney for its characters on cards had become a colossus of brand enterprise in the ensuing 40 years.

The first title for GameCube was "Super Mario Sunshine." It quickly sold twice as many units in Japan as the earlier "Luigi's Mansion," yet was not the industry stopper that "Super Mario 64" had been. Miyamoto, having spent two decades with the character, promised that it would not be his last trip to the Jumpman well, but helping Nintendo find its way with new consoles and games had become top priority.

"I am 50 years old this year. The Mario series has pretty much become my life's work. From now on, every year I will still work on it and hope more people will play it."[10]

A Company Man

Miyamoto's Mario, Donkey Kong, Zelda, and StarFox series helped to earn more for Nintendo than any comparable Hollywood studio star. Nonetheless, despite his contributions to Nintendo's success, the scope he was given to nurture his talents, and his responsibilities ranging from games to museum development, the Kyoto prefecture native preferred to appear a humble and loyal company man. In an era of self-promotion and transient vocational commitment in pursuit of a big payday, Miyamoto likely could have gained greater returns elsewhere, or even founded his own Mushroom Kingdom. However, he remained true to Nintendo as his patron, while realizing in his early Mario years that he was lucky to find the profession and such life circumstances.

"It was while coming up with graphics that fit nicely with the technology that I began to think: 'You know what? This is a pretty fun job!'"[11]

Yamauchi—known as a player of people, not games—seemed also to recognize the young man's skills by the mid-1990s. However, the boss never allowed confusion as to Miyamoto's place in the corporate pecking order, eschewing public praise as out of line or a waste of time:

"Miyamoto is an employee of Nintendo and I am president of Nintendo, so I feel it's not appropriate to say how I feel about him."[12]

In the character's first 25 years, over 140 Mario-related games appeared, selling some 185 million copies.[13] Yet some efforts flopped, notably the 1993 film *Super Mario Bros.,* which starred Bob Hoskins and sported a tagline of "This Ain't No Game, It's a Live-Action Thrill Ride."

The actor called it the worst film of his career, and box-office returns confirmed that audiences were not ready to trade in love of one gaming icon for two hours wasted. Miyamoto admitted something was missing:

"It became a movie that was about a video game, rather than being an entertaining movie," he said later. "I didn't collaborate with them a whole lot."[14]

With more computer-generated effects in film, cinema was also increasingly used as a marketing delivery platform for game debuts or a commercial outlet for games, story lines, and effects, with hopes that the small-screen audience would follow. Steven Spielberg, George Lucas, and other big directors and producers homed in on the new business, some more successfully than others. As *Super Mario Bros.* had shown, not all games could transfer easily to the big screen despite their popularity. Meanwhile, television was a less-expensive venture, if not more compelling.

Zelda

Miyamoto's "The Legend of Zelda," which began with the "*Famicom*" in Japan and as an NES cartridge globally from 1987, built a core following of designers and gamers who pursued the chimes of its puzzle solving. Team members Toshihiko Nakago and Takashi Tezuka joined with Miyamoto to develop the hit and its successors, becoming known as the "*Kansai Manzai*," or Western Japan Comedy Trio.

Using open-ended role-playing and exploration, Miyamoto for over two decades helped lead changes in Zelda's game nuances with subsequent teams, which used his initial vision as a benchmark of quality in an industry often derided as merely serving up short-term consumables. In later updates, such as "The Ocarina of Time" in 1998, Miyamoto took Zelda from 2D to 3D, drawing on his own childhood home's *shoji* (paper screen) hallways and cedar walls to create an intuitive maze world. While "Ocarina" was not technically a role-playing game, some industry-watchers said its cinematic quality offered the Nintendo 64 console its last hurrah.

Miyamoto's passion for the natural wonders of his youthful home—its rice fields, lakes, and caves—had provided the inspiration for a wealth of settings. He even navigated the occasionally rough waters around Yamauchi by once replying to a question about Zelda's characters that they were not based on the Nintendo president.[15]

Zelda, Link, and the stories' myriad mythic settings further evolved over the years, while the issue of puzzle solving and sustained game experience continued to be tended as faithfully by Kyoto production staff as if it was the *Book of Kells* or a Zen garden. Miyamoto included in the game, and other creations, a value for previous play experience and learning, while advancement after solving a puzzle or surmounting a challenge allowed a brief respite for gamers, so they weren't instantly confronted with increasingly difficult play at each new stage.

For GameCube, "The Legend of Zelda: Four Swords Adventures" was released in 2004, an offshoot of Game Boy Advance development and connectivity. It was seen by gamers as interesting but not among the more memorable efforts of the long-running series, and it was often lumped with the many disappointments tied to the console.

Future designers aimed for Zelda to offer the apparently contradictory traits of realism in a dream world, while the various versions of the franchise had sold some 47 million copies by late 2006. Zelda made a brief debut on North American TV before the decade ended as part of *The Super Mario Bros. Super Show,* but was canceled quickly with the syndicated series, and had yet to make a movie appearance as of 2010.

NEW GROWTH

If the GameCube era was depressing for Miyamoto, it did prompt a packaging of his gardening hobby into "Pikmin," a real-time strategy space game featuring carrot-like seedlings as the main characters. First demonstrated and sold in 2001, "Pikmin" was one of the console's few original hits, as well as a precursor of many future hobby-oriented games from Miyamoto, using his own Kyoto neighborhood and garden for some of the game's floral backgrounds.

The other-worldly environment with the player as astronaut interloper on a 30-day life clock was envisioned as potentially expanding the game market to young women. Yet the game actually saw the Pikmin battle enemies that resulted in death or destruction, a yoking of Miyamoto's traditional cute approach with a darker edge. It sold more than a million copies in less than a year, and spawned a sequel by 2004. It also had its own hit song—"*Ai no Uta,*" or "Song of Love," by the virtual group Strawberry Flower—an offering that despite its overtures toward a new demographic purportedly was, in perfect illogic, purchased most by middle-aged men.

Miyamoto said it may have just been coincidence that his hobby morphed into something more marketable, as it wasn't planned.

"We were doing a lot of experiments on GameCube by some concepts that eventually resulted in 'Pikmin,'" he said. "I was doing gardening at that time, so I thought 'Maybe this might fit into the concepts we are experimenting with now.'"[16]

The Kyoto gardener admitted that he was still searching for a full-immersion opportunity that Pikmin had not fulfilled.

"In the end, Pikmin wasn't the kind of game everybody could pick and play easily," Miyamoto noted, although the series ran for the rest of the decade. "It turned out to be a great game for people who are good at games. What I would like to see is games that are a relaxing play for anybody."[17]

Miyamoto was hinting that gaming needed to go beyond mere button-pushing and screen dynamics, while his hobbies would lead development further in this vein. His love of bluegrass and Beatles music helped to define the audio functionality of later consoles, while passions such as pets and fitness would eventually lead to other business lines. Asking Miyamoto about his hobbies became a way to guess what kind of software or game kit was coming next from the company, and later in the decade, Nintendo reportedly asked him not to talk about his pastimes for fear of giving away future intellectual property rights.

He had married a fellow Nintendo staffer, Yasuko, who worked in the general administration department and never had a real interest in gaming, and the couple lived a mountain bicycle ride from the company's headquarters in Kyoto. Concerned their own children would spend too much time gaming, he restricted play at home while designing new software aimed at encouraging children to draw and animate characters themselves. Miyamoto said later that he was trying to spend more time with his family, circumstances that would ironically also lead to new software development.

"I was a typical Japanese husband who had been neglecting my family life, but I am now spending more time with my family. I am now interested in how a family can enjoy [recreation] in one house."[18]

The GameCube period might have been disappointing for Miyamoto, but he soon lifted himself and Nintendo to new heights. The company began to back away from what was turning into its worst-selling major console ever, and to develop new creative products for gamers and non-gamers alike.

Miyamoto and all Nintendo staff were busy trying to return the shine to the video game giant, and the designer, as Yamauchi did, put aside his own rivalries, including that with Toru Iwatani, known as the father of the "Pac-Man" series. Iwatani now led game incubation at Namco, a company that had returned to the Nintendo fold after a period of exile. In December 2003, the two men rolled out a "Pac-Man Vs" series for the beleaguered GameCube, appearing together at a Tokyo museum event honoring the NES on its 20th anniversary, while the legendary dot-eating game had just reached its own two-decade mark.

"Our rivalry is part of history. . . . Now we have to create game titles that lead the industry," Miyamoto said.[19]

By 2004, the creative visionary most responsible for Nintendo's sustained success over decades was actually mentioning retirement. He noted his expanding outside—but related—interests and hobbies, with his usual quest for humor and new adventures: "I don't see anything changing drastically in the near future. I might leave Nintendo to retire someday. I'll have to consider what I'll be doing when that day comes," he said.

"My children are now 17 and 18 years old. Soon, they'll be off to college. . . . One thing I've been doing nowadays is practicing my musical instruments. . . . My wife sings sometimes, so maybe she'll join me in a band. It's my secret mission."[20]

MONSTER SUCCESS

Nintendo, meanwhile, had enjoyed its own monster success with the Pokemon series, which was first launched in Japan in the mid-1990s. It sold over 193 million games in 13 years and became the No. 1 trading card game in history for a company long steeped in the entertainment, pushing creator Satoshi Tajiri into the upper echelons of designers.

Tajiri designed software with his own hobby of bug collecting in mind, making trade as well as connectivity with other players integral to capture all characters and complete the game's tasks. The man behind

Pokemon, nicknamed "Dr. Bug" by friends, was born in a Tokyo suburb in 1965, and attended the Tokyo National College of Technology.

He first worked in the industry in the 1980s, producing the game "Quinty" for Namco. Tajiri joined Nintendo ahead of the Pokemon launch, where he worked with Miyamoto on the initial games, and with friend Ken Sugimori, who illustrated the characters.

Among a younger generation growing up on *manga* and Japanese *anime*, Tajiri had also watched *Godzilla* movies and the adventure hero TV series *Ultraman* before becoming a "Space Invaders" junkie in the late 1970s. He had started the revered industry magazine *Game Freak* with James Hanzatko, ultimately heading a company of the same name.

Focusing on the Game Boy's cord connection, Tajiri saw the potential to shift game objectives from competition to sharing information or rewards, as well as developing individual personalities and character traits for his creations such as Pikachu and Ash. The game's reach, or "tentacles" as some critics described it, included films and an animated TV series that aired in over 150 nations in 25 languages, making Pikachu arguably a Mickey Mouse of its era, along with an initial 150 comrade characters.

Retailing ultimately extended into apparel, toys, and even food-stuffs, while some company-watchers saw this as the perfect bookend to Nintendo's *hanafuda* card origins.

CARDS TO CARDS

Japanese gamblers of the 19th century had slowly become the pre-teens of modern homes across the world, hurling their "pokeballs" in an effort to catch, train, and own more game characters. Most important, like their forebears playing the older game, global youth often needed a new pack of cards for each session.

The original games—"Red and Green"—became a launching pad for a franchise that spawned over 30 games and a "Pokedex" that eventually exceeded 500 species. The franchise did not lose momentum in its second decade, with such stars as "Pokemon Platinum" character Giratina.

In Japan alone, Nintendo has sold more than 35 million Pokemon games, according to industry-watcher *Enterbrain,* while in the United States, sales had already hit $5 billion by the year 2000. There was also a Pokemon movie that quickly returned $116 million on a $4 million investment.

By late 2006, the Pokemon franchise was estimated to have sold 106 million games, compared to about 51 million for "Madden Football," which launched some six years before it, and 50 million for "Grand Theft Auto," which debuted in 1998.[21] Tajiri's games had conflict without character deaths, another Disney-like trait offering potential residuals in perpetuity. Retail shrines like a Pokemon center in Tokyo's ritzy Ginza district also helped bring in millions of dollars in character goods sales.

A low point came in December 1997 when hundreds of children watching a Japanese TV version of a Pokemon program became ill, with some vomiting and seizures reported in what was determined to be a reaction to the flashing lights of a scene depicting a "vaccine bomb" blast in the broadcast.

One media report called the cases "optically-stimulated epilepsy," but Hiroshi Yamauchi immediately proclaimed that Nintendo was not responsible, putting the blame on the production by broadcaster TV Tokyo. The network apologized but did not cancel the popular cartoon show, instead just removing the offending episode from future broadcasts.

The Pokemon boom continued relatively unabated, and despite predictions of a trip to the "Cabbage Patch Kids" ward for the terminally overmarketed, by mid-2008, sales hit 186 million copies. The franchise had immediately given a jolt to the Game Boy console in the 1990s and kept software sales going through the Game Boy Advance, essential as Nintendo's larger consoles struggled.

However, Nintendo was now in deep preparation for its next wave of software and hardware, which would help rewrite its history in a push with Miyamoto at the forefront. The company and its chief creative force looked to usher in new games and players, as well as find an entirely new dimension and definition for the nearly 30-year-old pastime.

NOTES

1. "Total Sales from September 14, 2001 to December 31, 2006," Nintendo Gamecube, May 6, 2007; available online: www.japan-gamecharts.com/gc.php; access date: August 16, 2010.
2. Entertainment Software Rating Board, "ESRB Game Ratings," n.d.; available online: www.esrb.org/ratings/index.jsp; access date: August 16, 2010.
3. Regina Joseph, "Q&A with Nintendo's Howard Lincoln," *Forbes*, June 22, 1999; available online: www.forbes.com/1999/06/22/feat.html; access date: August 18, 2010.
4. Zev Borow, "Why Nintendo Won't Grow Up," *Wired* 11.01 (2003). Available online: www.wired.com/wired/archive/11.01/nintendo.html; access date: August 28, 2010.
5. Kevin Gifford, "Miyamoto 'Very Sad' During GameCube Era," 1up.com, March 11, 2009; available online: www.1up.com/news/miyamoto-sad-game-cube-era; access date: August 16, 2010.
6. "Iwata Asks: New Super Mario Bros. Wii," n.d.; available online: http://us.wii.com/iwata_asks/nsmb/vol1_page1.jsp; access date: August 16, 2010.
7. Ibid.
8. "Iwata Asks: New Super Mario Bros. Wii; The Reason Mario Wears Overalls," n.d.; available online: http://us.wii.com/iwata_asks/nsmb/vol1_page2.jsp; access date: August 16, 2010.
9. "Interview: Shigeru Miyamoto," *Edge*, June 2, 2010; available online: www.next-gen.biz/features/interview-shigeru-miyamoto; access date: August 18, 2010.
10. "Miyamoto's Message to Everyone," July 19, 2002; available online in Japanese: access date: www.nintendo.co.jp/nom/0208/sms_miya/index.html; access date: August 28, 2010.
11. Yuri Kageyama, "Video Wiz All Business Entertainment," Associated Press, April 21, 1997; available online: http://articles.latimes.com/1997-04-21/business/fi-50844_1_best-video-game; access date: August 28, 2010.
12. Ibid.
13. David M. Ewalt, "The Superstars of Video Gaming," *Forbes*, December 14, 2006; available online: www.forbes.com/2006/12/10/bestselling-video-games-tech-cx_de_games06_1212franchise.html; access date: August 28, 2010.
14. "Miyamoto: The Interview," CVG, November 27, 2007; available online: www.computerandvideogames.com/article.php?id=176422; access date: August 16, 2010.

15. Laura Evenson, "Zelda Develops Character," *San Francisco Chronicle,* May 30, 1998; available online: http://articles.sfgate.com/1998-05-30/entertain ment/17721972_1_shigeru-miyamoto-virtual-world-game-business; access date: August 18, 2010.
16. Nintendo Corporate Management Policy Briefing, p. 3, n.d.; available online: www.nintendo.co.jp/kessan/060607qa_e/index.html; access date: August 18, 2010.
17. Steven Kent, "Steven Kent Discusses Miyamoto and Online Gaming," *Chicago Tribune,* March 25, 2002; available online: www.nintendoworld report.com/news/7177; access date: August 18, 2010.
18. Nintendo Corporate Management Policy Briefing, p. 3, n.d.; available online: www.nintendo.co.jp/kessan/060607qa_e/index.html; access data: August 18, 2010
19. "Nintendo Creates New Game Plan," *Nihon Keizai Shimbun,* March 1, 2004.
20. Hasan Ali Almaci and Heidi Kemps, "Interview: Shigeru Miyamoto," The Next Level, August 20, 2004; available online: www.the-nextlevel.com/ feature/interview-shigeru-miyamoto/; access date: August 16, 2010.
21. Ewalt, "The Superstars of Video Gaming."

CHAPTER 4

The Console Wars

N INTENDO HAS SET ASIDE A SMALL CORNER OF AN undistinguished office building in Tokyo's Asakusabashi district to display the hardware and software benchmarks of its low- and high-tech history. It covers the period until the handover from Hiroshi Yamauchi to Satoru Iwata, although without mention of either man. The company has no public showroom or product chronology at its Kyoto headquarters, and this meager arrangement in one of the most drab corners of the nation's capital is almost its only Japanese landmark—offering a few physical clues about the company's entertainment origins in *hanafuda* cards, along with its later history in software and hardware until the first years of the new century.

At this site, possibly never seen or endorsed by Yamauchi, the centerpiece of the dusty display is the console that proved Nintendo's most unsuccessful ever: the GameCube, with its empty boxes lining the room like Santa's undelivered gifts. They create a sense of where time could have brought down Nintendo had it not found a new path, and underscore the point that Yamauchi never expected a wing at the Smithsonian as a maker of kids' games—and found little merit in building or curating one himself.

The arc of advancement from the most basic devices was driven both by Nintendo's stable of developers and parts suppliers, which created new and more sophisticated CPUs, screens, and essential components, and by fierce global competition and consumer market demand. From Gunpei Yokoi's tiny timekeeping Game & Watch (G&W) consoles in 1980, Nintendo battled in an industry often known for its fighting games in what was dubbed "the Console Wars," with winners occasionally declared but victory laps short and apt to prove embarrassing.

The G&W units, the oldest items in the Tokyo showroom—with the exception of the card and board games preserved in a nod to the era before battery-powered fun—were small handheld LCD screen devices. Their most notable feature is the D-Pad, a cross-shaped controller that gradually eliminated the joystick and became for gaming what the mouse is for the personal computer. Nintendo ultimately developed about 60 different G&W versions.

Yokoi, a Kyoto native and electronics graduate of its Doshisha University, became the revered godfather to a generation of techno-tinkerers who helped Nintendo slowly evolve into a company with a new artisan class. The son of a pharmaceutical factory owner, Yokoi started in Nintendo's card division in 1965 as a maintenance engineer, a period after the Tokyo Olympics when the fall in demand for playing cards had become obvious and Nintendo's future much less so. His first job was to maintain assembly line machines, a mundane task that gave him time to ponder new creations.

ULTRA-HAND

One of those, the "Ultra-Hand," a product initially not intended for sale, was spotted by Yamauchi on a factory tour, sent to retailers at a price of about $6, and ultimately became a million-selling toy in Japan by around 1970. Yokoi later took over the company's oldest product design department, Nintendo's Research & Development 1 team, the heart of the group—eventually including three divisions—that created the company's most enduring games and hardware.

The raft of gadgets Yokoi and his team designed included a "Love Tester," a miniature vacuum cleaner, a baseball-throwing machine, an electric bongo drum, and a cube puzzle that predated Rubik's Cube.

Collaboration with one of his first recruits, Masayuki Uemura, who had joined from Sharp Corporation, helped set a new road for the company with the more advanced "Beam Gun." Yokoi and Uemura (who had been selling solar cells to Nintendo) rode the product's success, leading a migration toward more sophisticated software and arcade game production and ultimately helping push Nintendo from making games for other companies to working on its own business.

A central philosophy employed by the teams was the use of mature technologies to make inexpensive products in new ways, such as the Game & Watch console with its tiny but effective LCD screen. The finished products, under a theme of affordable fun, were often unpretentious and surprisingly capable, considering the price and technology of the day. They owed their origins to Yokoi's call for "lateral thinking of withered technologies," which made "retro" cool and profitable long before its time.

The G&W's rudimentary directional pad allowed movement change with minimal effort; the D-Pad remained a staple of portable consoles through the 1980s. G&W, meanwhile, becomes home to many of Nintendo's top characters, such as Mario and Zelda, and particularly its own Mr. Game & Watch. Its later screen, no longer employing LED simplicity, lent itself to more complex games and graphics, including basic human representation, while using less battery power.

Before the G&W console series reached obsolescence, even a multiscreen handheld was produced, a development more than 15 years ahead of its time. In later years, fans of the series could play a reissued G&W Gallery game on a handheld console, recognition of the team's pioneering work and the first of many updates. Yokoi's impact grew with the console's success, while he also produced the Metroid game series, which began in 1986 and landed shortly before his hardware masterpiece came to market.

GAME BOY

Game Boy, the cartridge-based handheld console first previewed for Yamauchi in 1987, was unveiled in the company's centennial year, a defining moment when the game industry turned from novelty to

Gunpei Yokoi's long-lived Nintendo Game Boy handheld console (1989).

ubiquity. Its April 1989 launch was backed by the game "Tetris," which proved a global gold mine, while its Methuselah-like longevity became a startling phenomenon in an industry infamous for short attention spans.

As it set sales records, Game Boy bowled over technologically superior handheld offerings from competitors, such as Atari and Sega, with Yokoi's vision of affordable fun going for under $50. Its 2.6-inch display, a 160x144-pixel LCD screen with admittedly bland colors, could run for 30 hours on two AA batteries.

Yokoi had engineered longer battery life and mobility, while Nintendo and other software makers supplied innovative games that would be the company's financial backbone even after he left the firm. In 11 years, sales topped 100 million consoles, while its appeal included simplicity, utility, and a surprisingly low price that one reviewer said made it both a game and a console.

Virtual Boy

Numerous tweaks occurred over the console's long run, such as Game Boy Brothers in 1994 and Virtual Boy in 1995, which aimed at creating 3D-like visuals through single-color technology. However, it was Yokoi's Virtual Boy that ultimately came to be seen as flawed as well as short of complementary software, leading to poor sales in Japan and a quick scrapping even before its global debut.

Some gamers even complained of nausea after playing, and even with three decades at Nintendo, Yokoi decided to resign on August 15, 1996. He quickly started his own Kyoto firm, Koto Laboratory, saying he would design and develop on a smaller scale. His future looked bright, given his track record of billions of dollars in game sales already and a devout following of juniors, or *kohai,* still at Nintendo, but it was not to be. Yokoi's life tragically ended when he was killed in an automobile accident on October 7, 1997, at the age of 56.

Impact

After Yokoi's death, Nintendo released later versions of the console, starting with the Game Boy Color, a radical overhaul of the flagship that truly added color and even greater battery life, but it was his call for satisfaction from the gaming experience that carried the greatest weight. Hiroshi Yamauchi said Game Boy's long success was not due to bells and whistles but to software, which—as Yokoi had noted throughout his career—had to be entertaining.

"Pokemon, which ran on an 8-bit machine carrying far less memory than PlayStation 2, was the world's top-selling software last year," Yamauchi said. "Sophisticated features, such as beautiful visuals and heart-stopping sounds, are not what gamers are really looking for. They just want to have fun."[1]

The Game Boy Advance, near the final chapter in Yokoi's epic hardware line, was unveiled in August 2000 and released in March 2001, pushing processing firepower to 32 bits with a screen that was 50 percent larger. It was priced under $100 and saw an initial release of a million units with 10 game titles. While basically without handheld rivals, some analysts saw the Advance as a warmed-over version of earlier Nintendo consoles, with unexceptional and more expensive game titles, and they wondered if the company was losing its way on all hardware fronts.

Advance was 17 times as fast as its predecessor and offered some 32,000 colors on its screen. Compared with larger TV-linked consoles, costs to make software for Game Boy were still low—only about $600,000, while PlayStation 2 games could run up to $3 million—although pricier than their predecessors.

Thus, some consumers would buy cheaper Game Boy Color titles and play them on the Advance, taking advantage of the new console's ability to offer four-person play. One Advance application allowed conversion of the handheld console into a musical instrument for jam sessions or musical composition, a technology not finding greater utility until later in the decade, when Nintendo hardware doubled as band kit.

Supporting Nintendo's still-nascent attempt at e-gaming, the Advance also had the ability for wireless downloads, mobile phone messages, or even e-mail, as well as linking to the GameCube. The intent was to allow children, or even some adults, playing outside the home to upload a game in progress from their handheld consoles to the TV-linked box on their return.

Game Boy took a turn for the small in 2005, with the release of the Micro, a mini-console weighing less than three ounces, playing Advance games with a near 10-hour battery life, and selling for under $100. However, the company was already focused on promoting its latest handheld console, figuring that device would expand the number of consumers as the Micro could not.

FAMICOM

For the large consoles, Nintendo found great success from the early 1980s with Uemura's line of television-linked hardware. Uemura, who grew up in Kyoto during World War II and attended the Chiba Institute of Technology, eventually headed the Research & Development 2 group, which focused on hardware and created the landmark Nintendo Family Computer, as well as the Super Nintendo Family Computer console.

Nintendo released the Japanese-nicknamed "*Famicom*" in July 1983, and the console rode its hit "Super Mario Bros." software to become an 8-bit mega-success. The hardware, which arrived on store shelves as Coleco and Mattel products were exciting the market, ran on a cartridge that was externally controlled and used a CPU and a picture processing unit that pushed its video, graphics, and sound output to connected TVs.

Yamauchi negotiated a rock-bottom chip deal with Kyoto-based Ricoh that made mass production as well as reasonable cost possible. At just under ¥10,000, or around $100, consumers were also plugged in. After torrid sales in Japan—2.5 million units—its overseas launch became the cornerstone of a U.S. marketing onslaught from 1985. It helped that the Nintendo Entertainment System received a rare guarantee to worried retailers that unsold consoles would be bought back.

Ultimately, Nintendo did not have to make good on the promise, as strong demand made all the playing card sales of the first 96 years pale in

The 8-bit Nintendo Entertainment System, known as the "Famicon" in Japan (1983/1985).

Source: Public domain.

comparison. By the time the "*Famicom*" was officially mothballed in 1994, some 700 NES games and over 500 million software units had been sold.

Even with a rather primitive two kilobytes of video memory, NES games and nostalgia continued over the ensuing years. A recent auction of an NES console with the rare 1987 game "Stadium Events" was purchased for over $13,000, a more fitting approximation of worth and user devotion than Nintendo's own Asakusabashi showroom.[2]

An upgrade came in 1990 with the 16-bit Super Famicom, also known as the Super NES. Nintendo had eschewed higher power with the NES, keeping CPU memory low to conserve costs. Still, Nintendo sold 62 million NES consoles across the world without pushing the technological envelope, allowing it to control about 90 percent of the global video game market, estimated then at about $13 billion. However, other consoles, particularly those from Sega, were gaining on the industry leader.

Uemura's Super Famicom, replete with "Super Mario World" and other games, doubled processing speed and saw demand continue to skyrocket. However, the hard-charging Sega (with its Genesis console) grabbed half of the gaming pie by 1993, later to be replaced by Sony, which again changed the market dynamics with its PlayStation franchise.

The Super NES, or Super Famicom (1990).
Source: Pixel8, Wiki Commons.

Uemura retired in 2003, a few years after the GameCube's release, to teach digital entertainment at Ritsumeikan University in Kyoto, while also working as an adviser to Nintendo. On leaving the company at the age of 59, Uemura said he never liked working on computers, but at Nintendo he had no choice, adding that his new focus on entering academia would be his former profession: "My greatest interest is finding out why 'Famicom' sold so well. Solving the problem is my lifetime challenge."[3]

Historically, the answer was software, with "Mario," "Zelda," "Pokemon," and "Tetris" all undeniably essential. Consoles—big and small, stationary and mobile, one-player and multiplayer, cartridge-based and SD card-driven, mega-hits and mega-flops—would come and go, but a great game or iconic character had real industry longevity.

Nonetheless, consoles remained the benchmark for technological advances in the industry—and a company's financial position in it. Until Nintendo actually followed its own call to focus on software first and hardware second, its position continued to be threatened.

NINTENDO 64

Nintendo Research & Development 3 Chief Genyo Takeda said the Nintendo 64 (N64) console, developed in the 1990s in cooperation with Silicon Graphics and offering twice the processing power of the PlayStation (PS), had been like asking "game creators to make their feet fit [our] shoes." Originally titled "Ultra 64," the console confounded as well as amazed with a CPU dubbed a "Reality Co-Processor," and some industry-watchers said it suffered because of an emphasis on quality over quantity in the more expensive cartridge-based system, which had storage issues that other rival CD-ROM consoles did not.

"When we developed the Nintendo 64, the thought was that software development for games would naturally become more difficult," he said.

"When we made Nintendo 64, we thought it was logical that if you wanted to make advance games, it becomes technically more difficult.

The Nintendo 64, named for its 64-bit CPU (1996).

We were wrong," he said. "We now understand that it's the cruising speed that matters, not the momentary flash of power."[4]

Nintendo had sold more N64 consoles in four months after its debut in 1996 than the upstart PS in a year, but the cost of game production had pushed away independent developers, such as Square, which later made the hit "Final Fantasy" for Sony. Shigeru Miyamoto, whose 3D "Super Mario" title for the console became a major hit with over 11 million games sold, did not pull any punches about the console:

"In each aspect of N64, we found difficulty," he said. "People are putting so much energy into giving games beautiful appearances and boosting the high-performance of the hardware, but unfortunately they are too busy to work on something that is more important—the creative side of the matter."[5]

Other games—"The Legend of Zelda: Ocarina of Time," Rare's "GoldenEye 007," and "Wave Race 64"—found enthusiastic audiences, but without a broad software stable overall, consumers bought Sony's PS and its games, often $20 less expensive. N64 would eventually sell about 33 million consoles, but its software-to-hardware sales ratio was low; it simply had too few games to drive a virtuous cycle of demand.

The industry was shifting from cartridges to chip-based software loaded on CD-ROM discs, as it was less expensive, reduced risk if games proved unpopular—as many had endured with earlier technological upgrades, and ultimately could provide more content storage. Nintendo had missed the trend, or rather had assumed it would always set the trend. By the time the Kyoto firm added a "double-drive" (also called a "bulky drive") to accommodate N64's more complex games, the console's days were numbered and Nintendo's market share was ebbing further.

Takeda had hoped to offset the N64's difficulties with the introduction of the GameCube, again bringing in designers from Silicon Graphics, many of whom had worked on the earlier console and were acutely aware of its failings.

"We told them, 'Let's achieve what we could not do with Nintendo 64,'" he said.[6]

WHEN IN ROMANIA

Takeda, credited with designing Nintendo's first game (the 1975 "EVR Race," a horse-racing arcade title using videotape), was born in Osaka in 1949. As a child, he created miniature toys and vehicles, later taking his growing interest in technology to Shizuoka Government University, where he studied the first wave of semiconductors.

Takeda answered a Nintendo newspaper advertisement, and after interviewing with Yokoi, he joined the team and worked with Uemura as they planned the great console onslaught of the next 20 years. He quickly rose to become general manager of Nintendo's Research & Development 3 team, overseeing technical development for arcade and home consoles for the next three decades, as well as a limited production of titles such as "Sheriff" in 1979 and the two-screen "Punch Out!!" in 1983.

Takeda's team was often charged with designing the chips in cartridges or technologies that would make other R&D teams' consoles more functional and user-friendly or their software more compelling. His development of supplemental memory allowed early games to be continued even when power was cut off or their cartridges were removed from the consoles.

The division, nicknamed "Romania" for its isolation from other parts of Nintendo, was renamed the Integrated Research and Development group in 2000. At that point, Takeda was placed in charge of introducing the new console, to be called GameCube, in August that year at a private industry event in Japan. Along with 128 bobbing Marios, one for each processing bit in its system, Takeda extolled the new console's merits while apologizing with "reflective regret" for the N64, saying the focus was now on game play.

The main aim behind the new console's development, with the code name "Dolphin," was to create a hardware platform that made it easy for developers to write cutting-edge games, bringing the best of high-tech to Japan. Using an IBM Gekko CPU, Matsushita's optical game disk, and 3D

The ill-fated GameCube, Nintendo's worst-selling large console (2001).

graphics from Artix Inc., NEC fabricated an existing chip that contained
SRAM-embedded memory. Nintendo was so enthused with luring IBM
to join its console team that the "Big Blue" logo was stamped on the
GameCube box.

"It shows we have the best technology in the world," said Takeda.[7]

The one-transistor SRAM (from MoSys Inc.) increased system performance over traditional six-transistor models and simplified code
requirements to write games. SRAM technology had earlier been used
with the main memory for the NES and Super NES consoles. N64 and
other consoles had used DRAM chips as the main memory source, but
designers found that game performance was not optimal because of issues
such as latency, or the time between commands and performance. Takeda
said DRAM chips actually caused developers to write code for lower-level
performance to ensure real-time functionality.

The SRAM chip cut latency to less than 10 nanoseconds for memory
operations, in the hope that it would expedite game production. However,
some analysts noted that the small disc capacity could cap its utility, while
proprietary storage technology for games stopped short of early plans to
offer standard-size 12-cm DVD functionality, despite an earlier plan with
Matsushita to do so.

DAY OF THE DOLPHIN

Nintendo said the console's small 8-centimeter disc, which was not called
a DVD, was a proprietary format to prevent piracy, while Takeda made
his own prognostication that the format would have lasting utility as
Nintendo broached the digital convergence question.

"When you consider the merging of TV and games in the home,
we are confident that this fashionably-sized disc will lead the way for
entertainment in the 21st Century, and become the *de-facto* standard
size," he said.[8]

However, as with the N64, Nintendo shortly thereafter announced a
delay in GameCube's release in Japan and the United States, while the new

disc never rewrote the components handbook. Other factors such as the lack of initial Internet Wi-Fi connectivity also chilled interest. Nintendo's view at the GameCube launch was that more options for users repre-sented greater competition—and less time spent on gaming, although the console did have SD card slots through the link-up with Matsushita, ports that could be connected to high-speed broadband networks, as well as a cable to connect with the Advance.

Yet without absolutely compelling software, GameCube was fighting to avoid third place among major consoles and certainly had not become the intended panacea for Nintendo's fortunes. Consumers quickly came to see GameCube as a toy, not a next-generation console worth the intense R&D investment that had gone into its creation.

Nintendo's CEO Satoru Iwata, looking at poor year-end season results in 2002, was already touting the next generation of consoles to come from the company, the earliest perhaps by 2004. No immediate code names were given to the future products, but sobering statistics for GameCube—missing its sales target by a million boxes and its software sales falling below a goal of 55 million units—made their arrival imperative.

HAND-TO-HAND COMBAT

A new front had emerged with Sony's intention to challenge Nintendo's handheld dominance, with its PlayStation Portable (PSP) set to debut in 2004 and open a new front in the console wars. Portable machines made up 50 percent of Nintendo's operating profits in 2002, and the prospect of an end to its uncontested dominance was another reason for Nintendo to find a game-changer soon. However, Iwata, flashing rare confidence and composure for a young company president, said he was merely apprecia-tive of Sony's heads-up on the PSP development.

"People ask me, 'Are you worried?' That kind of questioning troubles me most," he said in early 2003. "We should be thankful that Sony has given us such a long notice—one year and a half ahead of the launch—

so we can make preparations, if necessary," he said, admitting Nintendo had already started work on its next handheld model. "This new console must have some seeds of surprise—unprecedented surprise—for the game player."[9]

The PSP, equipped with MP3 and portable video players, would ultimately be larger and heavier than the Game Boy Advance, and forecasts that the console had 3D delivery technology for games that had not yet been created would prove premature. Launched in Japan in December 2004, the Universal Media Disc–based console was dubbed the "Walkman of the 21st Century" by Sony Computer Entertainment President Ken Kutaragi.

The console wars may have again expanded to the handheld front, but as Iwata had predicted, this time Nintendo was far better prepared to hold its market share and compete ferociously, and the PSP would not allow Sony to claim the portable console crown when it finally landed in U.S. stores in March 2005.

Separately, Nintendo—not necessarily in a sign of desperation—had entered the Chinese market, a source of software counterfeiting woes but now seen as a potentially huge sales and manufacturing center. Its initial focus would be on less-sophisticated machines and software, some of which derived from the earlier N64 console and games.

Pirated software and consoles notoriously existed in China, but Nintendo had already used the country as a manufacturing center. Its sales entry was thus a first official shot across the bows by a major console maker, as the battlefront now spread to China. Nintendo introduced its new console, the iQue Player, in October 2003, selling for about $60.

The iQue Player was marketed through Chinese retailers with Mandarin-language games distributed via the Internet and loaded onto flash memory cards at the stores. The joint venture, capitalized at about $30 million in a deal with former Silicon Graphics Vice President Wei Yen, had an operational base in Suzhou, home to Nintendo's software manufacturing in the country. Yen had worked on both N64 and GameCube development with Nintendo.

"We have targeted people in developed countries such as Japan, the U.S., and Europe with sophisticated machines," Iwata said. "To reach a wide range of people in China, especially those inland who are not as rich as those in coastal areas, we thought we needed to deliver a cheaper console,"[10] with the nation's online gaming market then estimated as being worth only $250 million.

CUBED

Iwata announced the move just hours after cutting the GameCube's U.S. price by $50 to $99 ahead of the holiday season, as console demand faltered further. Nintendo had earlier in the year halted GameCube production due to a backlog of unsold stock.

By 2004, GameCube was the No. 2 console in Japan, mainly because of Microsoft's only half-hearted efforts in the home country of its rivals, while Nintendo was bringing up the rear in North America. Iwata blamed the GameCube's release delay, while promising that Nintendo's next handheld would be special.

GameCube's "biggest shortcoming was that we were late in launching," he told industry-watcher *GameSpy* in 2004. "Because of that delay, our competitors were able to create a large install base for their consoles, and even though it was easier for software developers to create games for GameCube, because of the delay . . . in the end, we could not match that advantage.

"In the future, we may be able to combine the technologies of Game Boy and GameCube in a unit that will be small and light, with a long-enough battery life and a low-enough price for the market. Competition is tougher than ever before, and in the short run, we have seen declining profitability."[11]

Some investors and analysts still expected Nintendo to follow Sega and exit the hardware business, but the company's very deep pockets—more than $6.5 billion in cash—offered latitude that Sega never could enjoy.

SEGA'S SAGA

Sega had taken aim at Nintendo in the early 1990s and won substantial allegiance with a line of cutting-edge consoles and games. Entering the 8-bit world with the Sega Master System in 1986, and then the Genesis in 1989, Sega saw its market share rise dramatically in North America by 1993.

Then the PlayStation hit Japanese store shelves, while Sega's Saturn console in 1995 proved unsuccessful. Its high-resolution GD-ROM Dreamcast console debuted 12 months before Sony's PS2, but soon was in its shadow. Increasingly tighter financial constraints prevented a rollout commensurate with the Dreamcast's technical capabilities as an online console. In addition, certain game makers, such as Electronic Arts, did not make titles for Dreamcast, a crucial reluctance that developers blamed on its complicated design architecture. They were also waiting for the console to become a hit before investing in the project.

Dreamcast was shut down before a possible software rescue.

One story about its demise involves Sony's Kutaragi, who is said to have demonstrated his upcoming PS2 for Sega boss Isao Okawa. Okawa had made the earlier Saturn and then the Dreamcast consoles his personal projects in a sworn battle against rival Sony, pumping in half of the Dreamcast's launch cost of $820 million by himself. Shortly after the meeting with Kutaragi and Okawa's look at the PS2's bells and whistles, and coupled with a less-than-vigorous year-end sales effort, Sega pulled the plug on its console business in January 2001, later reporting a $435 million loss and axing a third of its Japanese staff.

Okawa died in March 2001 of heart failure, having only come back to the company the previous June as official boss to try to stave off greater woes. Before his death, his CSK Corporation was Sega's largest shareholder, and he donated $692 million in stock back to the firm when Dreamcast production was discontinued to help soften the blow.

Sega was later purchased by game and *pachinko* slot maker Sammy in 2004 in a $1.1 billion controlling stake deal, with joint Chairman Hajime Satomi overseeing an initial staff of 50 employees on completion of the merger.

KING OF THE HILL

Sony's rise had been rapid after spending $600 million in initial production costs in the 1990s. The original PlayStation's clever design and broad software support, including exclusive publisher deals, as well as its own disc-based games, took it to the top of the gaming heap. Nintendo quickly cut the cost of its software and advertised heavily, but Sony gobbled up market share, which it did not cede through the second-generation PS2.

Sony's game disc format had allowed greater cost-cutting freedom, and despite Nintendo's cries that this was flooding the market with cheap, low-level software, in the battle of quantity and quality, consumers were speaking with their wallets. Kutaragi said the secret of Sony's profitability had been making its own memory chips, but this was a technological avenue that ultimately involved spending billions of dollars in the hope that the in-house semiconductors could one day be used across the spectrum of the company's consumer electronic products.

Financial results had become so strong and market share so solid that Sony Computer Entertainment U.S. President Kazuo Hirai was prompted to declare to hundreds of industry executives and PS2 fans at a Los Angeles movie studio: "Officially, the console wars are over."[12]

Sony, like other companies before it, would come to rue that pronouncement. Nintendo was not ready to surrender the flag, Microsoft was slowly finding its way, and difficulties at the Japanese consumer electronics monolith had begun to emerge very publicly.

The "transition" period—when console makers in near uniformity phases in their next-generation consoles—had started, and software makers and retailers were making assumptions about continued sales of older units and the space and resources needed to sell the new ones. The three-decade fight was about to swing Nintendo's way again, while Sony was about to stumble in nearly every facet of its business.

"Nintendo is working on its next-generation system," Iwata said in April 2004. "What Nintendo is currently discussing is not about state-of-the-art technology for enhancing processing power, but what I,

Miyamoto-*san*, and Takeda-*san* are discussing is what should be done to entertain people in a new way."[13]

For Sony and the now over $30 billion industry, Nintendo's new entertainment would change the game. Sony's ultimately unsuccessful attempt to hold the industry crown is the topic of the next chapter. In brief, Sony ultimately found itself knocked from its top hardware perch, where it had enjoyed a 5-to-1 advantage, while it was also plagued by a string of hardships across many of its consumer electronic businesses. In its more than five years as console leader, and decades more as the flag bearer for Japan Inc., Sony had developed a hubris that was set to be humbled.

"There is a place for other consoles, and that happens to be the rear-view mirror," Sony's Hirai told an E3 industry audience in 2003.[14] This was a year after Sony had declared the "console wars" officially over after leading the industry for two generations of hardware.

However, in what would prove to a prescient reply for both Nintendo and his own Microsoft as they began to seriously challenge Sony, J Allard countered:

"Objects in the rear-view mirror may be closer than they appear."

NOTES

1. "Nintendo to Unveil Game Boy," Reuters, March 19, 2001.
2. Mike Smith, "Old Nintendo System Sells for $13,105," Yahoo: Plugged In, February 10, 2010; available online: http://videogames.yahoo.com/events/plugged-in/old-nintendo-system-sells-for-13-105/1389101; access date: August 28, 2010.
3. "Nintendo Mastermind Enters World of Academia," *Nikkei Weekly*, March 10, 2003.
4. "It's Hip to be Square: Nintendo Unveils its GameCube", P2, September 4, 2000; available online: www.newsweek.com/2000/09/03/it-s-hip-to-be-square.html; access date: August 29, 2010.
5. Steven Kent, "Zelda Creator Talks GameCube," Shigeru Miyamoto, September 24, 2000, MSNBC Interview transcript; available online: www

.zdnet.com/news/zelda-creator-talks-gamecube/110669; access date: August 19, 2010.

6. Yoshiko Hara, "Designers Bring Practical Touch to GameCube," *EE Times,* September 7, 2000. Available online: www.eetimes.com/electronics-news/4163480/Designers-bring-practical-touch-to-GameCube; access date: August 28, 2010.

7. Spencer E. Ante, "IBM Isn't Cashing In Its Chips," *Business Week,* September 17, 2001; available online: www.businessweek.com/magazine/content/01 _38/b3749103.htm; access date: August 19, 2010.

8. "Nintendo's GameCube Will Launch in July, Using 8cm Disc," *DVD Report* 5, no. 34 (2000; available on Factiva).

9. Kim Peterson, "Q&A: Nintendo Exec Shrugs Off Sony's Talk," *Seattle Times,* May 16, 2003; available online: www.gamecritics.com/forums/showthread. php?t=3794&page=3; access date: August 19, 2010.

10. "Nintendo to Enter China's Video Game Market with a New Console," Bloomberg, September 23, 2003; available online: www.bloomberg .com/apps/news?pid=newsarchive&sid=a1xe1_OtjGFA;accessdate:August 28, 2010.

11. Steven L. Kent, "Nintendo's New Direction," *GameSpy,* April 11, 2004, p. 5; available online: www.gamespy.com/articles/505/505234p1.html; access date: August 28, 2010.

12. Ben Berkowitz, "Sony Out to Claim Victory as the Game Giants Battle," Reuters, May 22, 2002.

13. Steven L. Kent, "Ninendo's New Direction," *GameSpy,* April, 2004, p. 5; available online: www.gamespy.com/articles/505/505234pl.html; access data: August 28, 2010.

14. Dean Takahashi, "Firms' Rivalry Is Gamers' Gain," *Pioneer Press,* May 19, 2003 (available on Factiva).

CHAPTER 5

The Sony Shock

T HE FIRST DECADE OF THE NEW MILLENNIUM saw a tremendous change in fortunes for Nintendo, and these developments were magnified by the humbling of its main rival. No success or failure occurs in a vacuum, and this chapter attempts to trace the rise and fall of Sony's dominance, after almost a decade at the top, to put the Nintendo story in perspective.

Sony—founded by Akio Morita and Masaru Ibuka in 1946—had long been the literal image of Japan's cutting-edge manufacturing and innovation. It was home to a growing library of films and music, and it had stormed to the front of the game industry by the late 1990s on the back of its PlayStation franchise.

Sony's entry into the video game arena had actually been in partnership with Nintendo. A joint venture around the beginning of the 1990s looked to combine the potentially superior graphic capabilities of Sony's proprietary CD-ROM drive with the 16-bit Super Nintendo Entertainment System console. Nintendo later walked away from the arrangement in disagreement on how royalties would be collected, instead joining forces with Philips to make a console CD-ROM drive that never left the launch pad, and—ultimately—remaining with a cartridge-based system long past its heyday.

The break in relations between the Japanese giants was followed by legal fireworks and President Norio Ohga's declaration that Sony would never walk away from the video game business. That decision was far from rash, but neither was it popular within a company priding itself on production of highly engineered consumer electronics.

Ohga, who had been selected by Morita, had to override board protest to proceed with what would become the tremendously popular and profitable PlayStation (PS) franchise. Despite that resistance, the console quickly won allegiance from software designers due to Sony's attractive profit-sharing arrangements, as well as some 4,000 development tools. Once launched in the mid-1990s, the PS quickly became a key profit center for the conglomerate, intended to lead its other business silos toward the 21st century in a process eventually dubbed "vertical integration."

Initial marketing of the PS kept the Sony brand at arm's length, as some within the company still saw the product as a toy that would have no image cachet for its TVs or electronics hardware. Eventually, though, Sony fully embraced video games and made the PS a lifestyle accessory found in living rooms as well as kids' bedrooms. Sony's executive vice president for development, Phil Harrison, said the game industry and consumers had been waiting for an upgrade in technology and links to other products.

"The market was dominated by two aggressive competitors: Sega and Nintendo. Although both companies had done a great job growing the market, it was still effectively a toy business and there were real commercial and technical issues with the cartridge-based business model they had adopted," he said. "The industry was extremely supportive of our attempts to bring new thinking."[1]

Some PS gamers, or those marketing to them, would later brand their demographic the "PlayStation Generation," a group some social scientists would also assert had traits bordering on dysfunction or maladjustment. Nonetheless, the appellation was mainly a touchstone for shared experiences via the 32-bit monster, Sony's most important product since the Walkman.

FATHER OF PLAYSTATION

Ken Kutaragi, the *enfant terrible* who led Sony's video game charge, joined the company in the mid-1970s, as gaming began to advance technically and dovetail with other products. He worked on a variety of hardware before the Nintendo project emerged, but with the launch of Sony Computer Entertainment (SCE) and its sales and marketing team, Kutaragi quickly had over 1,300 titles of generally lower-priced games in hand.

The PS sold one million hardware units in its first six months in Japan, while its first U.S. holiday season saw sales exceed 800,000 consoles in less than three months. By January 1996, Sony had sold some 3.6 million consoles, often to "early adopters" who cared little about its lack of pedigree and more about its 3D arcade feel and breadth of game choice.

Nintendo complained bitterly about the software deluge, saying low-quality games would lead to a repeat of the industry's earlier collapses. However, by 2002, more than 4,000 Sony titles existed and 120 million PS games had been sold, and Nintendo was struggling to mount a comeback—without eliciting much industry sympathy.

Kutaragi's strategy for profitability bypassed the company's traditional consumer electronics base, linking instead with software and hardware developers overseas and exacerbating his fights within Sony. The PS was sold at a loss, even at nearly $300 a console, which became another alarm bell for Sony executives, who were generally risk-averse except when it came to eye-popping movie studio purchases.

Ohga had created SCE as a joint venture with Sony's music arm to shelter Kutaragi's project internally and foster both units' disc procurement and audio aims. However, Nobuyuki Idei, who succeeded Ohga as Sony president in 1995, eventually dissolved the joint venture, bringing SCE back under the conglomerate's umbrella—now with billions of dollars in profit.

Sony aimed to own the home entertainment space, but had become fully reliant on the PS, and subsequent PS2, while investing $2.5 billion and tolerating a huge loss in the year 2000 from the new console. Sony's other products and the content in its arsenal—Vaio PCs, TVs, and Walkmans, as well as movies and music—would also be roped into the campaign, but success would depend on whether all the individual teams developing and manufacturing products could step outside their silos as the digital media era dawned.

That proved to be a huge and painful undertaking, and Kutaragi himself never fully embraced team play. He even took the stage at a meeting of hundreds of Sony executives in 1999 and advised senior management to resign: "The old boys should step aside to make way for the young."[2]

He also implied that Sony's headquarters was afflicted with Alzheimer's disease, but the Japanese gentry running the company—Idei, in particular—had to endure, beholden to Kutaragi and his backer, Ohga, knowing more than 70 percent of Sony's profits then came from game revenues. Late in the 1990s, Idei had encouraged talks with Microsoft about a possible gaming tie-up, but Kutaragi and CEO Bill Gates did not find common ground and each company went its own way, with the U.S. giant ultimately launching its own Xbox console.

PS2

Kutaragi's next-generation console, the 128-bit PS2 that had been code-named "Godzilla," yoked more of Sony's electronics expertise in the $299 product, including a DVD player and interconnectivity via an "emotion engine" chip. Initial supply problems—Sony only had 500,000 PS2 consoles for the October 2000 North American launch despite plans for one million and thousands of pre-orders—led to eBay auction prices exceeding $1,000, as well as frenzied year-end demand.

Kutaragi, born in 1950 as the son of a printing plant owner, had done little to quell the media hype, comparing the new console to a popular next-age film in a *Newsweek* cover story titled—not so subtly—"The Amazing PlayStation 2": "You can communicate to a new cyber city. This will be the ideal home server. Did you see the movie 'The Matrix'? Same interface, same concept. Starting from next year, you can jack into The Matrix!"[3]

His importance to Sony now fully established, Kutaragi continued to push the envelope of his boss's patience while cementing his game industry street credibility. If Miyamoto would be Nintendo's genius *"sarariman,"* Ken Kutaragi would become both Sony's bane and its savior.

"Synergy is 120 percent not my dream," he said. "Sony has Sony's agenda, but I want a very open platform, equal for every person."[4]

One element of equality was price, and by cutting the PS2 cost in 2002 to $199, as well as having a plethora of available games, Sony achieved sales of 50 million consoles by January 2003, and 100 million in 2006. It had more than 1,500 titles available for the backward-compatible PS2 within three years, a result of sending out over 10,000 development kits to software makers.

The PS2's tremendous success led some to believe Kutaragi was the next corporate answer for a company losing its way in traditional business lines, needing only Idei's blessing to become his successor. However, Idei was not convinced, telling the *Wall Street Journal* in November 2002: "If his personal ego is stronger than his will to keep Sony prosperous, then he will fail."[5]

The kinetic Ken declared with tremendous clairvoyance that the job was not for him. "My health would be ruined. Some people may find it interesting, but not me," he said.[6]

However, despite every politeness he dispensed with and every well-dressed company executive he insulted, Kutaragi had Sony in a hammerlock. The PS2's record sales only encouraged him to pour on the pressure, demanding that the conglomerate that had sanctioned his enterprise get its act together, in particular putting its engineering and entertainment divisions on the same page.

Managing

Idei's problems were piling up. Even though Kutaragi and Sony's gaming division weren't the cause, they hadn't been part of the solution either. Contemplating Kutaragi provided no balm for a CEO hoping to forget the day's troubles.

Idei, a French- and English-speaking career employee, was not a trained engineer—unusual in a company dominated by the profession. Rather, after joining Sony in 1960, he climbed to the top of the corporate ladder through business acumen and people skills. Handpicked by Ohga over 14 older managers for his marketing and international polish, as president Idei tried to make Sony a more media- and digitally-advanced company and, as with Kutaragi, had been emboldened by the PS franchise's success on his watch.

Yet the legacy of Sony's acquisition hubris was a $20 billion debt, albeit with a sizable content library and profitable studio business churning out such huge hits as *Spiderman* and *Men in Black,* as well as their sequels. Other dot-com media rivals, such as Gerald Levin's AOL Time Warner, Thomas Middelhoff's Bertelsmann AG, and Jean-Marie Messier's Vivendi Universal, had spent more money on Internet-related pursuits and fared poorly. Sony, instead, had been more focused on content and protection of intellectual property rights than on the Internet, although occasionally confused on how to prioritize, as with its music business.

Ohga continued to loom large in the background as Sony chairman, helping to shoot down Idei's plan to buy Apple Computer in the 1990s, and later torpedoing such deals as selling Sony Life to GE Capital in 2002, which would have raised needed funds. All such moves sent the message that his successor was not in charge. Meanwhile, Ohga offered undeniable support to Kutaragi despite his frequent insubordination, such as when he rejected an Idei emissary to the SCE unit, Masayuki Nozoe.

With few options, Idei decided to expedite internal management transition as problems intensified, selecting Kunitake Ando to be the company's next president, looking to address the woes of the consumer electronics division, in particular. Ando, known for his sense of humor, recognized Kutaragi's contributions but also the risks involved in managing a man who predicted gaming would take over Sony.

"Kutaragi is too much make-believe. I'm more realistic," said Ando, the man behind their Vaio personal computer.

Realism was essential for Sony now, as its downturn had first become tangible in a sliding share price, then in earnings reports showing it had been wallowing for some time in unprofitable business lines. All of this came to a crushing denouement as losses began to mount and competitors such as Samsung Electronics and Apple increasingly gobbled up its market share or beat it to the technological punch.

TRANSFORMATION 60

The internal crisis went public with "the Sony Shock" of April 2003, a stock plunge of 25 percent over two days that followed an unforeseen $1 billion quarterly loss. Investors cited the corporate bickering that had prevented Sony from utilizing its tremendous content library, as well as missed market trends (such as online music delivery) caused by an obsessive focus on its own technology, and—most damning for Idei—the perceived absence of a strong leader to rein in the multibillion-dollar goliath's many divisions.

To display such leadership, Idei and his team of executives announced 20,000 job cuts, with about a third lost in Japan as the company shuttered 30 percent of its factories and moved more production overseas. The aim of his post–Sony Shock plan, dubbed "Transformation 60" as the company's 60th anniversary loomed in 2006, was to cut more than $3 billion in costs by restructuring, efforts that would ultimately need repeated revisiting and refining over the decade.

With a push from the now officially "retired" Ohga, Idei tapped PS guru Kutaragi to lead Sony's electronics and semiconductor business, a move described as a trial run, but for what fate was uncertain. The 73-year-old Ohga had become honorary chairman three months earlier, when Sony announced a U.S.-style governance panel with outside directors.

Some 39 years earlier, Ohga had set up a product-planning group and design center, aimed at putting Sony's brand and technology in one box, a feat the company was finding difficult to manage or repeat now. On his way out the door, Ohga blasted those he had selected to follow him.

"Earnings have fallen due to a decline in profit margins, which is partly due to the management system led by three executives who are university graduates with liberal arts degrees," said the man who himself had graduated from the Tokyo National University of Fine Arts and Music.[7]

The opera-trained former president, whose 13-year run as Sony boss had seen sales triple to $45 billion, cited ill health as prompting the move; he had suffered a brain hemorrhage in November 2001, collapsing while conducting the Tokyo Philharmonic Orchestra in Beijing. Ohga's $13.5 million retirement package was donated to the Nagano Prefecture town of Karuizawa, known as a playground of Japan's elite, who would now have his pentagon-shaped Karuizawa Ohga Hall in which to enjoy music performances in comfort.

Idei, who had tried for years to right Sony's ship without success, pledged that operating profit margins would rise from 3 percent to 10 percent after his massive transformative effort, which would meld brand and business silos. However, Sony was still working on the pledge for the remainder of the decade, and Idei later backed away from the 10 percent margin figure, saying it was not a firm commitment but a guideline to improve corporate performance.

Most saw it as a goal that would—or could—never be met, as Sony margins wavered below 2 percent, a benchmark of its missing the digital convergence boat that it had once boasted of driving, despite a full cupboard of video and music content, as well as ample hardware at its disposal. The clock was ticking and Idei was running out of options, while even Sony's new video game consoles faced problems.

High Noon

Ohga's departure drew comment from Sony of America top executive Howard Stringer, an Idei loyalist. He said the moment was a chance for his boss to shine, an obvious implication that this had been denied him in the past. "At some time when you pick a CEO, you have to give him ultimate power," Stringer pointed out when still the relatively unknown head of Sony's U.S. entertainment business. "There are conservatives in the organization who say Idei is dangerous, but if there was ever a time for visionaries, this is the time."[8]

Vision had not stopped a 30 percent Sony share slide to a five-year nadir, while consumer electronics sales in the year ended in March had declined 6.5 percent. Video game sales then made up 61 percent of Sony's operating income, but even that cash cow was now under siege.

As part of his new title and duties, Kutaragi set out to yoke Sony's hardware with its gaming strategy. One of his first efforts emerged in 2003. The PSX, an omni-system designed for home entertainment domination, contained all the bells and whistles Sony could offer Japanese consumers: PS2, DVD, MP3, TV, and recording functionality. The company had hopes of a global launch. The world, however, was not ready for the 160- or 250-gigabyte PSX and its ¥80,000 (then $720) price.

Some of the consumer complaints in Japan were as mundane as having no TV antenna output jack, or that the DVD recording function was too slow and could not record directly from a television. An all-in-one console that Sony hoped to be the bridge to its next-generation PS3 became a precursor of its weaknesses.

Undaunted, in May 2003 Kutaragi turned his attention to Nintendo, which still dominated the handheld console space, impetuously announcing Sony's plan to create a portable unit. The PlayStation Portable (PSP) debuted 18 months later and was intended to be a body blow to its rival's increasingly fragile business position, but ultimately it glanced off target.

Released in December 2004, the PSP quickly sold 500,000 units in Japan due to its wireless capability and its high-quality video and audio. Many in the company saw the $250 PSP leapfrogging rivals in portable gaming, video, and music, even Apple's Steve Jobs complimented the console on its release.

It was Sony's attempt to knock the Game Boy—or even Nintendo's next handheld console—from the top of the pedestal or out entirely, but it sold at a higher price, which Kutaragi said reflected a more refined lineage and better multimedia capabilities.

"PlayStation and PS2 are like my sons," he said in October 2004. "PSP is a daughter with a different mother. . . . Game Boy is nice, but it's only for kids playing games. . . . We introduced this product to change the world."[9]

The PSP was initially made in Japan and later in China, and its real stepfather, Shinichi Ogasawara, designed the device to look nothing like a toy, while offering the same player mobility as with the Game Boy. Its 32-bit CPU and separate 32-bit "Media Engine" ran content using Sony's UMD, an optical disc format smaller than a DVD but capable of holding up to 1.8 gigabytes of memory. He said making the PSP as small as possible was essential, and that gamers were expected to become its main audience, using its Wi-Fi functionality to connect with each other, the Internet, and retailer Sony itself.

Kutaragi, seeing another Walkman with the handheld PSP, envisioned sales of three million units by the end of March 2005, then a trajectory of PS2-like numbers afterward. Idei, meanwhile, was in desperate need of a winning product.

"The PSP is an integration of the whole technology accumulated at Sony," Idei said, adding the potential flagship machine could process "anything that crosses your brain cells."[10]

Although the console reached its March 2005 sales target and lasted through the decade, it faced criticism for weak battery power, so that movies of more than two hours risked not reaching their conclusion. It was also criticized for its IP rights protection standards, which were so confining that they irked movie studios—including Sony's own. Gamers, meanwhile, said software titles were PS2 knock-offs that did not take advantage of the handheld's delivery capabilities.

Ultimately, the PSP earned the dubious distinction of becoming the most-successful handheld not made by Nintendo. By late 2006, Sony admitted that PSP sales had underperformed expectations, revising down the year forecast by three million consoles.

E-Dreams

Sony's electronics unit had focused so intently on proprietary technology that it had been slow to create content download services or even compatibilities within its own product line, as well as ignoring interoperability with other firms' platforms. At the same time, consumers rejected paying more just for the Sony name, eyeing a wealth of choices that either led—or barely lagged—the technological curve at lower cost.

Some of the groundswell for change came from analysts and investors who wondered how Sony products, such as its legendary Walkman or Bravia TVs—easily confused with its earlier high-end Qualia line that was discontinued by 2006—could become compelling, or even compete, as its MP3 music format and flat-panel TVs trailed miserably in sales to giants Apple and Samsung Electronics, respectively.

In a tacit admission that a proprietary rethink was needed, Ando even appeared at a Macworld event in January 2005 with Jobs to promote a new handheld Sony camcorder that was compatible with its rival's video-editing software. The appearance, though, only underscored the changing fortunes of the two companies, as the success of the iPod had made the Walkman seem like a product of another century—which indeed it was.

Early in 2005, another perfect storm of bad news blew in, expediting the end for Sony's embattled leaders, who promptly fell on their swords like disgraced feudal lords. A 31 percent drop in profit, caused by an ongoing price war for flat-screen TVs and poor year-end sales, brought Idei's tumultuous tenure, as well as that of his No. 2, Ando, to an abrupt end, along with that of several others.

Resistance within Sony's business silos had hastened their departures, only two years into a three-year plan to overhaul the sprawling conglomerate. Sales had fallen 5 percent below forecasts, slipping to the lowest level in five years at $68 billion.

Idei had intended to retire in 2006, on Sony's 60th anniversary, but the need for a corporate overhaul with extreme prejudice—as well as the likelihood of more red ink ahead—had put his "Transformation 60" in limbo. He called the man he had hired in 1997, Sir Howard Stringer, who was attending pre-Oscar parties with entertainment industry heavyweights in Los Angeles, with the news of his likely appointment as Sony's next boss.

SIR HOWARD

New leadership was deemed imperative to make Idei's vision reality. Morale at Sony, still the world's biggest consumer electronics company and home to some of the elite graduates of Japan, had fallen into a deep tailspin since its "Shock," with even more job cuts expected.

Along with the PS franchise, Sony's most profitable business had become entertainment, and thus it was not a major leap for the company to tap the foreign head of the unit responsible for its block-busters to lead the rest of company out of its protracted malaise. Stringer became that leader, taking the titles of chairman and chief executive, the first non-Japanese to hold the positions, though not the first non-engineer.

A naturalized American citizen who had spent the previous seven years running Sony's movie business, Stringer used a word in his Tokyo debut that would later become a clarion call on the political front, saying the Japanese company must "change," adding that restructuring alone would not lead to expansion.

"We would accelerate cross-company collaboration, thereby revitalizing the company and promoting creativity," he said. "Growth cannot be achieved just through cost reduction. We need new projects, new ideas, new strategies, new alliances, and a shared vision. All of our managers must have the authority and the will to manage."[11]

The major management shake-up, Idei's farewell play, was intended to show how serious Sony executives had become about its dire business conditions, as six senior leaders joined him in stepping down. But for many Japanese, what was most staggering about the transition was not the napalm strike on the leaders' own position, or even Stringer's nationality, but his mere seven years of service with Sony, compared to nearly 30 for Kutaragi.

In an interview published in April 2005, Stringer said he had not campaigned for the job. Instead, Idei had offered it to him because of a "new kind of widespread frustration" at Sony. "Whether I can harness that frustration constructively is really the question of the hour," he said.[12]

The foreign CEO strategy was not without precedent in Japan. It was a hopeful move, though it had not been universally successful. Nissan Motor, which Renault bought a third of in the 1990s as the Japanese carmaker flirted with insolvency, was now led by Carlos Ghosn, who took the embattled company to earnings recovery and ultimately record profits. Meanwhile, Rolf Eckrodt, CEO at Mitsubishi Motors Corporation (MMC), came to the helm after DaimlerChrysler invested in the automaker; he resigned in April 2004 as MMC was on the verge of collapse and the German investor had decided to end its support.

Ghosn was an outside director on the Sony board at the time of the leadership change announcement and opposed an initial Idei proposal to split the CEO position with another appointee, urging that it remain in one man's hands.

Stringer, 63, an ex-journalist born in Cardiff, Wales, had been a CBS media executive, once working as a producer for Dan Rather in a 30-year career that took him to the top of its news division. His background was multinational, multi-industry, and he may have been the only Oxford-trained Welshman to fight in the Vietnam War, as well as being knighted for his career in 1999.

After joining Sony and helping cement its entertainment links, Stringer and Chief Strategy Officer Robert Wiesenthal made a number of lucrative deals and investments, including merging Sony Music with Bertelsmann and acquiring MGM's movie library for $5 billion. They also launched a $700 million cost-cutting campaign before the "Shock" that had pared 9,000 jobs and trimmed the U.S. workforce by one-third, becoming a template for the restructuring that Idei tried to undertake.

Stringer quickly let it be known that Sony should prepare to endure the unendurable: "Sony is a kind, fair-minded, and intelligent company," he said. "But is it a tough company? It is time to find out."[13]

No Japanophile, Stringer was seen within Sony as someone capable of straddling both Hollywood and Tokyo, while achieving the company's aim of digital convergence. Selection of Stringer left Kutaragi, 54, once touted as a possible future leader of the conglomerate, off the radar.

A Better Listener

In a rare display of deference, Kutaragi was relatively quiet during the entire palace intrigue, which left him with the title of Sony Group executive officer but had essentially nixed any near-term chance to run the still powerful consumer electronics giant. Irascible and deemed responsible for at least some of the feuding among Sony's business teams, his demotion and exit from the corporate upper echelon elicited few tears, yet neither did the departures of Idei and Ando.

A second prize was also denied Kutaragi, and instead Ryoji Chubachi, an engineer focused on plant efficiency and comfortable with a low-profile approach, took the post of president. Chubachi had the job of turning around the electronics division, once responsible for 70 percent of Sony profit but now trailing other industry players such as Samsung, Panasonic, and Apple. When asked to compare Chubachi with Kutaragi, and implicitly why the latter had not earned the No. 2 slot at Sony, Idei said with no element of irony that Chubachi was a better listener.

Chubachi, from northern Japan, had spent nearly three decades at Sony managing its audio media technology, once running a Sony tape plant in Alabama. Stringer said early in his tenure that "Kutaragi-*san*" was very important to Sony, but the history and stark divide between the diplomat and maverick, as well as their supporters, left few expecting rapprochement in the near future, as the management makeover was intended to minimize troubles.

In comparison, Chubachi was deferent—if circumspect—in speaking about Kutaragi after the shakeup: "I respect him as an engineer," he said. "In the area of semiconductors, I consider him my teacher."[14]

In that vein, Kutaragi had inherited Sony's partnership with Toshiba and IBM to produce a next-generation "Cell" chip, committing $400 million over five years, not including the costs for factories to produce the marvel. The chip was intended to power more than the cutting-edge game consoles that the company had until then known only success with; it was scheduled to become the network link for all Sony's consumer products. Reports referred to the hoped-for marvel as a "supercomputer on a chip."

The key deadline to ensure that the next-generation PS3 console would debut before the year-end shopping season was autumn 2005. In the interim, Microsoft had contacted IBM about building a chip for its next Xbox 360 console. While still working with Sony, IBM sold the technology to Microsoft, meaning some of the Japanese firm's research and development money had ultimately been spent to aid a competitor.

Because of production delays, Microsoft received its chip before Sony, making the crucial November 2005 launch date for the Xbox 360 possible, while Kutaragi's team spent the holidays planning a spring debut and wondering what could befall the giant next.

By February, speculation mounted that Sony would also miss its 2006 target date, after Merrill Lynch analyst Joe Osha reported the delay could be as long as 6 to 12 months because of problems with Cell chip technology and the Blu-ray drive. The analyst also said production costs of the console could far exceed the announced $500 per unit, rising as high as $900, with the Cell alone costing over $230 at launch.

The technology that Sony had put so much faith in was potentially making its products prohibitively expensive, although Cell costs were estimated to decline to about $60 in three years. Manufacturing video game consoles at a loss was not new, but the size of the potential hit, the lateness of the PS3's delivery, and the technical issues weighing on the console again sparked a market sell-off.

Digital Convergence

Sony, the first Japanese company to list its stock on the New York Stock Exchange and one of the first to invite foreigners to sit on its board, was capitalized at about $72 billion at the time of the handover from Idei to Stringer, with foreign investors holding about one-third of its shares. Huge as this was, what people noticed was that during Idei's tenure, Sony's market capitalization had shrunk more than 60 percent. The firm—once twice the size of South Korean rival Samsung—had become less than half as valuable.

Some sector analysts greeted the new boss, who called himself a "Sony warrior," as an outsider who could implement the reforms and tough business decisions necessary for the conglomerate to right itself. Lehman Brothers hiked its price outlook for the stock, once seen as the bluest of Japanese blue chips, by 25 percent to ¥5,000, or a little over $50.

Some analysts believed that under Stringer, Sony needed to divide its content and electronics businesses into separate listed entities, potentially making their management—or sale—easier. To some degree, this was an East-versus-West proposal, with the Japanese company keeping the hardware business while selling off the Hollywood and music assets.

That did not occur, but by late September, Stringer had launched his own $2 billion cost-cutting plan, called "Sony United." He closed 11 of 66 plants, slashed 10,000 jobs of the then-150,000 global staff, and Japan again shouldered the largest share of soon-to-be-unemployed with 4,000 staff restructured. Some of those were retired executives who kept offices as paid advisers, while others were engineers who said the firm's turmoil reflected the growing divergence between being a leading technology company and an iconic global brand.

In September, Sony forecast its first annual loss in over a decade, but in the wake of the restructuring moves, its stock in the early months of Stringer's tenure gained more than 20 percent, along with a strong surge in the Japanese equity market. Eventually, the rise helped Sony to book a $1 billion profit due to its own significant holding of shares, but the electronics division continued to lose money, keeping operating margins still well below a new target of 5 percent.

Cost overruns for the delayed PS3 became enormous, while Sony decided to slash the number of its retail products from 3,000 to about 2,400. Even Aibo, the robotic canine that sold—on occasion—for about $2,500, was sent to the A-I kennel, in a massive restructuring effort that had no holy cows, or dogs.

Stringer, looking to history for inspiration, compared the consumer electronics giant's plight to early 19th-century Russia fending off the French, in what is known in Moscow as the "Patriotic War of 1812."

"We must be like the Russians defending Moscow from Napoleon, scorching the earth ahead of our competitors," he said. "We will galvanize group-wide resources like never before to ensure success."[15]

It was uncertain what empire Sony was now fighting, but many analysts saw its biggest foe as itself. Sony shares, which had mounted a comeback on some of Stringer's initial moves, saw their biggest two-day decline in 10 months in February 2006 on the prospect that the PS3 would be slower than expected to make it to global store shelves.

The next-generation machine, offered in separate units priced at around $500 and $600, respectively, finally arrived in Japan on November 11, 2006. A mere 100,000 machines were available, and sold out immediately to thousands of people who had queued for hours.

Some of that disappointment was offset by the availability of its rivals' consoles, Microsoft's Xbox 360 and the latest and most important monitor-linked hardware from Nintendo, now riding a winning streak after the success of its new handheld, launched in 2004. That portable unit had been designed for a mission of expanding the gaming demographic and broadening the definition of the entertainment, which Iwata said was imperative to Nintendo's future and that of the video game industry.

"The game has changed, and the way the game is played has to be changed."[16]

NOTES

1. "Origins of PlayStation: A Chat with Phil Harrison," *Guardian*, December 2004; available online: www.guardian.co.uk/technology/gamesblog/2004/dec/14/originsofplay; access date: August 19, 2010.
2. Robert A. Guth, "Sharpshooter: Sony Is Grooming Games Maverick for Next Level," *Wall Street Journal*, November 18, 2002, p. A1.
3. Steven Levy, "The Amazing PlayStation 2," Newsweek, cover story, March 6, 2000; available online: www.accessmylibrary.com/coms2/summary_0286-27621232_ITM; access date: August 28, 2010.
4. Ibid.
5. Robert A. Guth, "Sharpshooter: Sony Is Grooming Games Maverick for Next Level," *The Wall Street Journal*, November 18, 2002, p. A1.
6. Ibid.
7. Waichi Sekiguchi, "What's the Problem with Sony," *Nikkei Weekly*, July 7, 2003.
8. Ken Belson, "At Sony, a Quest for Convergence," *New York Times*, April 4, 2003.

9. Steven Levy, "Sony Gets Personal," *Newsweek,* October 25, 2004; available online: www.newsweek.com/2004/10/24/sony-gets-personal.html; access date: August 28, 2010.

10. Ibid.

11. Lorne Manly and Andrew Ross Sorkin, "At Sony Diplomacy Trumps Technology," *New York Times,* March 8, 2005; available online: www.nytimes .com/2005/03/08/business/worldbusiness/08reconstruct.html; access date: August 17, 2010.

12. Brent Schlender, "Inside the Shakeup at Sony," *Fortune,* April 4, 2005; available online: http://money.cnn.com/magazines/fortune/fortune_archive/2005 /04/04/8255921/index.htm; access date: August 17, 2010.

13. Marc Gunther, "The Welshman, the Walkman, and the Salaryman," *Fortune,* June 8, 2006; available online: http://money.cnn.com/magazines/fortune/ fortune_archive/2006/06/12/8379216/index.htm; access date: August 20, 2010.

14. "Demoted Sony Electronics Exec Still Outspoken," Associated Press, April 4, 2005; available online: www.ctv.ca/CTVNews/CanadaAM/20050404/sony_ KenKutaragi_20050404/?s_name=&no_ads=symbolic; access date: August 28, 2010.

15. Martin Fackler, "Sony Plans 10,000 Job Cuts," *New York Times,* September 23, 2005. Available online: http://query.nytimes.com/gst/fullpage.html?res=9C 06E0D61730F930A1575AC0A9639C8B63&sec=&spon=&pagewanted= all; access date: August 20, 2010.

16. Chris Morris, "Innovate or Die," CNNMoney.com, May 21, 2004; available online: http://money.cnn.com/2004/05/20/commentary/game_over/ column_gaming/; access date: September 3, 2010.

CHAPTER 6

Manifest DS-Tiny

N INTENDO'S DOMINATION OF THE HANDHELD MARKET HAD been its saving grace as its other growth engines had stalled or failed from the mid-1990s. Master inventor Gunpei Yokoi, departed but not forgotten, had not lived to see his Game Boy franchise exceed normal hardware longevity by more than three business cycles, but his brainchild kept Nintendo profitable and purposed even through its most difficult hours.

Yokoi's Nintendo handheld console, called a battery-powered pacifier by some, had sold around 110 million units by May 2001, despite over-all shrinking gaming demand in Japan. That trend continued in the first years of Satoru Iwata's tenure, with the home video game market standing at only 60 percent of its 1997 peak as of late 2004.

The implications were clear, with competition likely to intensify on Sony's entry into the handheld space that Nintendo had dominated for 15 years. Hiroshi Yamauchi had long maintained that cutting-edge graphics, studio-quality sound, and greater processing power were not resonating with consumers, or at least with Nintendo's consumers, and new boss Iwata and his team tried to crystallize that philosophy. They wanted to create an easy-to-use "third-pillar" console that would draw a larger audience and reverse the "gamer drift" phenomenon, which Iwata defined in these terms: "A declining number of people playing with games because they required too much time and energy, and because the skill gap between first-time players and veterans had become too wide."[1]

Nintendo wanted to gain light players and keep its traditional core consumers, as well as bring back the sleeping users—defined as "those who used to play but have not played in the last year." In a perfect world, Nintendo saw the demographic of gamers as ranging from 5 to 95 years old, yet what single console or software could win their allegiance? Given the myriad of options for their time and money, that was the multibillion-dollar question.

Iwata said to become bigger, Nintendo needed to think smaller and outside the box, as well as cut the exorbitant development fees for the console's software makers. Nintendo still had a 90 percent handheld market share with the Game Boy Advance, prior to the debut of Sony's PlayStation Portable, which allowed some latitude for less than immediate success.

Like Norio Ohga at Sony, the always feisty and still looming Yamauchi told the *Nihon Keizai Shimbun* in July 2003 that the rival firm would not ultimately become a handheld competitor, but—instead—would help Nintendo in the end by focusing its energies. "There have been analysts who think Nintendo has a monopoly over the handheld market and Sony may be able to break it—I don't think they understand the game business," he said.

"Software for both machines will be much different, and it would be a mistake to consider them in direct competition."[2]

DS IMPACT

Still, Yamauchi threw down the gauntlet for his successor, saying that the new "Nintendo DS" console—named for its dual screens and clamshell casing—would be absolutely critical to company recovery and advancement. Failure, following the GameCube, was not an option, while the

President Satoru Iwata (left) and design wizard Shigeru Miyamoto display the DSi console.

untapped potential of millions of non-gamers was the manifest destiny—DS-tiny—for the new console.

"If we are unsuccessful with the DS, we may not go bankrupt, but we will be crushed. The next two years will be a really crucial time for Nintendo," Yamauchi said.[3]

Financial markets had no greater confidence in Iwata just because of his youth and background in gaming. On the eve of the new handheld console's debut, Nintendo's stock stood around the ¥12,000 level, or about $100 at the time, a mild recovery from 2003 lows, but still down 40 percent since the Yamauchi handover.

In Nintendo's 2004 annual report, Iwata said he knew the score:

"In Japan, the software market has been shrinking for the past few years, and the North American market, which used to experience significant growth year after year, is seeing a slowing of that trend. . . . A revolutionary approach to video game creation is required more than ever."[4]

The portable Nintendo DS, proposed by Yamauchi before stepping down, debuted at the E3 game industry show in Los Angeles in May 2004, and was initially intended to complement the Game Boy series, not to replace it. Unlike any other Nintendo console, the DS first went on sale in North America in November that year, with a Japan launch in early December. The initial price was about $150.

Iwata ensured that the timing of the debut would not miss the key holiday season, nor be handcuffed by limited supply or public awareness, with retailers pre-ordering 2 million consoles. However, using the same carrot-and-stick approach of his predecessor—or at least the stick part—Iwata threatened to disband development teams such as Nintendo's "Jam with the Band" if they could not deliver titles by the DS launch date.

In Japan, a dozen titles were available by December 2004—five from Nintendo and seven from outside software developers, while a remake of Square Enix's "Final Fantasy III" would soon find its way to the DS's smaller screens. To show Nintendo appreciated the core gamer as well the new blood it needed to attract, the DS offered the first-person-shooter game "Metroid Prime: Hunters" from March 2006.

On the hardware side, Nintendo expanded production to a third factory in China, with over 1 million DS units shipped by the end of December, and a "Touch! DS" campaign allowed potential owners to play the console before purchase. The touch-screen, aimed at giving a more intuitive control interface, aided game developers by eliminating the need to rely on pre-set control mechanisms, while the use of a stylus for writing or for games such as golf as a swing simulator added a new utility.

The traditional A and B control buttons were also on the DS, but the thin film transistor LCD panels, interactive wireless capability, and voice recognition via a built-in microphone immediately found interest from players and designers alike. Powered by two separate 32-bit processors, the DS displayed game visuals from two perspectives simultaneously. The one gigabit of memory storage meant that, eight years later, the handheld had more processing power than the Nintendo 64, although not marketed as a high-tech portable.

Game guru Shigeru Miyamoto countered an early market view that the DS was just a Nintendo strategy to counter Sony's PSP, saying the in-house handheld was actually something new, unlike the other unit:

"I have not seen the PSP. The screen, I believe, is bigger than a DS screen and I am sure it will have excellent graphic quality," he said. "The PSP will not be able to play anything you cannot do on a current system . . . We want to do things that you could not do before. We are looking at the creative end."[5]

DS advertising in Japan centered on trend-conscious gamers, trying to make the console a ubiquitous lifestyle product like a mobile phone. Japanese pop singer Hikaru Utada led the publicity campaign at home, while U.S. commercials showed couples messaging each other with their small DS units in a form of 21st-century courting, which marked a major change in promotional direction for Nintendo and a statement that the product would not just be for children.

Other overseas ads became even more provocative, touting the DS's wireless and networking capabilities, and one commercial featured a woman's voice-over saying, "Someone, somewhere, wants to play with you," with the DS catchphrase, "Touching is good." The DS was definitely not your father's handheld console.

Game Changer

Iwata, in full PR mode, promised that the console would redefine the meaning of "game," noting the diverse demographics of those who took part in user demonstrations, as well as how its messaging functionality had altered the potential of wireless entertainment and community.

"Nintendo DS is the road map to the future of video games, and most clearly demonstrates the type of innovation that players demand."[6]

The 10-ounce console, which looked like a personal digital assistant (PDA), used an initial program loader displaying a menu for game choice or a program such as PictoChat that worked like an operating system in a personal computer. The British-produced CPUs were originally intended for cellular phones and not considered state of the art, but performance could be enhanced if desired.

Industry analysts saw this as Nintendo's step back from throwing all financial resources toward cutting-edge hardware, a legacy of the Yokoi

The author introduces Nintendo's Satoru Iwata and Shigeru Miyamoto at the FCCJ (April 2009).

era when decisions on arcade design occasionally stemmed from having leftover TV monitors to use. Battery life, an essential consideration since the invention of portable electronic devices, was designed so that a 4-hour charge offered about 10 hours of play, while switching off a backlight or using lower volume or brightness levels extended that period.

"We thought we would need to renovate the user interface if we wanted everyone to start playing from the same start line, and the DS ended up having a very unique configuration with dual-screen, touchscreen, and microphone command inputs," Iwata said.[7]

Closing the DS put it into a sleep mode, with games suspended midplay and resumed on reopening; the sleep mode would become disabled if other DS users or data feeds were in close proximity, allowing communication in established chat rooms. Such download connectivity was envisioned as letting users visit museums, movies, restaurants, or even Seattle Mariners' games, enjoying community experiences, as well as creating retail inroads for Nintendo; eventually, ad campaigns intimating greater socialization by using the console actually found traction with use of the messaging functionality.

Iwata said a planned Pokemon movie would have anime character information distributed during the film to those with DS consoles in the theaters. Later, McDonald's Japan established a "Nintendo zone" that offered DS connectivity as children and parents ate their meals, while again promoting new games or retail offers.

The DS could download game data wirelessly, play it back, and offer multiple-player contests, an advantage over the now $80 Game Boy Advance SP, and sparking user migration. Backward compatibility with Advance games also facilitated new console buying.

Download capability allowed Nintendo to debut or tease new titles coming to market, granting free short-term play and then requiring purchase to continue. The strategy was intended to see more than game sequels become best-sellers, while most game titles were priced under $40.

The DS also made a profit on hardware from its debut, unlike its rivals. Nintendo prepared 2 million consoles for the worldwide launch, with half intended for North America. By early December, the company had already hiked its shipment forecast 40 percent after stores in the United States and Japan sold out in the first week.

One *Wall Street Journal* headline called the DS the "Tickle Me Elmo of 2004," as desperate parents resorted to online auction house eBay to buy consoles at twice the retail price. An eventual plan to sell more than one DS per family would have to wait, at least until the first console was in-house.

Moving the Product

Reggie Fils-Aime, who joined Nintendo of America as executive vice president for sales and marketing in 2003, was seen as the driving force behind the earlier U.S. launch. His public debut with Nintendo at the E3 show in 2004 was known for the memorable lines:

"My name is Reggie. I'm about kicking ass, I'm about taking names, and we're about making games."[8]

With equal bravado, Fils-Aime had requested additional hardware for North America with a guarantee similar to NoA's gutsy peddling of the Nintendo Entertainment System in the 1980s: It would move every console. His confidence proved well-founded, as by the E3 game summit in May 2005, Nintendo had sold 5 million DS consoles and estimated its handheld market share at 94 percent.

As with the glory years under Minoru Arakawa and Howard Lincoln, NoA with Fils-Aime again began to dictate to North American retailers the terms they must meet to receive product supply, all indicative of having a must-have for stores and consumers. At the same time, Nintendo allowed free DS demonstrations and game downloads at participating retailers, with play possible until the console was turned off.

Fils-Aime also took the point in countering criticism from Sony and Microsoft that Nintendo still only had a single target audience.

"Our competitors are more interested in trying to pigeonhole us, versus articulating a clear strategy amongst themselves that differentiates where they're trying to do in the marketplace," he said. "This industry can

The newly-launched DSi console.
Source: Public domain.

no longer rely simply on more and more young men coming of age to try gaming. . . . The fact is that that demographic is shrinking and the next cohort, their younger brothers, is even smaller."[9]

Amid the sales onslaught, the former Cornell fraternity president, whose parents had immigrated to the United States from Haiti in the 1950s, was promoted to NoA president and chief operating officer in May 2006, with Tatsumi Kimishima becoming chairman.

The business environment leading up to the DS had been far from encouraging, particularly in Japan, as domestic software sales had shrunk more than 10 percent in 2003 alone. However, with the new console's arrival, in 2005 the market grew for the first time in five years, hitting almost $5 billion, while hardware sales alone soared over 50 percent to near $2 billion.

The DS had only just begun to take prisoners. The push to untether the video game experience from a basically young and male demographic was led by Miyamoto, as Iwata merged all company software designers under Miyamoto's Entertainment Analysis and Development group, which became the largest division in Nintendo.

Software makers did not rush to call the small DS the next "big" or "small" thing for the industry, as many said that making existing games compatible for the dual screen arrangement would take time. Still, holding the crown of reigning handheld champ helped, and games such as "Spider-Man 2," developed by Vicarious Visions and published by Activision, based on Sony's tremendously successful film series, were available at the DS launch.

NEW CONCEPTS

Nintendo's ambitions, though, went far beyond movie sequels or Roman numerals. Miyamoto created a number of early DS games with no equivalents. For example, "Nintendogs," which launched in April 2005, let people pet and bathe their virtual canines. Players could use the microphone to give commands and employ the device's Wi-Fi connectivity to communicate with other virtual pet owners.

Nintendogs

Somewhat similar to the egg-based "Tamagotchi" of the 1990s, a virtual pet from Bandai that needed to be raised by humans, "Nintendogs" set the stage for a more inclusive DS demographic, finding interest from pet owners and non-owners alike. In its first month in Japan, the game sold 400,000 units. By May 2006, with an avid market among young and older women, global sales reached six million.

In Japan, people in large cities sometimes paid for a brief opportunity to walk or play with others' real dogs or pets, and the video game was an obvious avenue to attract those who owned—or wished they owned—animals, without some of the time and resource commitments. Overseas, consumers were also waiting to rub the virtual bellies of the 18 dog breeds available, while events such as a Nintendogs Fashion Show in New York helped send demand soaring.

Miyamoto, considered a semiprofessional dog breeder, owned a Shetland sheepdog named Pick. His years with his Sheltie helped initiate the game designer into the nuances of inter-species communication and essential commands. Nintendo, meanwhile, had decided on only canines at the launch because cats were not renowned for their ability to perform tricks, a facet of the game, and a feline version remained in the virtual pet kennel for more than half a decade.

Nintendo localized the game for respective regions, based on the location's dog breed ownership breakdown, while Miyamoto himself introduced a new bloodline to the game, the Jack Russell Terrier, in a U.S. promotional event. Meanwhile, the game's "Bark Mode" led to social networking for virtual pet owners, who were alerted if nearby players wanted to discuss or swap animals, an option almost never pursued in the real world.

Miyamoto said the game might have looked better running on the soon-to be-mothballed GameCube, but the touch-screen ability as well as the voice recognition functionality gave more cyber-intimacy with the virtual pups. "Nintendogs" was initially cast as a Japan-only game, but by late 2006, sales exceeded 10 million units worldwide, in an industry where 1 million was commendable.

"The general view toward Nintendogs . . . was that there won't be a big market for such software in Europe and the U.S.," Iwata said, adding, "Nintendogs has become more popular abroad than in Japan."[10]

Another key new market segment that Nintendo would cultivate during the decade was dubbed "Serious Games," self- or professional-training software that nurtured skills or facilitated professional ties to companies, schools, and governments. Nintendo's own "serious" titles would still be fun—while having a targeted audience and purpose, such as using English-language software at Japanese schools, a setting long prohibiting game consoles. However, the centerpiece for DS expansion across generational lines was a game also seen initially as Japan-centric: "Brain Age."

Brain Age

Seldom do senior board members, even at a video game company, sit at corporate meetings and inspire potential software product ideas, but Iwata liked to joke that "Brain Age" found its roots at just such a gathering at Nintendo, when an inquisitive executive asked why there were no games for older people.

"When Atsushi Asada was a member of our Executive Committee, he complained that he knew no one his age playing video games. Because Japan is an aging society, he thought a game for seniors just might work," Iwata said. "I agreed it was a good start, but I said it might be a mistake to target only seniors."[11]

Professor Ryuta Kawashima's *Train Your Brain: 60 Days to a Better Brain* had taken Japan by storm, and Nintendo's chief financial officer, Yoshihiro Mori, was a daily devotee of the book's prescribed practices. In a move that might have raised some corporate eyebrows on the console's Japan sales debut in December 2004, Iwata went to Sendai to convince Kawashima, who taught at Tohoku University, to help develop games using his books on mental training.

Kawashima insisted he had but one hour to meet on that day only, so Iwata, even with the DS launch, headed to the northern Japanese city, hoping for a quick acceptance and then a return to promotional events.

The meeting took three hours.

"We showed our prototype brain training software and explained how his book might translate to other media. He was enthused," Iwata said. "His assistant came in with a strange bowl with wires attached. He placed it upside down on my team member's head. It looked like a 1950s' sci-fi movie. He could prove that the game was changing the blood movement on the surface of the brain."

"I'm sure people at Nintendo wondered how I could spend so much time on this meeting on the day of the DS launch, but I think it turned out to be a good idea."[12]

Iwata tasked a small team with game development in three months, and "Brain Age," based on the neuroscientist's writings, proved immensely popular. People responded eagerly to its potential to improve mental acuity, a self-help issue for middle-aged and senior players, many of whom had never touched a game console. The duration of play, long a major factor in why adults would not—or could not—commit to gaming, was addressed by designing the IQ builder to take only two minutes per session.

The potential to work certain areas of gray matter with math and comprehension games that potentially countered memory loss proved a "no-brainer" for sales success, as of course people wanted it. The daily training regimen, which involved drawing pictures using the stylus and even interfamily contests, also made the professor himself a character—his expressions denoted player progress.

Iwata, two years after contacting Kawashima and bringing the product to market, said the DS software was driving hardware sales.

"In Europe, already more than 1 million copies have been sold through, and sales are likely to reach 1.5 million units by the end of this year. We are also expecting North American sales to top 1 million. Just like it did in Japan, we know this software is driving the sales of hardware abroad, and the global sell-through figure is expected to top 10 million by the end of this year."[13]

The Big Board

The long-touted strategy for software to lead to console sales, cited as one of the reasons Yamauchi picked Iwata as his successor, had actually materialized. Meanwhile the PSP, also as predicted, had not become a real rival.

Of the top 10 games sold in Japan, the DS's "Animal Crossing" and "Brain Age" dominated, while 6 other titles were for Nintendo consoles. The Japan External Trade Organization calculated domestic DS sales alone at over 11.5 million by September 2006, and 15.3 million consoles overseas. The DS had outsold Sony's handheld, and by early 2007, Sony cut another 15 percent from the PSP's sticker price.

DS game sequels, including for "Brain Age," became a rapid by-product. The professor had rejected a number of proposals, but "Brain Age 2" made the cut and debuted in 2007, followed by "Brain Age Express," which split the franchise into Math and Arts editions. Still, even Iwata was surprised at the game's success.

"It's not like everyone at Nintendo who saw 'Brain Age' said, 'This will be a hit,'" he said. "Lots of users recognized the fun of trying to beat the clock, much as you might do in a racing game."[14]

Some players stopped using the software when their in-game brain age reached the peak performance of 20 years, but the split-in editions highlighted a player's strong suits, keeping consumer interest.

Overall, at least 16 different DS titles sold 1 million copies or more, and that surge pushed Nintendo's domestic software market share over Sony's and back to the top by 2005, with 54 percent of all game sales, mainly for the handheld console. "Animal Crossing" (or "Animal Forest," as its Japanese name said) had debuted with the N64 and evolved over the next eight years to games for the DS, selling an astounding 15 million units, while game titles such as "Photo Memory" and "Kanji Invasion" yoked retro "Space Invaders"-type shooting imagery with the modern demand of exact picture position and stroke order.

"Professor Layton and the Curious Village" became a top-selling puzzle title for the console after its release in early 2007, with its Sherlock

Holmes—like and young Watson detectives appealing to adults as well as children; by the end of the decade, the Layton series had sold 1.4 million games in the United States alone, while resulting in a feature film produced by Masakazu Kubo, who was also responsible for the Pokemon movies.

The DS's information mobility penetrated formerly game-free zones such as schools and museums, which enticed greater personal and professional ownership. At Tokyo Joshi Gakuen, a women's junior high school in the Japanese capital, students used school-supplied DS consoles to study English with software created by New Horizon, one of Japan's leading language textbook companies.

Not surprisingly, the young women liked using the stylus and comprehension features more than the rote-learning and drills of a usual lesson, which were primarily aimed at preparation for examinations and not communication. Teachers touted the push for more engaging and fun lesson plans, while the game consoles, which remained prohibited for anything but English class, were kept at school, although software could be taken home for later study, raising the need for another DS at home.

At Japan's 15,000 junior and senior high schools, school curriculum is decided for the most part by local education boards, but the DS debut had the potential to institutionalize a console presence, a windfall similar to the one Tokyo Disneyland received when it became a popular destination for school excursions. Schools did not uniformly adopt the DS as a learning tool, but even making a beachhead in a former sanctuary of seriousness was an important start.

"It's fun and helps me remember English," 13-year-old Kanako Takahashi told me during the school demonstration. "There's also math software that would be great to try."

Nintendo and its suppliers planned more than 60 teaching software titles by decade's end, covering subjects including English, Japanese, and mathematics. Paon, Plato, Ubisoft, and even Berlitz were among companies creating DS English-language training games, with the voice-recognition software becoming essential.

The DS in three years had broken through conventional sales expectations and saturation levels to force Nintendo to devise strategies on how to raise ownership beyond one handheld unit per household. Iwata said the aim was individual—not home—ownership.

"We are aiming to make DS the biggest-selling hardware in the history of video games," he said, with no trace of hubris.[15]

Overall, console sales in Japan were still shrinking as the three giants prepared their next-generation TV-linked monoliths, but handheld sales had jumped, and for the first time, portable software sales exceeded those of the larger consoles. Overseas, the DS's main competition quickly became Nintendo itself, as the large installed user base for Game Boy took time to migrate.

"Of all the territories around the world, it was taking the longest time for portable sales to shift from Game Boy Advance to DS in the United States," Iwata said.[16]

By September 2006, DS software finally outsold GB Advance games in the United States for the first time, and European numbers were also firming up. Nintendo forecast a net profit of $850 million in the business year ending in 2007, as sales of the DS had jumped nearly 20 percent. That estimate proved to be conservative.

As part of the strategy of ubiquity and beyond, Nintendo began introducing different versions of the console to spark sales and different functionalities with a particular focus on women. The Pokemon software line had put Game Boy consoles into the hands of young girls, but the DS was essential to lift the age bracket to adults.

Long ignored or underappreciated by the video game industry, women were estimated to make up 30 percent of the gaming population in 2006, with the DS ownership share substantially higher. The migration to the portable console grew as games diversified from the usual characters, cars, or conflict, while the shape and look of the DS also changed.

DS LITE

Nintendo unveiled the DS Lite in March 2006 in Japan, a slimmer version of the initial console, with female gamers and their aesthetic demands in mind. The 21 percent lighter console appeared even more similar to a PDA. Its colors (including teal or coral) might not have been intended solely as a gender statement, but Nintendo was banking that a sizable number of women around the world would think the DS indeed looked prettier in pink.

Some recognition of "what women want" could be considered sexist or a gender stereotype, such as a pink Swarovski DS Lite console, but most content creation was deemed respectful and engaging.

Lite's footprint ultimately proved bigger than its name, as women saw the console as a lifestyle utility with status, not a comment on age, gender, or hobbies as with Sony's PSP or the earlier Game Boy. Domestic game titles included "My Household Expense Book," which offered basic accounting and planning, and "Stock Trading Lessons," which made home management and investment clear benchmarks of empowerment—not condescension for profit.

However, Konami's "Dream Skincare," which gave advice on makeup application, as well as moisturizing and epidermal elasticity tips from Japanese skin expert Chizu Saeki, was undeniably an attempt to offer gaming its own $40 facial. The software from the same company making "Metal Gear Solid" used data such as body temperature and hormonal balance, as well as a desired date for peak skin condition like a wedding or graduation ceremony, and delivered daily cosmetic tips.

The game was a prelude to even more health-oriented software that would make Nintendo's financial complexion positively radiant, while Intelligent Systems' "Face Training," with tips from expert Fumiko Inudo for the *au naturel* crowd, eyed a clientele more interested in warding off wrinkles or other signs of age through facial exercises and smiling than appearing like a model on the first floor of a Japanese department store.

Other DS-targeted games included "Sight Training," or "Flash Focus," which was aimed literally at better eyesight functionality and created under the oversight of Dr. Hisao Ishigaki, a professor at Aichi Institute of Technology and known for training athletes. For those wanting personal change from the inside, Japanese magazine *AnAn* offered "Female Power

Emergency Up!"—a game that tried to cultivate personality improvement in three months; it suggested a list of 50 character types to choose from in 15-minute workouts.

Implicit in such games was the users' need to change their ways or persona, but Nintendo deftly navigated any introspection by continuing to give imperfect people what they wanted. Tokyo-based Dimple Entertainment's "DS Therapy" game lent a kind ear—or actually four virtual ears—of doctors Kota, Saya, Shun, and Reina, to listen to what ailed consumers, male or female. Topics for analysis included love, relationships, and money, while players received a daily evaluation of their mental stability and health, without need of a virtual second opinion.

Nintendo created more gender-oriented content such as etiquette training as well as cuisine guides and cookbooks, while also running global advertisements with Nicole Kidman, among other prominent women, in an attempt to further widen the DS demographic. In some nations, the DS push to women had taken root, with a TNS Worldpanel Entertainment survey in the United Kingdom showing software sales to women up 67 percent over a four-year period. (This helped to secure a one-third share for women in the game market.)

In South Korea, DS Lite sales were initially firm as Nintendo used the console as its sales catalyst into the country, shortly after establishing a local office in July 2006. Despite Korea's status as one of the most wired countries per capita in the world, Nintendo had not released its first Korean-language console until January 2007, using the Lite as a conduit to an upwardly mobile society locked into the trappings of the new century.

Tapping popular actors to promote the console in a nation known more for online gaming, the DS Lite in four months sold some 270,000 units, hitting 1.4 million by the following April and averaging about 100,000 a month. However, pirated software sales began to limit its growth, and Nintendo's Korean subsidiary demanded in September 2007 that the Seoul prosecutor's office crack down on pirate websites and the government tighten its customs controls.

Industry-watchers said Nintendo's practice of limiting its consoles to only Korean-language games in a regional "lockout" system inherently discouraged greater DS purchase; as many as 40 percent of owners were estimated to have modified their consoles to support other games, but Nintendo would not comment on the issue, only saying it would not provide user support for consoles that had been altered.

DS Makeover

Technically, the DS Lite had 20 percent more battery storage capacity, while offering four different brightness levels. However, Iwata, in one of his first Yamauchi-like moves, had actually torpedoed a larger-screen DS Lite shortly before mass production, saying global demand for the smaller version was overwhelming.

"As someone who has long been involved in manufacturing products, I knew how difficult it would be for the people involved in making this to accept that the product they had created wouldn't be released," he told a design team later. "There were a significant number of customers at that time who were waiting to purchase the DS Lite, and we were unable to keep up. I had to make the decision that this should remain 'pending' and would not be released."[17]

Nintendo's next version became the DSi console, with Masato Kuwahara of Nintendo's Development Engineering Department leading the project from late 2006. By the time the console landed in 2009, the company had already sold 100 million DS consoles globally.

The brief of Kuwahara's team was to make the next DS mesh with the existing kit's games, but somehow be different enough to lure consumers into purchase. Where had the DS not gone already?

His team added two cameras, one externally to take photographs, and another internal camera enabling self-viewing or taking pictures while playing games. As with some Japanese social networking sites, photos could be doctored for fun, compared, or just saved, but the utility initially would only allow sharing with fellow console owners.

A swivel camera mechanism as with cell phones was dropped due to durability and cost concerns, while photo clarity was capped at a minuscule 0.3 megapixels to allow sustained processing. The low resolution was also an inherent admission that DSi was not aimed at serious photography.

Iwata, though, accentuated the positive:

"We cannot boast about the resolution, as the camera for DSi has a 0.3 megapixel resolution. On the other hand, the DSi software includes 11 types of special camera lenses."[18]

Nintendo contended that the memory required for higher pixel count would limit overall functionality and that the photo quality sufficed for its purpose. Iwata maintained that the real intent of the cameras was to add quasi-human senses to the console:

"Originally, the DS touchscreen was its sense of touch and the microphone input was its ears," he said. "I remember hearing someone suggest that [we] give the console eyes. It has two—one on the outer shell and one inside when you open it."[19]

The DSi offered functionalities rivaling a smartphone—with the major exception of actual telephone use. Its larger LCD screen and higher price— near $200—featured new modifications, such as more refined sound delivery using speaker apertures. At the encouragement of Miyamoto, Nintendo added an SD memory card slot, which became a key feature for its audio.

The quick changes to the console's design, known as "upending the tea table," had been a historic facet of Miyamoto's approach to work and ensured the DSi would be different. Internet connectivity had long been touted for Nintendo kit, which had made stock trading possible with the "*Famicom*" of 20 years earlier, but its speed and range were admittedly poor.

Nintendo had made attempts to offer a browser for the DS and Lite from October 2006, but these proved cumbersome and unsatisfying, even with an extra 8 megabytes of RAM and $40 cost. With its new console, Nintendo would try to make the common provisions of e-mail and search more accessible and immediate, another reason to buy the latest DS iteration.

Browsing

The free browser, made with Norwegian firm Opera, was an acknowledgment that the original DS unit was slow. Eventually, a team led by Eiichi

Shirakawa of the Software Design & Development Department expedited the DSi's response time to 1/60 of a second.

The third DS version's marketing strategy ran commercials with Beyonce, while offering over 850 games for the thinner console. To attract younger users, the DSi's browser was presented as a kind of "Internet primer," to which parents could add a content filter. For older users, its "Shop" function may have been more attractive, as well as an inherent money spinner for Nintendo.

"[If] many people use their Nintendo DSi systems more often, and add packaged software, our business opportunities will expand and chances for new customers to play our games will increase," Iwata said.[20]

Options included creating a console layout that Nintendo touted as "My DS," shorthand for a handheld that reflected the personality and interests of its owner. Overall, the DSi did not rewrite the DS formula, but it did contravene the marketing pattern in which a new console would not be unveiled until interest in its predecessor had started to wane.

Iwata said the DSi had kept the handheld fire burning, with sales of 300,000 units in both Europe and the United States in its first two days, and new features such as museum maps, guided tours, and utilization of shopping coupons possible.

"The cycle to present—by which in a five-year cycle a piece of hardware is released, its price gradually falls and its demand disappears—has been the standard. There is no need to say we must continue on with this cycle. With the launch of the Nintendo DSi . . . we have been able to gain back the momentum of the Nintendo DS business to a certain extent."[21]

The DSi LL, unveiled late in 2009, offered larger screens that were comparable to Sony's PSP and larger than Apple's iPhone. A DSi XL console was launched in the United States in March 2010 for $190. Some speculated that the bigger screens were aimed at older users with weaker vision, while the package included "Brain Training" and "DS Easy Dictionary" came preinstalled, which was more popular with older users. Nintendo, however, contended the screen size was for multiple-player use, with two styluses and a design aimed at facilitating Web browsing.

CREATIVE DS-TRUCTION

In overall numbers, from April 2006 to March 2007 alone, Nintendo sales exceeded $8.1 billion, compared to $4.3 billion the preceding year. For the business year ending in April 2008, the Kyoto powerhouse saw profits of nearly $4.8 billion, growth of over 70 percent year-on-year, with earnings now exceeding sales of only two years prior. Nintendo anticipated profit of over $5.1 billion the next year, as money continued to fall from the sky like virtual rain.

The numbers underscored how Nintendo's DS had and would dominate as no other handheld before, including the legendary Game Boy, as it expanded and—statistically—became the market. Handheld consoles made up 52 percent of global business in 2005, and some market-watchers began to say the outlook for the larger monoliths, which Nintendo and its rivals were in the process of delivering, would no longer be the industry benchmark, potentially following fixed telephone lines into small corners of the home, while portable game consoles that rivaled cell phones in utility and size became the standard.

In Japan alone, one in five people—in a nation of 125 million—now owned a DS, while the ratio was lower in the United States, but still staggering at 1 in 10—in a nation of 330 million. Nintendo's success with the DS had sent its stock price soaring, doubling in value in fiscal 2006 alone, and making Hiroshi Yamauchi and a horde of international investors a windfall.

That investor ride was far from over, as Nintendo prepared a "Revolution" for the game industry, with its next TV-linked console. If successful, Nintendo could reclaim the hardware title lost to Sony in the 1990s, although competition would be on three fronts, as its main rival prepared its PlayStation 3 console. In addition, a now energized Microsoft would be the first to stores with its next generation Xbox 360, as the culmination of billions of dollars in research and investment finally began to pay off—the topic of the next chapter.

NOTES

1. Satoru Iwata, address to Foreign Correspondents Club of Japan, December 7, 2006. Courtesy of FCCJ Archives.
2. *Nihon Keizai Shimbun,* July 2003; available online: http://spong.com/article/5186/ Yamauchi-on-Famicom-PSP-and-more; access date: August 20, 2010.
3. Olga Karif, "Nintendo DS; Got Game, Will Travel," *Business Week,* January 27, 2005; available online: www.businessweek.com/technology/content/ jan2005/tc20050127_8481_tc117.htm; access date: August 28, 2010.
4. Nintendo, *2004 Annual Report,* June 29, 2004, p. 5; available online: www .nintendo.com/corp/report/fiscal2004.pdf; access date: August 18, 2010.
5. Steven Kent, "Nintendo Unveiling a New Portable," USA Today, May 11, 2004; available online: www.usatoday.com/life/lifestyle/2004-05-11-nintendo-ds_ x.htm; access date: August 20, 2010.
6. Craig Harris, "Official Nintendo DS Launch Details," IGN, September 20, 2004; available online: http://ds.ign.com/articles/549/549919p1.html; access date: August 28, 2010.
7. Iwata, address to Foreign Correspondents Club of Japan.
8. IGN Staff, "The Nintendo Reggie-lution," May 13, 2004; available online: http:// cube.ign.com/articles/514/514769p1.html; access date: August 20, 2010.
9. Peter Rojas, "The Endgagdet Interview: Reggie Fils-Aime," Endgagdet, February 20, 2006; available online: www.engadget.com/2006/02/20/the- engadget-interview-reggie-fils-aime-executive-vice-preside/; access date: August 20, 2010.
10. Iwata, address to Foreign Correspondents Club of Japan.
11. Satoru Iwata, GDC Keynote Speech, March 23, 2006; available online: http:// kotaku.com/162642/iwatas-gdc-keynote-transcribed; access date: August 18, 2010.
12. Ibid.
13. Iwata, address to Foreign Correspondents Club of Japan.
14. Yasuhiro Nagata; "Iwata Asks: Special Edition Interview: Turning the Tables: Asking Iwata," n.d.; available online: http://us.wii.com/iwata_asks/special_ edition_interview/; access date: August 20, 2010.
15. Iwata, address to Foreign Correspondents Club of Japan.
16. Ibid.
17. "Iwata Asks: Nintendo DSi XL: The Phantom 'Extra Large' DS Lite," n.d.; available online: www.nintendodsi.com/iwata-asks-chapter.jsp?interviewId =4&volumeId=1&chapterId=1; access date: September 5, 2010.

18. Nintendo News, "Nintendo Introduces Dsi," February 10, 2008; available online: www.nintendo.co.uk/NOE/en_GB/news/2008/nintendo_introduces_dsi_9691.html; access date: August 20, 2010.

19. "Iwata Asks: Nintendo DS: Chapter 1: Hardware; 1. Two Cameras and an SD Card," n.d.; available online: www.nintendodsi.com/iwata-asks-chapter .jsp?interviewId=1&volumeId=1&chapterId=1; access date: August 20, 2010.

20. Yasuhiro Nagata; "Nintendo DS: Volume 4; Asking Iwata; 1. Turning the Tables: Asking Iwata," n.d.; available online: www.nintendodsi.com/iwata-asks-chapter.jsp?interviewId=1&volumeId=4&chapterId=1; access date: August 20, 2010.

21. Satoru Iwata, "Financial Results Briefing for Fiscal Year Ending March 2009" (presentation), p. 4, May 8, 2009; available online: www.nintendo.co.jp/ir/en/library/events/090508/04.html; access date: September 5, 2010.

CHAPTER 7

The Third Way

F OR MOST MANUFACTURERS EXCEPT NINTENDO, MAKING hardware for the "console wars" had usually been a money-losing proposition, to be earned back by selling games . . . if you were lucky. To compete on that field, a corporation needed substantial economies of scale and a large war chest, as well as a tolerance of protracted losses for a bill that would take years to repay. Thus, it was telling but not particularly surprising when billionaire Bill Gates included Nintendo among the firms he considered as Microsoft's key competitors.

At the time (in the 1990s), Gates had just topped *Forbes* magazine's wealthiest list. He reportedly wanted to acquire a share of Nintendo, but Hiroshi Yamauchi would not sell then—or ever. Undeterred, by the end of the decade, Gates pushed Microsoft to begin work on its own game machine, extending its tremendous technological shadow still further in a quest for a home entertainment center that would lead the industry.

In truth, Microsoft, Nintendo, and Nomura Research Institute had dabbled in a small partnership in Japan to provide satellite entertainment and Internet service from July 1996, but this had fallen flat by 1998, and Nintendo had tried to proceed with other partners to no avail, even looking to bring gaming to mobile phones in 2001 with Japan's mobile industry No. 2, KDDI. Nonetheless, online gaming for Nintendo and the industry remained largely an untapped mine, full of potential synergies but onerous to implement and uncertain to yield much.

Meanwhile, Microsoft itself had earlier walked away from video game talks with Sony, but it continued to create and sell PC game software, most notably "Microsoft Flight Simulator," for a market that began around the era of the first home computer. Microsoft now looked to cement that purpose with a shift of even greater resources toward console-based gaming.

XBOX

In March 1999, a senior team at Microsoft proposed launching the Xbox, intending to have game strategy become integral to the company's five consumer divisions. A development plan called "Project Midway" emerged, named after the famed World War II battle that saw the United States regain control of the Pacific theater and begin to liberate occupied territories from the Japanese—a metaphor for the state of the game industry at the time.

The software giant's entry into the fray startled few who saw Microsoft's potential to own not only the content but also the complex delivery systems that could be truly multimedia and—if successful—omni-household. Sega, the other historically successful force in the modern console wars, decided to leave the field at about the same time, but Microsoft would prove a different breed of competitor. The firm, launched in 1975 by Gates and Paul Allen, had become a feared money-making machine, and its prospects for at least spending its way to success seemed strong, although it would be veering starkly from its historic strategy of creating software that would run on other firms' machines.

Even with an estimated $36 billion to find its way, making consoles with other firms as key suppliers was a new and expensive ballgame. However, the no-nonsense company ethos, which had made its college-dropout founders among the most successful businessmen in history while lifting the brand to ubiquity, was about to change, or at least wrinkle.

Microsoft had approached a variety of gaming, chip, and PC makers, as well as retailers, on its plans, with many predicting hardware losses that could exceed $3 billion in trying to catch up with the established industry leaders. Those forecasts, while correct, ultimately led Microsoft to delay its console launch as it prepared resources with a staff of about 1,000.

Gates, not originally a gamer himself, began to tout the entertainment's virtues, noting the hours he would play with his wife Melinda using beta versions of his company's games and hardware after putting their own children to bed. However, for the more cynical, Microsoft's growing interest was ascribed to corporate concerns that Sony's PlayStation 2 would find hegemony in homes, pushing the lowly PC—and many of Microsoft's relationships—to also-ran status, as digital convergence success grabbed home entertainment and office space.

To promote his company's claim on the living room, Robbie Bach, a Stanford MBA and Microsoft executive, was tapped in the year 2000 as senior vice president of the Games Division to head the push into PC, online, and video gaming. He had earlier spearheaded the Office product campaign, as well as the consumer software and PC game businesses.

Software to Hardware

Bach and others had convinced management that Microsoft had to build its own console, after attempts at having computer makers develop hardware for it failed. He was now armed with $500 million for a promotional campaign led by McCann-Erickson, and though not a gamer, Bach was technically well versed and exceptionally media-savvy.

He proved a strong public leader for his young six-group team, responsible for everything from developer kits and hardware to software contractual ties. By the E3 game summit in May 2000, Bach was already touting the new Xbox, which would debut a year later, as well as such opportunities as massive multiplayer games that potentially would involve hundreds or thousands of people in a sort of gaming Woodstock.

The Xbox, which did not run on Windows and was without keyboard or mouse, launched with about 20 software titles and sold for under $300.

"Our cost to produce Xbox will be significantly lower than Sony's, since the costs are off-the-shelf," Bach said.[1]

Still, analysts predicted the company would lose about $100 on every console sold, as Gates purportedly had demanded three times the graphics power of game competitors before release. In a not always flattering comparison to PCs, the Xbox had an Intel CPU with 64 MB of memory, a 10-gigabyte hard disc, an NVIDIA graphics chip, and a DVD player, as well as an Ethernet connection enabling networking. The online gaming connectivity that Nintendo eschewed would become fertile ground for Microsoft, which would push the console's capability toward launching its own "Live" service in late 2002.

Bach expected Xbox to eventually become the No. 1 home console, complementing Microsoft's history as a PC games publisher, as well as its MSN network and Windows franchise. Microsoft's PC games, however, would not cross over to the new console, although they could be rewritten to work on Xbox and become multiplayer experiences.

"Xbox brings Microsoft into the living room and den, where people are 10 or 15 feet from the television and there are two or three people playing at one time," Bach said. "The PC attracts certain types of users to certain types of games that are played mostly behind a desk. It is primarily a single-user experience."[2]

Some 1.5 million consoles were shipped by the 2001 year-end season, but the PS2 had a crucial 18-month lead, as well as key game hits in installments of "Grand Theft Auto" and "Gran Turismo." Some industry observers said few of the 20 titles Microsoft quickly brought to market offered a compelling reason to buy an Xbox in a market already saturated with choice.

Microsoft considered a slate of financial incentives for game developers, similar to what Sony had used successfully on the original PS platform, but at least one game helped to bring attention to the console and set the stage for its online gaming push.

A Shining Halo

Xbox's first winning title was Bungie Studio's sci-fi "Halo," which had been redesigned as a first-person-shooter game from an original PC-based game. To nurture its own content, Microsoft had purchased Chicago-based Bungie in June 2000, adding the game maker (founded in 1991) to a growing stable. "Halo 2" was announced by September 2002, coming to market a little over two years later and becoming an essential conduit to "Xbox Live" service migration.

Microsoft intended ultimately to produce about one-third of the games for its console while working with more than 200 third-party developers, who often produced different results and occasionally missed deadlines. Eventually, Microsoft would even invite small developers for its online retail business, but the giant also continued acquisitions, buying British game maker Rare in September 2002 for $375 million.

Rare had created some of the Nintendo 64 console's biggest hits, including "Golden Eye 007," "Banjo-Kazooie," and "Donkey Kong 64"; Nintendo had sold its 49 percent ownership in the family-run U.K. company as part of the acquisition deal with Microsoft. Relations between Nintendo and Rare had soured over game budgets, escalating to the point that Rare had purportedly sent a year 2000 Christmas card with a black box under a holiday tree.

Meanwhile, Microsoft recognized the potential sting that losing the firm could inflict on Nintendo, while it harped on differences between the companies, saying Xbox games would be designed across the demographic spectrum.

"We're not going to focus just on the kid titles, like Nintendo does," Bach said. "Xbox is going to change video games the way MTV changed music."[3]

It took Microsoft substantial time—and funds—to back up its initial pronouncements, while MTV by the end of the decade would be broadcasting more reality programming than music. Meanwhile, Rare's first Xbox title was "Grabbed by the Ghoulies," a game that did nothing to revive industry esteem. Many observers said Nintendo had been fortunate to extricate itself from the relationship, and it was Microsoft's problem to solve now.

Nintendo of America's Minoru Arakawa, on the eve of leaving the company after more than 20 years, said the other Washington state titan was still learning to walk in the gaming world: "Microsoft is spending a lot of money, but they are beginners."[4]

Nonetheless, Xbox launched almost simultaneously with the GameCube and quickly became a sales equal for Nintendo's moribund purple box in the units' first holiday season, as both companies tried to gain at least the market space left by Sega's hardware withdrawal.

While retaining its ties to Nintendo, Sega became a crossover collaborator with Microsoft, and then-president Peter Moore ultimately joined Microsoft in 2003. Sega (one of 70 software companies pledging support) signed a strategic alliance with Microsoft to bring 11 future titles to Xbox, as well as online games.

To enhance its prospects further, Microsoft cut the Xbox's price in certain markets in April 2002, quickly followed by a similar move by Nintendo. Microsoft hoped to kick-start greater enthusiasm while offering "thank you packages" of two free games and an Xbox controller to those who had purchased the console at the initial higher price.

eHome

To establish its beachhead, Microsoft had created an eHome Division with 200 dedicated engineers, who had Sony square in their sights with a similar home convergence strategy. The console, under the technical watch of Bach, Xbox Chief Technology Officer Seamus Blackley, and James "J" Allard, who went by J Allard, was a crucial element to implement and measure the success of that plan.

The barely 30-something Allard, who had joined the company in the early 1990s and quickly caught the attention of senior executives by highlighting convergence opportunities in the Internet Age, led its third-party game development and then its Xbox Live service, later managing the rollout of its "Zune" media player, Microsoft's woeful attempt to answer Apple's iPod.

Allard, in particular, frequently represented Microsoft's intense ambition and New Age confidence, as with his rebuttal of Kazuo Hirai's claims of Sony's dominance. His statements tended to launch verbal Molotov cocktails, often aimed at Sony or anyone in the company's way: "What gets me out of bed and into the office every day is the thought of Ken Kutaragi's resignation letter, framed, hanging next to my desk."[5]

Allard's "Live" service, launched in November 2002, had 1 million members within two years, as well as an arcade platform to retail certain downloadable games. However, the video game results for the Xbox were admittedly mixed, and Allard said Microsoft's first console came into battle at a disadvantage, adding it would not happen with its next creation, code-named Xenon.

"This generation, we were statistically out of the playoffs before we even laced up our shoes," he said. "Next season, there won't be an 18-month head start. We'll be neck and neck right out of the gate, and Xbox Live will give us a huge online head start."[6]

Unlike Sony and Nintendo, financial markets still saw Microsoft as doing little wrong, expecting over $9 billion in profit in fiscal 2002, and even more the following year. Its share price had shot up over 50 percent in a year. (And continued to do so; by late 2004, the stock was reinvigorated by Microsoft's returning some $32.6 billion to shareholders in the form of a $3 dividend, which it hoped would just be reinvested in the company. Chairman Gates, though, said he would donate his own $3.3 billion proceeds to his charitable organization.)

Gates had played cheerleader for Xbox at home and abroad, as he extolled the virtues of multiplayer games such as "Fuzion Frenzy," seen as a rival to Nintendo's "Mario Party." He unveiled the company's Xbox plans in Tokyo in early 2001 with a parade of Japanese production ties ahead of kicking off sales from February 2002 in the home of its two rivals.

The console sold for about $260 in Japan, higher than either the GameCube or PS2, and saw sales of about 123,000 consoles in its first three days. Microsoft spouted ambitious plans for the world's No. 2 economy, intending an ADSL broadband network alliance with telecom giant NTT Communications.

However, Japan remained the country where Project Midway appeared a losing battle, long after other tides were turning. Console sales were described as hitting only a few thousand a week after its launch, and Microsoft made a huge revision in its sales forecast—to between 3.5 million and 4 million units for the year ending in June 2002, down from as high as 6 million consoles. It blamed this revision on poor Japanese business as well as a slow start in Europe. However, many said the software lineup, with few role-playing games, was obviously not aimed at a Japanese audience.

LOSSES MOUNT

In what he denied was a related development, Xbox CTO Blackley resigned in early 2002, saying he would pursue his own software projects in the Seattle area; whether related or not, Microsoft was also seen as plagued by some of the same kinds of internal turf battles as the ones at Sony, exacerbated by the billions of dollars it had begun to lose on gaming.

Microsoft and Gates continued to endure substantial red ink, similar to Charles Foster Kane's bankrolling of unprofitable newspapers in *Citizen Kane,* with an estimated $3.7 billion lost on unsold merchandise, as well as on exorbitant development and marketing costs. By the end of the console's run, some loss estimates reached $6 billion, although U.S. quarterly sales had eclipsed the PS2's by the fourth quarter of 2004.

Microsoft's entry had proven largely a branding exercise in the console's first four years, but executives continued to talk about eventual market share of 40 percent. Still, its next-generation console was expected to lose at least $125 a unit, working toward a "gross margin neutral strategy," shorthand for eventually not hemorrhaging too obviously.

On the plus side, Xbox Live had become a mild hit, as the $50 service quickly surpassed Sony's PS2 online business and remained the leader through each company's next console. Xbox Live would approach sales of $1 billion online near the end of the decade, seeing an average of 6 million players a month.

Live's expansion dovetailed with considerable broadband growth in North America and a dramatic decline in spending on video game discs, estimated by the NPD Group to have tumbled in the United States alone by $700 million from 2004 to 2005; the online service's international footprint, meanwhile, extended to more than 20 countries where consumers downloaded often cheaper games or just used the service to interact with other global gamers.

Key to the growth may have been "Halo 2," which had a Hollywood-sized promotional budget and delivered launch sales equivalent to a block-buster film, or better. Opening day sales hit $125 million, which earned the period the nickname within Microsoft as "the 'Halo 2' quarter."

Sony Computer Entertainment's Kazuo Hirai said online gaming was important, but not a top priority for the industry leader: "When you're losing market share, you're tempted to talk about things down the road."[7]

Microsoft did not have substantial market share to lose, hoping that synergies and profits would emerge over time with the new console. The gradual approach gave Bach's team space to tweak the Xbox's successor, intending to come to market first this time. Dedicated game software production was also part of the plan, while increasing the number of online titles for Xbox Live to over 50 by early 2004.

SEAT CHANGES

Microsoft's changing of the guard, which began with Gates becoming chairman and Steve Ballmer CEO in 2000, was also seen as having driven its approach toward gaming, as the division gradually moved away from accepting substantial losses as a start-up enterprise, instead becoming a more profit-driven business. Indeed, Bach wanted the next-generation console to be delivered on time, with the unmistakable purpose of gaming, and—with a short grace period—to find profitability. Making it happen within the usual five-year life cycle for a major console was the plan, and Microsoft's next-generation console would come to market before either of its competitors.

Rattling the competition was also part of the strategy. Peter Moore said when he joined rivals Microsoft that Ballmer, known for his competitive nature as well as his temper, grilled him on aggressive tactics. "He wanted to know how I was going to win for Microsoft, how we were going to take on Sony," he said in an interview in 2008 after leaving the company. "We were just completely fixated on Sony—Nintendo didn't even come into the conversation . . . . We wanted to keep [Sony] out of the living room, from a software and services perspective."[8]

Microsoft had sold 20 million Xbox consoles, compared to 80 million PS2s; its successor, the Xbox 360, would have to best that figure considerably to be considered a success, after becoming the first cutting-edge unit of the industry triumvirate to debut in 2005. Allard wrote a long treatise outlining the next two decades of Xbox strategy, but his basic premise was winning over core gamers, who would facilitate selling more.

"If we can get the first couple million Xbox 360s into the hands of the serious gamers, we can get to 10 million first," he said, adding, "The first guy to sell 10 million units wins."[9]

With Allard leading the console's technical design, the 360 used a standard DVD optical drive with a resolution of 1080i—a high-definition TV mode nearly as sharp as what would be used in Sony's PlayStation 3— along with wireless controllers and a detachable hard drive. The console's connectivity to home PCs positioned it to be the on-ramp for all stored or portable multimedia content for home entertainment, Microsoft's plan for home ubiquity.

Moore, now vice president of marketing and publishing, orchestrated promotional events such as a "zero-hour" pre-launch in the California desert with 5,000 selected gamers and a 30-minute infomercial program on MTV, and gave public predictions of selling 10 million Xbox 360s in the console's first 16 months. He said one area that had to be tweaked was a softer design for the 360, including a color besides black.

"We went to Japan and worked with a company called 'Hers' to give us that concave shape," he said, adding, "We took all the sharp edges out; otherwise, we were going to get the same 25 million people and lose the same $2 billion again."[10]

Microsoft's home and entertainment division had lost $485 million going into its new console's debut. That loss grew to $1.26 billion on Xbox 360 launch expenses.

SELLING 360

In late 2005, I met Robbie Bach at a Reuters Technology Summit in Tokyo. He told me that Microsoft's climb to the game industry's summit remained the company's goal, regardless of past losses or its current market share. With a thin white Xbox 360 next to him, Bach said being first to strike with a plate of game titles would help Microsoft achieve this quest.

"We look at our launch lineup—about 15 to 20 titles for launch, and 25 to 40 by the end of the year. We've got the lineup, we've got the games, and I think that will be a very positive advantage," he said. "Our goal with Xbox 360 and the new games is to be the global-wide leader in this business. That's been a goal since we got into the business. Xbox was a great first step. This is the logical follow-on to be No. 1."

Bach acknowledged that Sony's PS3 was its main competitor, while seeing both of its rivals as one-dimensional.

"Sony is a great company—they'll be a tough competition, but we think we have the product and games to win," he said. "Sony and Nintendo really are a consumer electronics company and a toy company. They aren't a hardware, software, and services company."

Microsoft had recruited three leading Japanese game designers, responsible, respectively, for the "Final Fantasy," "Resident Evil," and "Lumines" franchises, to become exclusive 360 talents. Bach said Microsoft, which admittedly had found little traction with Japanese gamers or even its software makers with the Xbox, was starting to see mild interest after a first-round miss.

"Our first-generation of Xbox in Japan didn't have the right games for the Japanese market," he said.

"We've added a lot of support. They've seen our success in North America and Europe. They've seen the design of the box, they like the vision that we've created, and they see a great business opportunity."

"We've got the most powerful hardware coming onto the market, but in the entertainment environment we're creating, it's more than just hardware . . . Microsoft, obviously, has made huge investments in the online space and we think that is going to differentiate us."

Microsoft's Moore said video game historians would look back on the era of game discs—as the industry already did with Nintendo's cartridge business—and wonder what took so long to migrate to an online model.

"Years from now, the concept of driving to the store to buy a plastic disc with data on it and driving back and popping it in the drive will be ridiculous," he said. "We'll tell our grandchildren . . . and they'll laugh at us."[11]

Red Ring of Death

Microsoft engineers had begun on the 360 project later than Sony with the PS3, but the console reached market first as promised. However, the company—and consumers—later discovered flaws, which had further implications for loss—financial as well as in prestige.

The most expensive and notorious defect exceeded $1.2 billion in costs, as affected consoles had to be replaced or repaired at the factory—and the problem plagued at least a million consoles. It was dubbed the "Red Ring of Death" because its visible sign was a circle of red lights flashing near the power button, indicating a complete breakdown of the Xbox 360.

Testing during development had not uncovered the issue, which had been seen as self-correcting, an approach that some analysts said was similar to a long-time software company expecting "a patch" to cover system vulnerability. The hard-drive disc and wireless controllers were cited as partial causes, adversely affecting air and electrical circulation within the high-definition console, while some of its cutting-edge features had made the overall system fragile.

By the summer of 2005, output had reached only about 10 percent of plan due to technical glitches, but shutting down production to sort out the bugs would have resulted in missing the intended launch. The Xbox 360 landed on shelves on November 22, 2005, while estimates of returns by mid-2007 were as high as 10 percent of the 11.6 million consoles shipped.

Microsoft has not disclosed the ultimate replacement rate, only saying that the number of repairs for its free return policy was unacceptable and would not happen again. Some media reports estimated that up to one-third of the first-run 360s had broken down.

Bach, though, said customers had been forgiving.

"You would expect it to show you up in the customer reaction data. We just haven't seen that," he said, admitting that some owners felt it took too long to fix the console. "Does it frustrate them? Yes. On the other hand, they know we're taking care of them. . . . If it happened on a product that had less baseline customer satisfaction, it would have had a bigger impact."[12]

Microsoft preferred to accentuate the relative success of its new console and coming first to market, even with a troubled product.

"It has given us a leg up with game developers. It has given us a leg up from an economics perspective. It helped us to expand Xbox Live quickly. At a strategy level, if you asked if I wanted to be first again, I would say 'yes.'"[13]

A First Blow

In the 360's first year, Allard and Moore could boast that some 10.4 million consoles and 160 game titles were sold, which the company saw as a green light to double output and ramp up online subscriptions. Bach, meanwhile, had become co-president in charge of consumer electronics and entertainment industry ties at Microsoft.

Repeating the mantra of "connected entertainment," Bach pushed for partnerships with Hollywood studios and satellite TV companies, all of which potentially could be content for the console. A possible use of the then-20GB new console as a cable TV box for subscribers was rejected during development, but other functionalities, such as digital music, were tied to the Zune player, which debuted in November 2006.

Some entertainment firms were less than receptive to Microsoft's overtures over concerns about its distribution intentions and history. Gradually, though, studios including Paramount and Warner Brothers began offering rentals over an Xbox Live Marketplace service. Meanwhile, by early 2007, Bach's Entertainment and Devices Division had hired away senior officials from Sony and Sega, growing its staff to about 7,000.

XBOX TV

Yoking all its resources together, Microsoft started selling Internet protocol TV (IPTV) software that allowed delivery of program content through home telephone lines to Xbox. This circumvented cable or satellite providers, offering the possibility that the Xbox 360 could replace the traditional cable box.

IPTV numbers were under 10 million worldwide in 2006, but industry-watchers had estimated growth of five times that figure by 2010—to near 50 million. The actual total by the end of 2009, though, was under 30 million, according to research firm Informa Telecoms & Media, due to tough competition from established broadcast delivery firms.[14] In its expansion, Microsoft inked deals with British Telecom and other service providers, allowing broadband customers to use the Xbox 360 to download on-demand content and access libraries, along with "Live" services.

A larger processing capability was imperative to allow viewers to watch high-definition video, play DVDs, and access Live. As a result, the 360 was upgraded to 60GB and 120GB versions within three years. Exclusive games such as "Halo 2" and then "Halo 3" proved just as important as movie or TV content. "Halo 3" had received 1.7 million pre-orders, with its first-week sales ultimately hitting $330 million, becoming the first Xbox title to break the 10 million mark. In total, the Halo franchise alone sold more than 30 million copies from 2001 through August 2009.

Bach's division, which had made six straight annual losses, saw revenue jump more than 90 percent, and the total number of 360 sales hit 28 million by the end of 2008, some 8 million units more than the PlayStation P3, with $1 billion in Xbox live revenues alone. Still, Microsoft sold the 360 console at a loss, which affected its operating profit margin, but it was seeing bottom-line impact from hit games, with estimates as high as $120 in software profit per console sold. This proved that the decision to abandon the original Xbox a year before the end of its normal five-year console run had been astute.

Bach said turning Microsoft's loss leader to the black would be a victory, but began to ease the emphasis on becoming the industry leader, saying the business was big enough to have multiple winners.

"Having 40 percent market share to somebody else's 30 percent market share is less important than it might have been five years ago."[15]

Microsoft had begun to find financial equilibrium after bleeding red ink with its own start-up costs and problems over the years. However, many pressing issues besides gaming faced CEO Ballmer, including a $47.5 billion bid to buy Internet giant Yahoo. Revenues under Ballmer, who was the second-biggest shareholder after Gates, had tripled to about $67 billion, but Microsoft's stock price had again begun to decline.

The number of worldwide staff had grown to over 90,000, but internal changes and the first job cuts in the company's history pared thousands by the end of the decade. Bach's team saw its own share of movement, with Peter Moore leaving Microsoft in 2007 to run software developer EA Sports, and replaced in the gaming division by Don Mattrick.

Moore said later that Microsoft still did not see Nintendo as the company to watch, nor its next console (code-named "Revolution") as potentially intimidating as the PS3.

"Then, it was all about Sony; it was not about Nintendo because they were down and out," he said. "GameCube was just dying and the 'Revolution'—as it was called—we knew it couldn't be anything powerful."[16]

Nintendo's next console would indeed be less powerful than the Xbox 360, with NoA chief Reggie Fils-Aime saying it would not support high-definition delivery. However, the Revolution would also be less expensive and less obsessed with the core gamer, which had been an integral strategy of Microsoft and Sony.

Nonetheless, having products to sell first had clearly been an advantage for Microsoft over its rivals, and Bach said work on its next next-generation console had begun even before shipping the Xbox 360, noting the need for perpetual planning. It would not appear within five years of the Xbox 360's arrival, as the industry and Microsoft itself began to have a rethink about hardware.

"People are continuously working on new technology," he said. "Stuff doesn't become concrete until you get inside a window of when you have to ship, more than 18 months or so out."[17]

NOTES

1. Amy Doan, "Time Is Xbox's Opponent," *Forbes,* January 9, 2001; available online: www.forbes.com/2001/01/09/0109xbox.html; access date: August 28, 2010.
2. "New Game: Head of Microsoft's Games Division Outlines Strategy for PC and Console Games," Microsoft News Center, May 10, 2000; available online: www.microsoft.com/presspass/features/2000/05-10bachqa.mspx; access date: August 24, 2010.
3. Lauren Fielder and Shane Sattefield, "E3 2001: Microsoft Delivers Xbox Launch Details," GameSpot, May 16, 2001; available online: www.gamespot .com/news/2761182.html; access date: August 23, 2010.
4. Jay Greene, Steve Hamm, Catherine Yang, and Irene M. Kunii, "Bill Gates in Your Living Room," *Business Week,* January 21, 2002; available online: www .businessweek.com/magazine/content/02_03/b3766095.htm; access date: August 24, 2010.
5. Dean Takahashi, "The Rise and Fall of Microsoft's Xbox Champions: Robbie Bach and J Allard," GamesBeat, May 25, 2010; available online: http://games .venturebeat.com/2010/05/25/microsofts-longtime-entertainment-execu tives-robbie-bach-and-j-allard-resign/; access date: August 24, 2010.
6. Kemp Powers, "Showdown," *Forbes,* August 11, 2003; available online: www .forbes.com/forbes/2003/0811/086.html; access date: August 24, 2010.
7. Ibid.
8. "Peter Moore Interview: Part Two," *Guardian,* September 18, 2008; available online: www.guardian.co.uk/technology/gamesblog/2008/sep/11/play station.microsoft; access date: August 24, 2010.
9. Josh McHugh, "The Xbox Reloaded," *Wired 13.06,* 2005; available online: www .wired.com/wired/archive/13.06/xbox.html; access date: August 24, 2010.
10. "Peter Moore Interview: Part Two."
11. David Kushner, "The Infinite Arcade," *Wired 14.08,* 2006; available online: www.wired.com/wired/archive/14.08/nintendo.html; access date: August 24, 2010.

12. Dean Takahashi, "Interview with Microsoft's Robbie Bach, Part 2, on Xbox 360," GamesBeat, June 13, 2008; available online: http://games.venturebeat .com/2008/06/13/interview-with-microsofts-robbie-bach-part-2-on-xbox-360/; access date: August 24, 2010.
13. Ibid.
14. Michael Carroll, "IPTV Struggles for Global Market Share," Telecoms Europe, March 24, 2010; available online: www.telecomseurope.net/content/ iptv-struggles-global-market-share; access date: September 3, 2010.
15. Takahashi, "Interview with Microsoft's Robbie Bach, Part 2."
16. "Peter Moore Interview: Part Four," *Guardian*, September 18, 2008; available online: www.guardian.co.uk/technology/gamesblog/2008/sep/11/gamesin terviews.microsoft; access date: August 24, 2010.
17. Takahashi, "Interview with Microsoft's Robbie Bach, Part 2."

CHAPTER 8

Revolution in the Streets

T HE "REVOLUTION" WAS NOT TELEVISED, BUT NINTENDO did telegraph the coming of its next console from May 2004, when Satoru
Iwata tried to raise corporate hopes after the GameCube console
had dimmed them. Hinting of better days ahead, Iwata promised the
new hardware would be a certain game-changer while being a "small,
quiet, affordable console," characteristics seemingly at odds—but not to
Nintendo executives.

In the following two years, the blazing success of the DS handheld
raised expectations even beyond the usual hoopla for Nintendo's TV-
linked hardware, which carried the not-so-subtle code name Revolution.
Iwata admitted the console's working title might have been a bit over-the-
top, but said it matched the company's intentions; industry-watchers had
to admit it was more enticing than the media's appellation of "GCNext,"
a connection to its past console that the company likely wanted to forget
as soon as possible.

"Nintendo has taken with the idea of breaking with the past and
made a console with the somewhat overblown code name of 'Revolution,'
all in the hope of dramatically changing the way things are done,"[1]
Iwata said.

Invigorated by the DS, Nintendo increasingly recognized that a
compelling interface with new utilities could help it regain the top position overall, after becoming the No. 1 games seller and hanging onto the

portable crown. Moreover, it was a chance to catch its rivals flat-footed with an incorrect bet that core gamers with complex, multi-purpose machines would win the day. In the words of Shigeru Miyamoto, and earlier Gunpei Yokoi, gaming was all about fun.

As with the DS portable, Nintendo could realize the long-touted plan for a software-driven business model, in which a raft of new immersive titles expanded demographics and the actual definition of gaming.

The console itself had its own wizardry, utilizing micro electro-mechanical systems (MEMS) technology to empower a wireless handheld controller that would respond to changes in acceleration, direction, tilt, and elevation instantly. The tiny multi-axis linear acceleration and MEMS sensors were designed by Analog Devices and STMicroelectronics, providing real-time game recognition and untethered play.

Nintendo had previously used the technology in "Kirby's Tilt N' Tumble for Game Boy Color," and would make MEMS the console's cornerstone, along with ATI graphics. The controller was designed to be easier to hold and control than the real-world object it represented in the game, resulting in an actual play experience that would be less heavy and more manageable for efforts such as swinging a racket or rolling a bowling ball.

The Bluetooth-enabled Wi-Fi console allowed online or multiplayer games, eliminating most of the cables of the past. IBM's "Broadway" microprocessors, also used in Microsoft's Xbox 360, ran the console with 512 MB of flash memory internal storage, but the machine ultimately was intended to capitalize on standard and readily available technology, rather than to become a cutting-edge wonder. In short, priced at under $250, which was substantially below its rivals, the console would be profitable from day one.

GAME HYBRIDS

Rather than rev up CPU processing power, Nintendo focused on improving energy consumption while maintaining performance, aiming to create a 24/7 console that ran software spanning the range from sports and leisure to self-help and e-commerce. In automotive parlance, the console hardware, no bigger than three DVD cases, would down-shift power to ensure better—or continual—energy utilization without affecting duration or quality of use.

Tasked with development was Genyo Takeda, Nintendo's general manager of the Integrated Research and Development Division. He had been deeply involved with the last two failed consoles, and the Revolution had the potential to offer a kind of redemption for Nintendo—and for Takeda, who described the console as a video game industry hybrid.

"If automobiles can be used as a metaphor, our industry has always been trying to compete on horsepower, even though not all cars are made to compete in F1 races," Takeda said. "Some are trying to make faster cars; others are gathering public attention around the world with their hybrid engines."[2]

Takeda said part of the console's name status was derived by not following industry views on technology and product development, which normally dictated Nintendo's direction. These "roadmaps" usually offered prognostications about semiconductor technology and crucial issues like multimedia content and wireless delivery.

Nintendo again put its "less is more" mantra to the test, envisioning escalating demands and diminishing returns from a console strategy in which gigabytes and expectations had doubled every four or five years.

"If we had followed the existing 'roadmaps,' we would have aimed to make it 'faster and flashier.' . . . During development, we came to realize the sheer inefficiency of this path," Takeda said. "There is no end to the desire of those who just want more. Give them one, they ask for two. Give them two, and the next time they will ask for five instead of three. . . . Then, they want 10, 30, 100—their desires grow exponentially. Giving in to this will lead to nowhere in the end."[3]

Interface

That shift in focus had long been preached by former boss Hiroshi Yamauchi, and now Iwata was continuing to push for it, but it took the

DS, as well as capable engineers and software designers, to make it reality. Durability and safety were imperatives with the new console's small size, but Takeda said after the handheld DS, creating something intrinsically different was not easy.

"I really fretted over what kind of interface to follow up the DS with," he said. "We considered a touch panel on the controller. . . . We also thought of using a pointing device, like a computer's mouse or track pad."[4]

Nintendo opted for a thin rectangular console with a slot-loading disc drive that used a stand to avoid clutter around the TV, aiming for a sleek look that could fit in tight spaces. Development focused on a cutting-edge wireless controller that could beam commands to a linked TV. The next-generation remote went through over 100 concept proposals and prototypes, including one worn on the head and another known as the *gunbai,* after a fan used by *sumo* judges (it would have placed a game directional pointer in its middle).

But Shigeru Miyamoto would come to console planning meetings and pull out his cell phone or car navigation system pointer, asking the development group to try to make a controller in the same vein. Most game remotes had not changed significantly in two decades, requiring hunched-over, two-handed command execution. Meanwhile, TV and audio devices had for decades been employing single-handed "zappers," which had become increasingly ubiquitous in homes.

"I wanted to make something that would make people want to pick it up and try using it. . . . We started to question everything about conventional controllers, including the idea that a controller had to be held with both hands," Miyamoto said. "It was a good opportunity for us to think outside the box. . . . Once we decided on this shape and the control became one-handed, several problems were solved at once."[5]

Remote Developments

The Revolution's "Core Controller" had a larger "A" button for thumb action and a "B" trigger pulled by the index finger, as well as the traditional control buttons and the basic cross-shaped D-pad. Iwata initially wanted the unit to be called *rimokon,* the Japanese name for a TV remote, to underscore its functionality and design, but another name was selected ahead of the launch.

The controller could send information to a small sensor bar attached to a TV or monitor as far away as 30 feet (about 9.14 meters), and the wireless unit eventually could connect to a separate device called a "Nunchuk" for two-handed first-person shooter games as well as other game options. The remote and Nunchuk were shock resistant to a point similar to a 10-kilogram weight landing on it, in anticipation of heated games and the possible tempers of many future players who could send the controller flying or squeeze it with destructive grip.

Together, the controllers relayed data from sensors that utilized upgrades in transmission speeds from 60 signals per second to over 200, while a "virtual controller" option and ports for peripherals made the console backward-compatible with past games. Play was a multidimensional, multiperson experience using virtual weapons, sporting implements, musical instruments, or a myriad of new software possibilities. The strategy behind the remote and its applications was the same as the DS: Get more people to play.

However, unlike the DS, success for the console would be measured not just by player migration to Nintendo and its games, but by actual console relocation from children's bedrooms to the living room and the number of people gathered to play. The treasured location was also where Sony and Microsoft looked to pitch their tents, with visions of convergence and domination of the home entertainment center, but Nintendo's aims were humbler—and ultimately more achievable.

CORE CONCERNS

Even with eyes on the masses, Iwata said Nintendo understood the concerns of core gamers who had played "Zelda" games for almost two decades and wondered whether their expectations had become less important. In response, he called the new console a widening of scope, not a retailoring.

"It is true Nintendo is reaching out to non-gamers, but this does not mean that we are ignoring game fans," he said. "It's not as if we've become less committed to 'Zelda.' On the contrary, we've invested four years and a huge amount of effort into developing the new Zelda."[6]

Industrial design (ID) was a key element of the internal process. Nintendo's development team, tutored by Miyamoto, focused on how the console would—or should—utilize its new software across many potential applications. ID had been an essential element of success for Nintendo's consoles dating back to the Super Nintendo Entertainment System in the early 1990s, but Miyamoto said the new hardware interface needed to break down the usual software designer's resistance to change.

"We had to overcome how to convince users and game designers who had grown accustomed to traditional interfaces," he said. "I teamed up with ID people to fight against people creating the current market."[7]

The console's mainly white exterior, coming after the GameCube's often indigo color and toy-like handle, was intended to avoid confusing potential consumers about its utility and audience. Bundled software included "channels," which had news and Internet connectivity via an Opera browser, as well as family message bulletin boards and traditional game-play options.

Channeling Enthusiasm

A "Shopping Channel," an imperative as gaming increasingly expanded into the e-retailing space, was also included. The console's download service allowed purchase and use of classic Nintendo, Sega, and Hudson titles. Prices for older games from its first three consoles ranged from $5 to $10, similar to Microsoft's costs for its available titles on the "Live" online service, while the "Mario," "Donkey Kong" and "Zelda" franchises became some of the 30 retro favorites available initially for download, quickly rising to 60 titles.

Similar to cable TV, a "Forecast" channel for global weather updates was the first designed to ensure that the console would indeed be around-the-clock and interactive. Iwata initially wanted the console to shut itself off after a set period, saving game data but ensuring that parents could control total use. However, to the satisfaction of staff—and likely most children—the idea was not implemented, although usage history could be recorded and stored.

One channel offered game character design, which created the faces of virtual players in a follow-up to the idea of a *kokeshi,* or Japanese wooden doll player, which had been suggested by Miyamoto. Designers had toyed with a customized avatar-related game since Nintendo 64's "Talent Studio," as well as the "*Manebito*" concept for the GameCube, a title that never launched.

For the new game, they added foreign facial characteristics to the Japanese caricature library already on hand, with players designing their own avatars. The alter ego's body resembled the wooden dolls with the addition of the new face design, and the results could be used in the player's other games and later as a guest in anyone's game.

Separately, "Photo Channel" seized on the cell phone's popularity with photography and snapshot exchange, tapping the development team behind "Brain Age" for rapid deployment. Nintendo added slideshows and video, now standard features of many smartphones and digital cameras, cementing the multimedia utility of the new console.

Some channel suggestions had been dropped before console production in an attempt to keep from overwhelming traditional gamers, but the main intention of the 48 that made the cut was to reach a larger audience. By the November 2006 launch, 25 first- and third-party games would be available, priced at around $50.

Healthy Gaming

However, it was the wireless remote's potential to liberate users from the sofa that created the biggest buzz among new and old gamers. Movement and exercise could now happen in the house, a healthy makeover for a pastime historically linked to sedentary calorie intake, not active weight loss.

A Mayo Clinic report, published in the December 2006 edition of *Pediatrics,* said activity-oriented video games increased a child's energy expenditure between 20 and 40 percent over resting levels, and might actually be considered for obesity prevention and treatment. Other professionals began to give their blessings to gaming's health prospects after a long period seen as a bane, also noting benefits for seniors, even if just stress or boredom relief.

One study by Liverpool John Moores University said in theory, up to 27 pounds, or 12.5 kilograms, could be lost by young teenagers who played about 12 hours a week. The report lost some traction after it was revealed it was funded in part by a Nintendo-affiliated firm. Indeed, skepticism was just as healthy to some, who said touting the benefits of gaming was more marketing than makeover, as the virtual pursuit would never be more invigorating than the actual workout.

Regardless, a team led by Miyamoto designed a collection of active sports games as a bundled software package, linking with other pre-installed games, such as the message board, on which players could post results. As with "Pong" some 30 years earlier, one of the console's first designed sports games was tennis, adding extra remote controllers for multiplayer contests.

The first time I saw the console, late in 2006 in Tokyo, Iwata and Miyamoto played in demonstration tennis matches against each other. In the promotional blitz before the launch, the game and competition among its champions became a road show staple.

To make the experience resemble actual tennis play, the sensors registered the delicate differences in stroke speed and ball spin that a player could employ, while acceleration and timing in acts such as serves were calibrated. Games also measured skill progression, and virtual opponents could also be selected by talent ratings to ensure proper challenges even in auto-play mode. If players improved, the console and game software recognized the accomplishment.

Training options in tennis and many games offered instruction to master techniques, but with a bigger audience paramount, all had been designed to be simple enough for immediate use. By the time of the launch, the initial sports offerings had expanded from tennis, golf, and baseball to bowling and boxing.

That's what drew me in. My own first use of the console was a boxing match against a Nintendo public relations official who explained how to hold the wireless remote controller and play the game and then kindly entered the virtual ring with me. I still savor the moment: my avatar knocked out the PR official's avatar, and I proceeded to blow on my gloves and dance like a new flyweight champion, standing over the fallen game marketer until his fellow staff led me to a virtual corner.

The Mii Generation

In offering five sports instead of one, Nintendo altered its previous game release approach from one polished sports title, featuring a Mario or branded locale or professional player who lent their name and avatar to endorse it, to more games that used players' "Mii" caricatures as participants. Iwata said the approach was part of the gaming revolution.

"It's not a single lavish stand-alone game, neither is it a compilation of 100 different mini-games. It has no official licenses or endorsements, nor are there any famous people featured," he said. "It lives up to the initial concept of offering a revolutionary control method, a brand new type of game."[8]

The success of the DS, and its inflow of new gamers to Nintendo, added throw-weight to decision making about the console, although the product was admittedly a work-in-progress, Iwata said.

"I wasn't so blissfully optimistic to think that the Nintendo DS would be so well received . . . and the same is now true just before the [new console] launch," he added.

"When releasing a new product—whether or not it's a hit is beyond our control to a large extent. . . . We had to improvise a lot, and the finished product is the result of a lot of groping around in the dark for what was a workable solution at a given time."[9]

The console debuted in late 2005 at the Tokyo Game Show. Iwata played a video and then showed how to use the controller. Peter Moore, who was then at Microsoft, said his company was stumped by the new product, but it did not seem to be a game-changer. "I was in Tokyo when Iwata-san brought the controller out and said, 'Here it is!' And we were all going, 'What the hell is that?'"[10]

Iwata admitted the crowd's response at the show confused him. "I was up on stage as the keynote speaker at that event and I still vividly remember the silence that followed. . . . It was as though the audience didn't know how to react."[11]

Intuitive Gaming

The buzzword for the new console was "intuitive," but Nintendo had not foreseen the dropped jaws, and Genyo Takeda later joked that he was in the audience sweating. Miyamoto, though, said he compared the new console to other offerings at the event and remained confident that sales would follow.

"I couldn't help but wonder whether our message had gotten across or whether people thought it was too unconventional," he said. "Looking at the other unveilings at the Tokyo Game Show that day, I was very much relieved that Nintendo was the only one doing something new."[12]

In late April 2006, Nintendo unveiled the launch name of its console—the "Wii," pronounced like the first person plural "we," intended as an appellation signifying its family gaming orientation. Some media reports mocked the spelling, asking if "wee" or "whee" would have been more appropriate, while online comment ranged from saying it was a confused choice to calling it the worst console name ever.

But by the Electronics Entertainment Expo in Los Angeles two weeks later, Miyamoto was using the "Wii Remote" (or "Wiimote") wand to conduct virtual orchestras, while Iwata was playing tennis, as the gaming community began to rally behind the new console and its planned 21 game titles. According to media reports, the Wii completely left Sony's PlayStation 3 in its shadow at E3, if the long lines of fans who waited for hours to play its games were a sign of future sales.

Financial markets began to take notice of what could become Nintendo's second hit console in two years, and by May 2006, the company's shares had hit a four-year peak.

WII LAUNCH

Nintendo had the confidence of 16 million DS consoles sold, although Takeda kept up pressure on designers and developers to make the console more universal in its potential use. "Americans are, by nature, a group of people who will openly applaud anything that challenges the norm," he said. "I was pleased it had been so well received, but . . . we still had loads of work to do."[13]

A lack of third-party game designer support had crippled the last two consoles, and Takeda wanted to ensure no recurrence of that problem. He planned ample development kit distribution for third-party game makers.

"There was a fear that there would again be a divide between those who could successfully adapt to the new system and its implementation and those who could not," he said. "We wanted to share these ideas with developers outside the company to aid the development of new products."[14]

Pricing would be a key factor for the Wii, which first hit shelves in the United States on November 19, 2006, with "Wii Sports" games bundled in and a $200 million marketing wind under it. At $250, compared to $400 to $600 for one of the versions of the Xbox 360 or PlayStation 3, Nintendo had an advantage at the cash register in its first holiday shopping season, particularly with consumers focused on price.

Nintendo planned to ship more than 4 million consoles and 17 million games by the end of March 2007, and as with the DS, most of those would initially head to the United States. Marketing would center on an older demographic, with some 70 percent of U.S. TV commercials placed with programming aimed at a 25- to 49-year-old audience.

Previously untapped media like *Reader's Digest* and *AARP* (the periodical of the organization originally called the American Association of Retired Persons) saw Wii advertisements. Nintendo said it was not a "next-generation" pitch, but rather one for "new-generation gaming"— grandmothers and other first-timers.

FOR THE MASSES

For younger players, promotion included the then-popular social-networking site MySpace, as Nintendo of America President Reggie Fils-Aime joined the chorus exhorting a game change aimed at making it easier in practice and pocketbook to play.

"Our goal is to bring gaming back to the masses," he said in a statement. "You see that in our pricing, you see that in the number of units we plan to make available this year, and you see that in how we are positioning the Wii to appeal to every member of the household. . . . Our competitors are stuck in an old paradigm."[15]

After two console failures, Nintendo knew that consumers would soon be the final arbiter of what mattered most. Iwata promised to avoid the mistakes of the past, and without a hint of boastfulness indicated that a potential prize in his company's long comeback was in sight.

"We cannot win user support by offering only a few titles at the launch like we did for Nintendo 64 and GameCube," he said. "We are the only one who has clearly made it a mission to lure those who don't play games and those who have quit playing games, and to break down a wall in a household between players and non-players."

"If that goal is achieved," he added, "there is a good chance we can be No. 1."[16]

NOTES

1. "Iwata Asks: Special Edition Interview," n.d.; available online: http://us.wii.com/iwata_asks/special_edition_interview/; access date: August 24, 2010.

2. "Iwata Asks: Volume 1: The Wii Hardware," n.d.; available online: http:// us.wii.com/iwata_asks/wii_console/; access date: August 24, 2010

3. Ibid.

4. "Iwata Asks: Wii Remote: Part 1: Taking Control to the Drawing Board," n.d.; available online: http://us.wii.com/iwata_asks/wii_remote/; access date: August 24, 2010.

5. Ibid.

6. "Iwata Asks: Special Edition Interview."

7. "Iwata Asks: Wii Remote: Part 1."

8. "Iwata Asks: Wii Sports: Part 1: A Truly Ground-breaking Collection of Games," n.d.; available online: http://us.wii.com/iwata_asks/wii_sports/; access date: August 24, 2010.

9. "Iwata Asks: Special Edition Interview."

10. "Peter Moore Interview: Part Four," *Guardian*, September 18, 2008; available online: www.guardian.co.uk/technology/gamesblog/2008/sep/11/games interviews.microsoft; access date: August 24, 2010.

11. "Iwata Asks: Wii Remote: Part 3: Towards a New Standard," n.d.; Available online: http://us.wii.com/iwata_asks/wii_remote/part_3/; access date: August 24, 2010.

12. Ibid.

13. Ibid.

14. "Iwata Asks: Wii Sports: Part 4: Games That Even People Watching Can Enjoy," n.d.; available online: http://us.wii.com/iwata_asks/wii_sports/part_4/; access date: August 24, 2010.

15. Stephen Hamm, "Hot Chips and Cool Consoles," *Business Week*, September 14, 2006; available online: www.businessweek.com/the_thread/techbeat/archives/2006/09/hot_chips_and_cool_consoles.html; access date: August 24, 2010.

16. "EXPO-INTERVIEW-Nintendo May Not Launch Game Boy Advance Sequel," Reuters, May 11, 2006.

CHAPTER **9**

Wiining the Day

THE HANDHELD MANTLE REESTABLISHED, Wii was set up to prove that Nintendo's "new generation" gamer strategy could succeed beyond portable consoles in the now $30-billion video game industry. Satoru Iwata admitted the name "Wii" had faced criticism, but he maintained the title emphasized the console's group gaming utility, translating across international boundaries better than "Revolution."

"I have never thought the name was a mistake. Some people seem to have a problem with it now, but I think they'll grow to like it," he said.[1]

The $250 Wii was estimated by analysts to produce a $50 profit on each unit. Based on a normal sales lifespan of 35 million consoles, that would bring in astronomical returns, and bring them in very quickly if initial feverish demand for bundled games like "Wii Sports" continued. Numbers from Japanese industry-watcher *Enterbrain* showed Wii outselling PlayStation 3, as well as Microsoft's hardware, in its first 2006 year-end home season, despite debuting three weeks later than the PS3 and long after the Xbox 360.

In the United States, the NPD Group said less than 200,000 PS3s sold in the first 13 days on store shelves, under half of Sony's target, while Nintendo sold more than 475,000 Wii consoles. That didn't put it instantly on top, though; the Xbox 360 and Epic Games' "Gears of War" sold more than 510,000 consoles. The initially exclusive 360 title sold over 1.8 million copies by year-end, eventually helping to boost "Xbox Live" subscriptions by 50 percent.

157

Wii's appeal to all age groups helped drive sales up.

Iwata tried to downplay competition with the other firms' consoles, but Wii's sales performance would show whether stepping back from the "console wars" strategy had been the right call. At the same time, limited supply was plaguing Nintendo's Japanese rival; Sony had prepared only 100,000 consoles for Japan and 400,000 consoles for North America, while the PS3's European launch would not occur until 2007.

Price also became a key factor, as Wii sold for $50 to $350 less than its rivals' models, depending on the bells and whistles or add-ons purchased. Those who had never played games before had a limited amount of money to take a chance on the entertainment and opted for simplicity and lower cost, which often meant the Wii. For seniors living on a pension, a new gaming market that Nintendo made an extra effort to reach, extravagance and experimentation were even less likely.

Iwata and Shigeru Miyamoto spoke at the Foreign Correspondents' Club of Japan late in 2006 to promote the console, which was when I met these executives for the first time. With its global debut now just weeks past, Iwata said Nintendo had sold 600,000 Wii consoles in its first eight days in North and Latin America, some 400,000 in a day at Japanese stores, and more than 325,000 units in Europe in just two days. Stock had so quickly vaporized that making sales forecasts was becoming more difficult, he said.

"Nintendo aims to ship 4 million Wii by the end of this calendar year and 6 million by the end of the fiscal year in March," he said, adding that early success in no way guaranteed sustained sales.

"It is not uncommon for game machines to enjoy great sales during the launch period. More important is how we maintain our strong momentum."

The author (right) introduces Nintendo's Satoru Iwata (middle) and Shigeru Miyamoto at the FCCJ.

GAME CHANGERS

That "sales mo" depended on bringing more new players to Wii and Nintendo software, and—as DS had demonstrated—reaching women was an essential part of this goal. Women of all ages were now estimated to make up nearly 40 percent of game console users and an even larger share of PC-based players, as overall time commitment to the entertainment had been falling.

"Serious" games such as Nintendo's "Brain Training" had helped to stave off the "gamer drift" trend, and now—with Wii—playing video games was morphing into an accepted expenditure of time that was perceived as useful for personal development, stress relief, exercise, and family bonding. Certainly, intense and substantial marketing contributed to these images, but Wii quickly found footholds where gaming never had before: retirement homes, cruise ships, hotels, and even—ironically—sports clubs.

Nintendo had trumpeted gaming for those 5-to-95-year-old gamers, but a "Wii Seniors Bowling Night" must have seemed far-fetched when

Satoru Iwata (right) and Shigeru Miyamoto play Wii Sports' tennis at a product launch.

the idea was mulled in its development stage in Kyoto. However, the console's low cost and relative low management made a number of assisted-living facilities see the merits of the entertainment. The Wii's minimum of buttons and maximum of indoor wireless-play literally bowled over some gray consumers, as the percentage of U.S. citizens over 50 who played video games in 2007 hit nearly 25 percent, up from a mere 9 percent in 1999, according to the Entertainment Software Association.

The senior share of players grew further in 2008, while estimates for hardware sales to those near retirement age rose to 10 percent of Nintendo's total. The standard cry from "seniors-gone-wild," a group who had grown tired of board games and *mahjong*, was that the console offered a chance to get out of their chairs and actually play again, and Nintendo was only too happy to oblige.

Demand remained intense even after the year-end holidays, particularly from those unable to buy before Christmas or who had been exposed to "Sports" on friends' consoles. In the month of January 2007 alone, Nintendo sold over 490,000 Wii consoles in North America. Microsoft and Sony trailed by more than 30 percent, while the PS2 was the Wii's closest rival. In what would become a refrain over the console's boom years, Nintendo said finite supply had ultimately capped sales.

Lured by the success of the DS and now salivating at initial Wii numbers, third-party software makers, who often waited for early sales performance to dictate whether to make substantial research and development investment, began announcing that they would shift resources to Wii game production. After cool relations with outside developers had chilled demand for Nintendo's last two TV-linked consoles, the embrace was a welcome and essential development. Industry estimates pegged Wii game development at a cost of about $5 million, still just a small fraction of the cost of creating a PS3 title.

However, problems did emerge. Some people were breaking the straps on the Wii Remote controller, or really throwing the "Wii-mote" in games such as bowling when trying to recreate the sensation of a ball rolling from the hand. Iwata said Nintendo took the situation seriously, but was cheered that people had been using the controller aggressively.

The author (right) awards Honorary FCCJ Membership to Satoru Iwata (middle) and Shigeru Miyamoto.

"Even beyond our expectations people are becoming more and more excited playing with Wii," he said, noting measures such as sales of a special controller grip glove, free replacement straps, and the launch of a 1-800 number to look into any damage reports that emerged.

Share Rally

Pelham Smithers, head of a U.K. market and investment advisory firm and long-time Nintendo watcher, told me the Wii launch convinced global investors that the DS handheld console was no fluke, while the Wii's broad utility and demographic, relative to its peers, was affecting the stock's allure.

"The shares started to take off. During 2006, Nintendo's share price just went from strength to strength," Smithers said. "In June, the DS-Lite was launched in the United States, and sold 600,000 units in just 19 days, and Nintendo was struggling to keep up with demand. Just when you think it couldn't go more right, Sony dropped the ball on the PlayStation 3—there were production problems with both the 'Cell' chip and the blue laser diode, resulting in huge cost over-runs and production shortages. Sony can only launch in two regions, and did so with an over-priced product."

Microsoft, which came to market before its console rivals, was winning the core gamer battle with the Xbox 360 and some first-person shooter hits, but losing the overall war, Smithers said, adding, "Because of the Xbox's reputation as a hard-core gamer product, consumers opt for the Wii and like it, and soon the Wii becomes unavailable."

In January 2007, Nintendo hiked its operating profit forecast for Wii's launch year to a record $1.6 billion, also raising its stock dividend by 20 percent, as its share price climbed to over ¥29,000 (about $240), a near tripling in value from just two years before. By the end of the month, Nintendo attributed a 43 percent rise in profit to the new console, sending its shares through the ¥34,000 level, or about $280. The stock rallied even further by mid-year, putting Nintendo's market capitalization above Sony's, in a definitive statement on literal changing fortunes. However, the rocket ride that had begun in late 2005 with the success of the DS was far from over.

What had been a relatively moribund industry saw sales in the United States alone hit $12.5 billion in 2006, and then soar to a record $17.9 billion in 2007, according to the NPD Group. For Nintendo, the results were indeed becoming a revolution and its relatively new leadership was taking on rock star status.

Reggie-Lution

Some dubbed Nintendo's success and aggressive agenda in the United States a "Reggie-Lution," a play on the first name of Nintendo of America chief Reggie Fils-Aime, who offered the pitch with all the verve of a veteran salesman. The executive credited Iwata and Miyamoto with driving the transition in Nintendo that led to the Wii.

"We had to do something fundamentally different, so here we are at the mid-point of 2007, the total industry is up just under 50 percent; Nintendo is driving just under 70 percent of that growth, and we're launching new accessories," he said. "When you look at the U.S. business results for hardware and software for console, portable and PCs, there was a five-year time period where the numbers were just bubbling around $11 billion, more or less; they weren't moving—the market was stagnant."[2]

Some claimed the company was being intentionally parsimonious in Wii console and game availability, aiming to prolong demand and squelch calls for price cuts, but Fils-Aime said blistering demand, and not under-production, kept the Wii in relatively perpetual short supply.

"We're making huge amounts of products every single month. It's not a capacity issue, it's a demand issue. We're not trying to temper demand; what we're trying to do is figure how to add additional lines to meet a higher level . . . We're on a pace to drive installed numbers worldwide faster than any other home console box before us."[3]

Nonetheless, limited supply affected 2007 year-end sales, or rather some parents' ability to obtain the hot items as gifts, while complaints emerged that Wii retailers had tied sale of the console to purchase additional software, driving up the price by as much as two times. Demand for the Wii had become so intense that a black market valued the console at 10 times its list price, while in Europe, reports emerged that British consumers traveled across the channel in a mini-replay of the Normandy invasion on hearing that French retailers still had Wii consoles in stock.

Global holiday video game shopping at the end of 2007 reached $4.8 billion, a jump of nearly 30 percent on the preceding year. The DS was the most popular console, followed by the Wii, which hit 20 million in total sales by the end of 2007.

Nintendo's share price continued to skyrocket, while *Asiamoney* magazine named Iwata one of 2007's best executives, noting a market capitalization that had jumped from $25 billion to $85 billion. In April 2008, Nintendo reported a record operating profit of $4.7 billion and forecast another epic year ahead, even with the yen rising against the U.S. dollar.

Overall, Nintendo's combined console and software sales hit $16 billion, a staggering jump of over 70 percent on the preceding year and a result with which the late Fusajiro Yamauchi could have purchased the entire mulberry bark output of northeast Asia as well as all its *hanafuda* factories. The numbers came not from an automaker, financial institution, or petroleum giant, but from a nearly 120-year-old Kyoto-based entertainment firm that started by making playing cards.

Yet, in the mold of Hiroshi Yamauchi, none of this paper wealth was taken for granted by company executives or staff, even if they owned Nintendo stock, which would have briefly provided them untold riches. That restraint, as financial turmoil in global markets began to consume share value and threaten consumer video game demand, proved a defining characteristic. Nintendo's momentous achievements never dared to become a parade, as its focus become fixed on not surrendering the No. 1 spot again.

By the end of 2008, U.S. Wii sales alone hit 17.6 million consoles, with over 10.2 million purchased that year, more than the combined total of the PS3 and Xbox 360. Five of the 10 top-selling year-end games were designed for the Wii, while the DS also continued to sell at a record pace, likely to break the sales totals of the most popular game consoles of all time, as its software approached 100 million units.

Nintendo's rosy scenario was not universal for the industry, as a rash of software studio closures and layoffs hit such stalwarts as Microsoft's Ensemble Studios, a team that had helped on "Halo Wars." The layoffs continued the following year, including hundreds at Microsoft's Aces operation, which had produced its "Flight Simulator" franchise.

Blue Ocean

Meanwhile, Nintendo and Iwata accentuated the positive, which was unquestionably the success of his "Blue Ocean" strategy—laying nets where others were not fishing, or finding markets without competitors. Iwata said the idea was not universally endorsed when proposed once he become CEO, but the results had found many quick converts, including even Nintendo's rivals.

"Within Nintendo, among the shareholders, everywhere, there was resistance. When I first raised the idea in 2003, nobody believed it was possible to broaden the games market," he said. "There is no doubt our blue ocean will turn red. . . . Microsoft, for example has made it clear that it wants to follow our success."[4]

After "Wii Sports," Miyamoto, whose hobbies had often found their way into hit games such as "Pikmin" (gardening) and "Nintendogs" (pets), had a new obsession ideal for driving consumers to the console: Fitness. His "Health Pack" prototype game was renamed "Wii Fit," with origins in Miyamoto's own history of too little exercise and too much work. He said he came upon the idea after giving up *pachinko* and smoking for trips to the pool and subsequent weigh-ins.

"When I graduated from university and joined the company, I ended up putting on weight. We were so busy back then," he said. "I started regularly going to the swimming hall. My weight dropped quite a bit, and it felt like my overall fitness had increased as well. I started thinking that getting fit could actually be fun."[5]

Miyamoto said daily tabulation of the ups and downs of his own 62-kilogram frame, as well as studies of balance and health, led to development by colleague Takao Sawano's team of new fitness software contained in a "Balance Board" that acted as a kind of bathroom scale. The unit would now be placed in the living room or den, rather than the bathroom, if Nintendo became successful with the game.

Private scale makers could not develop a price-competitive alternative that met Nintendo's specifications, as the unit needed a sturdy but comfortable shell for software that could send out 60 game signals a second, not a box merely reading weight or body mass. Sawano's team created an in-house version, modeled on the pairs of scales Japanese *sumo* wrestlers had to use because their weight exceeded the limits of a single unit.

The system employed a rotary encoder from the Nintendo 64 thumb stick that could assess weight and other data to a precision of 100 grams, while shifts in position and balance could be calculated via four implanted sensors immediately detecting movement. The team went through various board shape designs, but at Miyamoto's suggestion changed a square board prototype to a rectangle.

The board's width—about that of human shoulders—also allowed skateboarding and a broader slate of games, as its design was intended to support feet of all sizes. Body weight, though, even in a game format derived from *sumo*, did have a limit: those above 150 kilos, or 330 pounds, would not be allowed on the board, although still accepted in the *dohyo*.

Games focused on posture and balance, with 40 fitness activities such as low-impact workouts. Like the Wii Remote, the peripheral Balance Board was cordless, while the price at near $90 was considered high, even with the many game options. The cordless status for the 3.5-kilo (or 7.7-pound) board came late in development, as an "upturning of the tea table," or "*chabudai gaeshi*," demand from Iwata, who recognized that Wii's allure had stemmed in great part from its minimum of wires and connections. At least 10 additional games were created to utilize the board even in non-"Fit" activities.

Fit as a Fiddle

"Fit" used a cartoon TV character commenting on individual development efforts, while players tried to reduce a gap between their actual age and Wii avatar, as calculated by the timed game. To some degree, Fit used the same dynamic of "Brain Training," but Nintendo hired personal trainer Kaoru Matsui to consult on key workout regimens and Miyamoto stressed the game's family focus, promoting group weigh-ins and body-mass index (BMI) charting.

Amid intense discussion, Miyamoto insisted that weight had to be calculated as a sign of healthy progress, as players would never celebrate BMI improvement, only lost kilograms or pounds. Admittedly designed for women, Fit's New Age approach resonated across the globe and genders as yoga, aerobics, and conditioning became the *Jane Fonda Workout* of the decade. Other software later replicated Fit's efforts with cardio workouts, Pilates, and personal training, but Miyamoto said there had been strong arguments at Nintendo against giving the game a green light.

"We had all sorts of reasons against the project—'What to do if someone accidentally dropped the weighty board on their feet?' 'Who would want to measure their weight in front of other people?' 'How could people accurately measure their weight with their clothes on?'" he said. "Yoga was undergoing an upsurge in Japan at around the same time as we were conducting the planning meetings, so there was a staff member who wanted to make yoga-related software."[6]

Company-watchers predicted Nintendo's U.S. promotional outlay for "Fit" would become its largest ever, launching at chains such as Target and Best Buy instead of the game-oriented outlets that had been essential in the past. NoA's Reggie Fils-Aime said the company's expectations were high for the May 2008 launch, after "Fit" sold a million units in Japan in its first month.

"In the United States the reaction will be just as strong, if not stronger, given the American focus and psyche on being fit, and the game itself is going to be localized for our audience," he said. "For the launch of Wii, we executed a number of non-traditional programs and that thrust will continue with Wii Fit. You can expect to see it on morning national programs . . . female-oriented programs. There will be a broad Internet program . . . and there will also be traditional prime time TV advertising. It will likely be our largest launch of the year from a total dollar spent standpoint."[7]

Nintendo opened "Wii Kiosks" in shopping malls and continued to promote the console widely in North America. Analysts estimated that 30 percent of the then 10 million Wii owners in the United States would buy the game. That estimate proved conservative, and by June 2009, Nintendo had sold 20 million "Fit" copies worldwide, nearing $2 billion in sales.

Meanwhile, sales of traditional video game staples like Take Two Interactive Software's "Grand Theft Auto," played on Sony's PlayStation franchise for a decade, began to slow—after the latest edition saw an amazing $500 million in turnover in its first week on store shelves. Industry-watchers said games often portraying women in a poor light for a mostly young male audience were now being outsold by titles designed with women in mind.

Retailers like Walmart and online markets such as Amazon.com used "Fit" to boost Mother's Day sales, quickly selling out in pre-order periods. By the end of the decade, the franchise had become, along with "Sports," among the most successful games ever created. Nintendo added to the line "Wii Fit Plus" for the 2009 year-end, touting personalized workouts and 20 new activities. Despite the potential for overkill of the health theme and the now-raging global financial crisis, "Plus" sold 340,000 copies in its first week in Japan, followed by strong U.S. and U.K. showings.

The innovative Wiimote, Nintendo's Wii remote, took gaming experience to the next level.

The month of December 2009 proved to be the greatest U.S. month for video game sales ever, in which the Wii and DS held the top two console spots, and "Wii Fit" the No. 2 game position, after the latest Mario title. In the key holiday month, Nintendo consoles played 6 of the top 10 games.

"Fit" had been a key reason, but some media noted incidents of foot-related injuries by people slipping off of boards, similar to the remote thumb pain known as "Nintendinitis" in the 1990s. The overall spin on the console's games, though, remained its positive health impact, and "Wii Sports Resort," Nintendo's update of the original bundled game, had the third-best launch in Japanese game history in June 2009, reaching 17 million sales globally in its first 20 weeks on the market.

Researchers at the American Heart Association in November 2009 presented a study showing that workouts in certain "Sports" and "Fit" games could contribute to the prevention of cardiovascular diseases. The study found that one-third of the games boosted MET energy expenditure to the 3.0 level, considered to be moderate intensity, with games like boxing clocking in at 4.5 METs.

Nintendo, in a recurring role, helped to fund the study and ensured that its results found circulation across all media arteries.

MARIO RETURNS

Until the GameCube, Nintendo had launched a Mario title with each new console, as the success of the franchise fed demand for the hardware. Within Wii's channels, the Mario avatar was widely available, but Nintendo looked to personalize and diversify the gaming experience, and to some degree, that meant distancing key software from its icons.

Nonetheless, "Mario Kart Wii" proved popular for the new console, adding a new "Wii Wheel" for virtual driving in its sixth update to a series that began in 1992, as well as 16 new courses and 16 retro raceways. The "Wheel" was also sold as a separate unit, meaning a potential windfall if the entire family wanted to race, while the game was added as a channel to the Wii directory, allowing online global racing challenges. By August 2009, "Kart" had sold more than 15.4 million copies.

"Super Mario Bros." returned for the Wii's 2009 year-end season, after an earlier revival on the DS, a version that had been criticized as a less than innovative update of the series, although still selling over 20 million units. The Wii version allowed 2D multiplayer use for the run-and-jump staple but not online gaming, which some industry-watchers said was less homage to a game that began over 25 years earlier and more indicative of Nintendo's misgivings about the benefits and experience of complete interconnectivity.

Iwata predicted sales of at least 10 million copies, while Miyamoto said the game had finally helped him realize its simple premise after more than 20 years:

"Fundamentally, 'Mario' is a game where if you fail and lose a turn, you'll be sent straight back to the start," he said.[8]

Nintendo was not sent back to the starting line, as his latest "Mario" edition reached its 10 million sales goal worldwide in an astonishing seven weeks and then broke the 15 million mark in little more than a half year.

However, the Kyoto firm and the entire industry began to see ripples as the worst retail environment in recent history began to force downward revisions and lower console prices.

Nintendo results announced in May 2009 showed a $2.8 billion profit, as sales jumped 10 percent to $18.5 billion with the DS breaking the 100 million console line and Wii the 50 million mark. However, Nintendo's forecast for the year ahead of flat to lower sales and profits was either exceptionally conservative or exceptionally prescient, and the Kyoto firm had never been known for wild exaggerations in its outlooks, while conditions both internal and external for its Japanese rival were even more challenging.

SONY UNITED

As Nintendo belatedly felt a downdraft after a slew of record-setting hits, Sony already had faced profound changes in its business environment. Gaming, the former source of billions of dollars in profit for the conglomerate, ran into critical development and delivery issues for its next-generation PS3, a combination that would knock the company from its top industry perch, and ultimately prove to be its fiery creator's Waterloo.

The console, equipped with Cell chip technology and a Blu-ray disc player, came to market a year later than planned, both limited in supply and substantially higher in price. Sony envisioned the Cell chip to be a multicore MPU delivering advanced computational power that would actually strengthen when linking with other chips in company products. Ultimately, this would create an interconnected network in which additional Sony purchases would further complement total performance, a convergence that it believed would yoke its hardware and content to sustained dominance.

Ironically, industry-watchers said games from Sony and other software makers for the PS3 did not fully utilize the Cell chip's capabilities, while some designers complained, as they had about Nintendo's GameCube, that development tools for the high-end console were too expensive and difficult to use, relative to rivals' offerings. Sony had charged over $18,000 for a PS3 development package, before eventually cutting that price by half when developer demand and game supply proved thin.

The Cell project further lost traction in December 2005, when Ken Kutaragi was forced to give up his role as head of TV and semiconductor operations, as well as losing his day-to-day leadership status for the gaming unit that he had founded. The PS3 had only debuted in November, and despite a relative track record of excellence—as well as one of insolence—he found his remaining tenure at Sony was a matter of months. A career spent waffling between maverick company savior and outrageous bad boy was coming to a close.

A Generation Too Far

The third iteration of Sony's console franchise, which had begun in the 1990s, became an expensive product with all the trimmings at a moment when consumer wallets were tightening and the electronics giant was listing to port from other corporate losses. Internally, calls over the years to get rid of Sony's "OB"—its "old boys"—had left Kutaragi with few friends and tenuous support when his own products ran into sales or delivery schedule difficulties, and some began to see him as now also representing a product generation too far removed from reality.

Kutaragi at one point in late 2006 blamed the electronics division's inability to deliver parts on time as key to a PS3 shipment delay, going so far as to say manufacturing quality at Sony had declined. Thus, the man once touted as a possible president of the Sony group made his farewell announcement at an afternoon board meeting, only with knowledge of the Sony chairman. It ultimately shocked few, as CEO Howard Stringer had effectively taken away all of his power already and Kutaragi had threatened to resign, while still talking about PS4, PS5, and PS6 in the same month as giving notice.

Sony said after the PS3 European rollout in March that Kutaragi had identified the June shareholders meeting as the ideal time to "pass the torch to the new generation of management," which would center on Kazuo Hirai, a Stringer ally known for the PS2's success in North America.

Hirai took over Sony Computer Entertainment in December 2006, finding a growing malaise that needed rapid attention.

Hirai, 46, made it clear that the PS3 was a gaming console, despite its many multimedia capabilities, while Stringer said that after establishing the console's "street cred" with players and improving its sales performance, other broadband-linked functionalities would then be promoted.

Kutaragi told the *Nihon Keizai Shimbun* on the day after his resignation that he would measure his achievements in terms of the console he pioneered: "From now on, I will think of myself as the grandfather of the PS, and continue working toward my dreams."[9]

Some compared Kutaragi's corporate travails to Steve Jobs's early rise and fall at Apple, predicting a possible return and implying that his departure would have a second act. By decade's end, the play was still stuck at Act 1, and his coda became a cross between a 21st-century disembowelment by a proud and long-feted *samurai* who had lost honor, and the impetuousness of an angry genius seeking greener pastures elsewhere.

Microsoft's J Allard, who had long maintained that his corporate dream would be posting Kutaragi's resignation letter by his desk, never actually saw the Sony game legend's farewell manuscript, but he had the satisfaction of knowing that the third installment of Kutaragi's franchise was now in the unfamiliar position of the bottom of its bracket.

PS3 Plunge

Sensing disaster at retail counters, Kutaragi had announced PS3 price cuts at the Tokyo Game Show in September 2006, only two months before the console's debut. Still, the PS3 never really regained lost ground to the Xbox 360 and Nintendo Wii, and Sony had to cut its price to under $500 within a year of the console's launch—increasing its loss per model sold.

Sony also introduced a separate PS3 with a smaller hard drive for $370, but that model—still $120 more than the Wii—initially could not play PS2 game software, launched under the premise that it would drive the older console's consumers to buy the new and more expensive hardware. Instead, many existing owners stayed with their PS2s and older game library, waiting for another PS3 price cut or more compelling games.

From 1994 to 2006, Sony's gaming business had made approximately $4 billion of operating profit, and now its losses were beginning to erode that legacy of success. Electronics industry firms in general average a 2.5 percent profit-to-sales margin, while the PS franchise had exceeded 4.5 percent—until the PS3.

Kutaragi had insisted that the sleek machine, powered by the Cell, was more than a game console, but potential alone could not restore the near $2 billion encumbered by SCE to create the console, as well as the research and development tied to its cutting-edge chip and its factories. By his departure, some media reports called the new console a flop—an ignominious distinction for a Walkman franchise of its day that had sold more than 100 million consoles and at one point held a 70 percent market share.

Meanwhile, Sony production of Cell chips for the PS3 had initially been considered essential, but by 2007, the company decided to sell off its chip business (into which it had poured $2 billion). The move was an attempt to drive down the price of other companies' chips, meaning Sony could pass on the savings to PS3 consumers in a lower retail price. In short, it was more cost-effective not to have their own technology, and the Cell project had proven an expensive exercise in do-it-yourself futility.

Some saw Kutaragi's departure as an internal checkmate by Sony's foreign CEO, Sir Howard Stringer, who had slowly taken the reins away from the *enfant terrible* since his arrival, essentially doing what his Japanese bosses could not—fire him. The Welsh-born Stringer had attempted to reverse years of silo business strategy that had limited sharing of technology, but the media and Hollywood-trained boss was overwhelmed by the tide of red ink facing him, and arguably by how little the consumer electronics giant could be changed.

By May 2007, Sony announced a near 70 percent drop in profit, which it blamed on PS3 price cuts and a lithium battery recall. The overall loss in the games division had grown to over $2.3 billion, especially devastating when compared to a mild profit the year before—and to Nintendo's billions of dollars in the black. In a search for new profit streams, Stringer pushed the gaming unit to offer a video-downloading service on the PS3, trying to broaden the console's audience and content.

Estimates of the potential Internet video market exceeded $5 billion by the end of the decade, with the potential to double within five years, aided in great part by Sony's in-house TV and movie content. Yoking the assets would be a test of corporate integration, which so far had proven to lack complete commitment. Stringer tasked Hirai with putting gaming and all Sony's electronics businesses on the same track.

Hirai, who once had said the "console wars" ended with the PS2's dominance over its rivals, was now deep in corporate triage, trying to restore the lifeline of Sony's video game business as well as its image globally. After two years in the job, he made mild headway and, to a small degree, sounded like Miyamoto and Gunpei Yokoi before him.

"It's been a very busy and hectic couple of years for me," he said. "We're in the entertainment industry. My question is, 'If you're not having fun, why are you in it?' We're not selling widgets, we're selling entertainment, and everyone needs to be entertained."[10]

Main rival Nintendo could claim to be having fun while making its remarkable comeback, but also was recognized in late 2009 by *Business Week* (in a compilation by management consulting firm A.T. Kearney) as the "World's Best Company". The title, requiring firms to have at least $10 billion in sales and at least 25 percent of business abroad, put focus on sales growth and value creation over a five-year period. Based on Nintendo's soaring market capitalization, it topped a "Who's Who" list that included Google and Apple right behind it. Sony and Microsoft were not on the list.[11]

Nintendo's $16.8 billion in sales in 2008 and 38 percent jump in value creation with its soaring stock had sparked tremendous changes in the recognition of its global footprint and brand beyond pre-teens and their parents, while its financial success had made its largest shareholder, the now quietly retired former *shacho Hiroshi Yamauchi,* an even wealthier man.

NOTES

1. "Nintendo Pres: No Regrets about Wii Name," Dow Jones Newswires, June 7, 2007.

2. Bro Buzz, "GamePro Q&A: Nintendo CEO Fils-Aime Talks Wii Production Woes, Online Plans," July 27, 2007; available online: www.gamepro.com/article/features/125669/gp-q-a-nintendo-ceo-fils-aime-talks-wii-production-woes-online-plans/; access date: August 28, 2010

3. Ibid.

4. Rhys Blakely, "Wii Are Swimming in a Clear Blue Ocean," *Times,* July 12, 2007; available online: http://business.timesonline.co.uk/tol/business/industry_sectors/technology/article2063714.ece; access date: August 24, 2010.

5. "Iwata Asks: Wii Fit, Volume 1: A New Creation," n.d.; available online: http://us.wii.com/wii-fit/iwata_asks/vol2_page1.jsp; access date: August 19, 2010.

6. Ibid.

7. Matt Casamassina, "Interview: Reggie Fils-Aime on Wii Fit," IGN, February 20, 2008; available online: http://wii.ign.com/articles/853/853258p1.html; access date: August 24, 2010.

8. "Iwata Asks: New Super Mario Bros. Wii," n.d.; available online: http://us.wii.com/iwata_asks/nsmb/vol1_page9.jsp; access date: August 24, 2010.

9. Akito Tanaka and Tomoyuki Kawai, "Analysis: Is It 'Game Over' for SCE Chairman Kutaragi?" *Nihon Keizai Shimbun,* May 2, 2007 (available on Factiva).

10. Tom Hoggins, "Kaz Hirai Interview: Start of a New Movement," *Telegraph,* June 24, 2009; available online: www.telegraph.co.uk/technology/videogames/5624022/Kazuo-Hirai-interview-Start-of-a-new-movement.html; access date: August 24, 2010.

11. Esme E. Deprez, "World's Best Companies 2009," *Business Week,* October 1, 2009; available online: www.businessweek.com/globalbiz/content/sep2009/gb20090930_066258.htm; access date: September 3, 2010.

CHAPTER **10**

Wealth and Legacy

Hiroshi Yamauchi retired as Nintendo chairman on June 29, 2005, after 55 years of employment, citing age and physical condition. He had only ventured to work a few times a month since the handover to Satoru Iwata in 2002, and the formal retirement was more an act of closure than a corporate revelation.

In his new status, Yamauchi would continue to serve as a company adviser, domestic ambassador, opinionated shareholder, and occasional philanthropist. At his Kyoto estate—not far from Shogoin Temple, which was built in 1676 and known as the "Guardian Temple of the Retired Emperor"—Yamauchi began a rare display of his own imperial benevolence on the cusp of leaving a legacy beyond his family business.

It was not a pronounced change in demeanor. The walls of his family home remained high, with added planks of wood and metal as well as barbed wire and spires to keep out prying eyes and unwanted visitors. On the outside of the family compound of a man who had earned billions of dollars from children's entertainment, a sign told neighborhood youth not to throw balls against the sides of his mini-fortress. It seemed to fit the image of a man who seldom found little of the "fun" that his company frequently preached.

A chauffeured car usually waited outside the gates, as the home had been built long before the carport era. However, in the 1,200-year-old city, the trappings of the multibillionaire and his family melted easily into a neighborhood and cultural basin long familiar with wealth and history.

If the Yamauchi estate ever became a tour bus stop, it would not happen with the family's assent or the local government's assistance, as no reference or reverence was apt to be bestowed upon the living in a town so embedded in the past. Even the neighborhood cultural site, Shogoin, now served as an inn for overnight travelers, none of whom were likely aware that the former head of the "House of Mario" lived nearby.

With its business history spanning little more than a century, the Yamauchi family possibly still seemed only *nouveau riche* to some in Kyoto, compared with certain scions of the ancient former capital. Kyoto, moreover, was not known as the friendliest of Japanese cities, and in that was a perfect setting for a man who likely saw networking as the trivial pursuit of those who could not create their own worth.

Born into wealth, the nonconformist Hiroshi had never felt the need to pay for class respect or entry, and—similarly—as noted, he and Nintendo had opted out of Japanese industry organizations and events, although many of his key game and parts suppliers took leadership roles. In the company's home city of nearly 1.5 million people, often characterized as at worst "snobby," and at best "mannered," Yamauchi perhaps saw efforts to ingratiate himself with local gentry or with the public at large as the chief of a kinder, gentler company as both foolish and disingenuous.

Business had always been a kind of warfare to make more and pay less, while his public service, as Yamauchi often noted, was evident every March 15, Japan's tax deadline.

"I think I'm involved in community service sufficiently," he told the *New York Times* in 1996. "I'm the biggest individual taxpayer in Kyoto, and Nintendo is the largest taxpayer overall."[1]

PLAY BALL

However, there had been moments when his actions appeared out of character, even spendthrift—the most memorable being his purchase of the Seattle Mariners in 1992, which allowed the baseball team to remain in the U.S. city. With obvious self-interest due to the proximity of

Redmond to Seattle, Yamauchi and Nintendo of America (NoA) bought the franchise for $125 million, after receiving local pleas to keep the woeful team from pulling up stakes for another city.

Yamauchi, no fan of baseball or sports in general, had been contacted by his son-in-law, NoA head Minoru Arakawa, about the opportunity, which was not without controversy and obvious cost. Some in baseball portrayed the potential acquisition of the team from its then owner, communications magnate Jeff Smulyan, as another landmark property grab by a cash-rich Japanese giant in the era shortly after the nation's "bubble economy." These critics asserted that the United States—in an economic downturn—would be potentially losing a symbol of its national pastime to a foreign invader.

Robert Whiting, author of the *Meaning of Ichiro* and a close watcher of baseball on both sides of the Pacific, called the acquisition enlightened self-interest.

"Yamauchi didn't know the first thing about baseball, but he did see the public relations value in rescuing the team for Seattle. Call it an advertising expense, as Nintendo's annual after-tax profits were enough to buy more than one Major League Baseball (MLB) club a year," Whiting told me.

The Baseball Commissioner and MLB franchise owners initially did not approve the deal but relented under pressure from Seattle fans, although requiring Yamauchi to hold less than 50 percent of team ownership himself, despite no similar rules on Canadian investors. Proving no good deed goes unpunished, Yamauchi's largesse was soon rewarded through no fault of his own with a players' strike that wiped out most of the 1994 MLB season and took the pathetic Mariners franchise off the field.

Since the team's origins in 1977, the Mariners had not enjoyed a winning season except for 1991, while their Kingdome stadium, which had been constructed for football and not baseball, was falling apart. Both the team and its stadium had become landmarks of futility at the time of the acquisition, certain to need even greater financial commitment and see further losses before developing any chance of maturing into profit centers.

Once MLB play resumed in 1995, astute hiring and talent acquisition over the next several years ultimately filled the team with stars, including the incumbent Ken Griffey Jr., Edgar Martinez, Randy Johnson, and Alex

Rodriguez, finally lifting the club to the status of playoff contender. Seattle achieved numerous highlights although never a championship, but keeping the team and allowing citizens to witness this metamorphosis with a slate of likely future Hall of Fame players had subtly endeared Nintendo further with locals.

Japan Imports

Yamauchi's impact may have been greatest in helping cultivate a major league beachhead for Japanese talent, as the Mariners became home to pitchers Kazuhiro Sasaki and Shigetoshi Hasegawa, catcher Kenji Johjima, and the greatest baseball export from the country so far, hitting and defensive phenomenon Ichiro Suzuki.

"Many Japanese players, like many Japanese fans, think of the Mariners as a 'hometown' team and Seattle as a 'Little Tokyo,'" Whiting told me. He added that the famously stingy Yamauchi may have overpaid for some of the imported stars.

With Ichiro's arrival in 2001, the Mariners tied the record for most victories in regular season history, although his Rookie of the Year and Most Valuable Player awards could not push the team any further. Ichiro's exploits in the new retractable-roof stadium grabbed headlines and helped fill seats, even when the Mariners again took a turn for the worse.

The team's Japan connection was intended to be cemented with a visit to the home country to start the 2003 MLB season, but the trip was canceled amid security concerns tied to the war in Iraq. Yamauchi, who usually avoided flying overseas if possible, intended to sit behind home plate at Tokyo's "Big Egg" stadium to watch the game, which would have been the septuagenarian's first chance to see his own team play in person.

Ownership had provided advantages and career opportunities for Nintendo's executives, some of whom remained on the Mariners' board or led the team. Yamauchi did not participate in this, however; few billionaire owners have ever been so hands-off with a sports franchise, particularly as the team remained in the red until the 21st century.

On paper, the Mariners lost another $175 million through the 1990s until building Safeco Field, named not for the franchise's guardian angel but a local insurance company that paid $40 million for rights on Seattle's 20-year lease on the sports venue. The state-of-the-art stadium opened in July 1999, but ran $100 million over budget and alienated some taxpayers because of the public debt burden created by the $517 million monolith. However, with the ballpark's fan-friendly design and stars like Ichiro, the team headed toward the black as Yamauchi prepared for his own move from the owner's box.

In November 2004, as his retirement approached, Yamauchi sold his controlling stake in the Mariners to NoA, while Howard Lincoln remained team CEO and Arakawa was chairman emeritus. Lincoln, who had stepped down as chairman of NoA on his 60th birthday in 2000, had been another of the 16 Mariner owners since 1992, along with Yamauchi and Arakawa.

Lincoln said on Yamauchi's resignation that the Kyoto boss had not interfered in team operations, only helped in Japanese personnel decisions. On the Seattle team homepage, no mention is given to Yamauchi or Nintendo, although Mariners' Web pages exist in Japanese as well as in Spanish. *Sake* and *sushi*—a $10 "Ichiroll"—are sold at Safeco, but the stadium has no temples or overt references to the team's international ties.

The temple for Ichiro was on the field, and as of his tenth pro season, he had made the MLB All-Star team every year, due in part to the now common practice of online international voting. Yamauchi, in his most unusual shareholder decision on ending his ownership, gave the superstar 5,000 shares in the Seattle Mariners, valued around $110 each at the time, which was extended after the Japanese player broke the single-season hit record in 2004, a feat many considered impossible.

Ichiro paid tribute to the outgoing boss as he began, to a small degree, to work for himself:

"We all think Mr. Yamauchi doesn't pay much attention to what is going on with us on the team, but when you talk to him, you find he doesn't miss anything."[2]

A Museum Piece

Overall, marketing of Nintendo's team relations has been limited over the nearly two decades of ownership, although those with DS handheld consoles had special game events organized, as well as chat functionality, at Safeco Field. Back in Japan, in Nintendo's lowly corporate showroom in Asakusabashi in Tokyo, one of Ichiro's jerseys hangs on the wall without framing, humbly stapled to a poster board. It looks rather like a project for a school "show-and-tell" session, put together by a student who never cared about the subject and just wished that the assignment would be over soon.

Other Nintendo sports interventions—also on display in the room— have been few, but often came with Kyoto in mind. The Kyoto Purple Sanga soccer team, now called Kyoto Sanga F.C., a franchise perpetually struggling to hold a place in the Japan Pro Soccer League's top division, received financial support from hometown giants Nintendo, Kyocera, and other firms.

Its brilliant purple jerseys and Sanskrit name reflect Kyoto's imperial and Buddhist ties, though Yamauchi himself and the ill-fated GameCube had also been known for a penchant for violet. However, similar to the console's struggles, the team's spotty sports history includes both an Emperor's Cup victory and the J-League record for most second-division relegations.

And, despite his protestations about his civic obligations, in November 2003 Yamauchi became head of a group that wanted to build a museum in the city for a centuries-old card game celebrating a nearly 800-year-old anthology of poems. The *Ogura Hyakunin Isshu* Hall of Fame Shigureden, along the bank of the Hozugawa in the Arashiyama area of Kyoto, opened in 2006 and became a subtle statement about the company's origins, *raison d'être*, and future.

Again, without blatant mention of his contributions at the site, Yamauchi invested more than $20 million into the high-tech wonder, while Nintendo senior staff helped design and develop the facility. Shigure-den, dedicated to Fujiwara no Teika's anthology of *waka* classical poems and the parlor card game *Hyakunin Isshu Karuta*, is a two-story site offering visitors a DSi console to tour the Kyoto Sky Walk virtually, as well as to view giant *karuta* cards and the compilation of 100 poems by 100 poets.

The "Autumn Shower Palace" hall was actually designed by Shigeru Miyamoto, displaying visual and audio wonders through a 70-screen LCD floor. The collection of the 31-syllable, five-line poems can be read or heard on the DS console's *ShigureNavi* museum navigation system, a relationship that Nintendo has also cultivated at other museums and cultural sites.

However, unlike those locations but par for the DS game course, visiting the site is timed. For those wanting greater insight or more playing time, though, Nintendo sells a *Shigure-den* game for the console as well as *karuta* cards online and at the museum gift shop.

Yamauchi, reflecting his interest in film, intended to make an animated movie on the ancient card game, which would dovetail with Nintendo's nascent plans to launch its own production studio in late 2004. However, most of the film unit's business stemmed from its modern game and card monolith, "Pokemon," and Miyamoto, known as the company's biggest dreamer, called building a movie studio in 2007 a "non-prospective" activity, a sign of how fiscal realism had become part of Nintendo's corporate ethos even in a company touting fun.

A LIFELINE

But for the retired Yamauchi, other acts of munificence in his hometown became more concrete, often stemming from personal or professional experiences that later merited his financial assistance. After undergoing hospitalization in June 2006 for treatment on his eyes at the University of Kyoto hospital, Yamauchi donated around $60 million to construct a new ward at the institution. The huge contribution for the neighborhood hospital at the national university was earmarked for patients needing multidisciplinary cancer treatment, and the new 82,000 square foot facility opened in May 2010.

Also in Kyoto, Yamauchi and Nintendo had begun to open their purse strings for old and new company landmarks. However, the work did not substantially address the buildings' chilly ambience, lack of amenities, and general disregard for visitors—if they had the privilege to be allowed in the building, which usually was not the case.

Nintendo sites steadily saw upgrades or at least sustained financing to keep them available if—and when—legacy tours or a more engaged corporate public relations approach began. The company's Meiji Era stone headquarters, little used for 40 years, continued to hold its place on Shomen-dori near a bridge over Kyoto's Kamogawa.

Early in the 21st century, the building still bore plaques and trademarks denoting its *karuta* card origins, along with more modern advisories warning "tourists" in unmistakably brisk English that trespassers would be "brought to justice." Only a sprinkling of staff actually worked in the long narrow building that had once been home to Nintendo's artisans and later its card-making machines. The building, instead, appeared to be a museum-in-waiting, or even a mausoleum for a not-yet-deified corporate emperor, unwilling to sanction greater pomp and circumstance in his lifetime but damned if the site would become a McDonald's or parking lot.

Nintendo's current corporate headquarters is on the south side of Kyoto station, having moved to the location around the beginning of the 21st century. The nearly 33,000-square-meter white building, designed by Yoshimura Architects and originally purchased from an electric company, features a single entrance surrounded by high walls and Japanese maple and cherry trees that enclose a paved courtyard.

The seven-floor complex with basement could be compared cynically to a large ivory GameCube with portholes to breathe, but the Kyoto-based architectural firm described its ceramic design as simple. A blue flag with Nintendo's name in Japanese characters towers over the building. The company's English-language name sits in the far right top corner of the façade, and there is little reason for anyone but an employee to find it. No on-site rooms boast of past or present achievements, and its reason for being is—quite literally—all business.

Staff members usually arrive each morning around 8:00, most traveling by foot or bicycle through a neighborhood dotted with convenience stores, high-voltage power lines, and industrial metal firms, which appears more an unplanned urban sprawl than a multibillion-dollar video game valley. A nearby R&D center that opened in 1954 at Tobakaido Station is slightly more inviting, but also offers no pretense that employment should in any way mean comfort or complacency.

In an effort to meld all its resources and link two separate R&D departments, Nintendo bought a golf driving range behind its white headquarters building for planned expansion. The 40,000-square-meter lot, purchased in December 2008 for almost $142 million, was intended to become

Nintendo's new R&D center, ultimately devoted to new game console creation and software development. Whether it would actually have a showroom remained in doubt, as long as Hiroshi Yamauchi lived in Kyoto.

PUBLIC RELATIONS

Nintendo, unlike most large companies and particularly unusual for one that has been making entertainment products for over 120 years, has kept merchandise display and visitor welcome to a minimum at nearly all of its business locations. This approach—which has avoided public self-recognition of the firm's meteoric rise to the top of the game industry, as well as a greater profile of its pantheon of heroes over the last three decades of invention—reflected the way Yamauchi's Spartan management style permeated the company and its Kyoto roots, which is only beginning to change slowly with his retirement and the company's even greater globalization.

Forays into new retail business models, including online retailing and promotion, emerged when the company launched its first modern retail store at New York's Rockefeller Plaza in May 2005. Nintendo World, a two-story mega-outlet, sells goods ranging from the company's *hanafuda* origins to its latest video games, consoles, and Pokemon cards and characters.

Nintendo World's opening, which included a Manhattan block party, was complemented by a website (www.nintendoworldstore.com) and an online shopping window, which dovetailed with Nintendo's increasing desire to go directly to consumers. The store, which remained without other chain outlets as of early 2010, was intended to be less a monument than a business, selling some merchandise solely at the store while also allowing consumers a chance to "meet Mario" or visiting pop stars, such as teen singer Justin Bieber, who happily showed up to revel in all things Nintendo.

The site offered special DS and Pokemon lounges and facilities and bridged the traditional division between manufacturer and retailer, which Nintendo had maintained since Fusajiro Yamauchi's first retail card shops in Kyoto and Osaka moved to mass production. More dramatic, though, was

Nintendo's online approach, which began to counter the historic culture of corporate quiet, or at least aloofness, with the change in deportment extending beyond its North American marketing arm.

The moves did not threaten to rewrite the Nintendo public relations story, as its corporate website still began a tersely worded company history in the year 1985 with the launch of the Nintendo Entertainment System (NES). The brief chronology concludes with the Wii console in 2006, omitting mention of Hiroshi Yamauchi or any other individual in the company's earlier 96 years of existence. The new boss, however, has begun to put his revolutionary imprint on the company's public façade.

Iwata Online

In a sign of the budding modern history for the company and a significant step away from the Yamauchi leadership era, transcripts of the CEO's "Iwata Asks" (www.nintendo.com/iwataasks) segments—discussions with Nintendo staff—are posted online. These sessions run the gamut of products and services, company history and myths, as well as internal heroes, and Iwata and a broad cast discuss software and hardware development for the two hit consoles and earlier monoliths. He exudes a self-effacing but upbeat presence forged in the confidence of technical perspicacity and interpersonal relationships.

The public series, which Yamauchi almost certainly never would have—or could have—participated in, details the developmental decision making and staff behind the company's hit products. Discussions often include Shigeru Miyamoto and Genyo Takeda, but also others integral to development, while the transcripts of interchanges with the CEO show not only internal recognition for expertise within the company but also the chief's profound respect for his staff's contributions and willingness to highlight them publicly.

In an engaging way, he also challenges staff to stand in front of their ideas and products, and to explain delays and hits or misses, as Iwata and Miyamoto had been doing for decades. His intent—in a company not known for public speakers or comfort with the spotlight—seems to be cultivating a new generation of potential leaders from within, which his own original selection basically outside Nintendo had shown the company to be lacking.

Another unspoken aim appears to be imbuing greater pride internally—and respect externally—for those who are creating the entertainment, and an outright admission that development is far from linear or solely dependent on any one individual. The subtext for Nintendo-watchers is that the company may target children of all ages with its wares, but in no way should it be considered childish.

While certainly a public relations effort, Iwata's willingness to laugh at himself as well as cajole his team to new heights in public show a company more than comfortable in its 21st-century skin. This is a quality that financial investors increasingly recognized as the DS and Wii took no prisoners.

Taking Stock

By 2006, Nintendo's return on investment, or ROI, was over 27 percent as Wii debuted, up from 11 percent, while its price-to-earnings ratio, or PER, rivaled Apple at about 40, underscoring an investment community image as both a toymaker and a cutting-edge technology firm.

In October 2007, its share value crossed ¥10 trillion for the first time, a jump of 15 times in two decades of trading, to almost $87 billion. In a two-week period during the month, its market capitalization jumped by ¥1 trillion. New record share highs became the norm, and portfolio managers lamented not having purchased Nintendo stock when it stumbled for lack of direction in the early part of the decade.

In the United States, Nintendo's American Depositary Receipt (ADR) peaked at $78.50, compared with a low of $9.50 in November 2004, a multiple of more than eight since Nintendo's console onslaught began. Nintendo briefly became the third most valuable company in Japan, trailing only auto giant Toyota Motor and top bank Mitsubishi UFJ Financial Group.

The historic ebb and flow of Nintendo's share price had initially matched Japan's own bubble economy orientation to some degree, peaking in 1990 as the NES had been followed by the tremendously successful

Game Boy handheld console. However, Nintendo's share price more or less languished until 2005, as the Nintendo 64, GameCube, and later handheld units did not generate enough investor confidence to give substantial upward loft.

Nintendo—and Yamauchi—were always known as cash-rich, with a war chest over $6 billion and little debt, but the firm had never been known for offering luxurious dividends or for quick stock gains. Yet with two tremendously successful products bringing in billions of dollars in profit, money also poured into Nintendo stock. Foreign and individual investors became the most notable buyers in the stock's record rally, while domestic institutional shareholding in Nintendo declined.

Darryl Whitten, managing director at Investor Networks in Tokyo, told me the Capital Guardian Group, Fidelity, and Franklin Templeton were among those piling into Nintendo shares, with each owning a stake of more than 5 percent at one time.

"The reason was the explosion in earnings and cash flow because of the huge success of not one, but two, major products," Whitten said. "At the stock's peak of over ¥70,000—as the Nikkei 225 was also peaking, Nintendo was priced for perfection, almost to the degree that IT stocks were in the year 2000, at the peak of the Internet bubble."

JAPAN'S WEALTHIEST

Yamauchi had refused his own retirement allowance, although he and his family still owned about 10 percent of Nintendo's shares, making him—for at least one year—the wealthiest man in Japan, according to the *Forbes* 2008 rankings.

In 2005, *Forbes* had pegged his wealth at only $1.8 billion, but the success of the DS console and later Wii took Yamauchi's paper holdings to $4.8 billion by 2007, trailing only Japanese real estate baron Akira Mori and Internet and mobile magnate Masayoshi Son on its annual list. As the Wii became a runaway hit, Yamauchi's personal fortune ballooned an estimated $3 billion the following year, taking him to *Forbes*'s top spot.[3]

Yamauchi in retirement, as well as many still in the video game industry, briefly created a VIP list of Japan's wealthiest current and former corporate chiefs. Of the top 40, five were executives of game-related firms, including Yasuhiro Fukushima of Square Enix; Kagemasa Kozuki, founder of Konami; Keiko and Yoichi Erikawa of Koei; and Hajime Satomi of Sega Sammy Holdings.

However, Satomi, head of the merged firm making Sonic the Hedgehog games, nearly missed the cut as his personal wealth shrank to an estimated $760 million with a plunge in Sega Sammy's share price.

Moreover, Yamauchi likely did not put great credence in the permanence of his bulging share fortune, always preferring cash on hand, and indeed, in the next year, the share market lost much of its gains. In late 2008 and 2009, substantial paper wealth vaporized, encouraging some investors who had missed the share's skyrocketing to sell it short—speculate on its decline—with the Nikkei's tumble and the onset of global recession.

The former president and chairman of Nintendo slipped from the rank of the nation's wealthiest individual to No. 3 in *Forbes*'s next annual list. The same $3 billion that had taken Yamauchi to the top of the fortune heap had mostly evaporated in the worst consumer and financial market environment since the Great Depression.

The Japanese taking Yamauchi's top spot on *Forbes*'s list ran a discount clothing chain, while others seeing their fortunes rise also owned substantial stakes in low-cost drug, furniture, and shoe businesses, as price—always a key point for Nintendo—increasingly mattered in the economic storm.

THE BOTTOM LINE

Nonetheless, business conditions for Nintendo under Iwata had improved sharply, while the transition showed the depth of staff talent as well as a productivity level that investment banks would envy.

A *Financial Times (FT)* report in 2008 put Nintendo's generated profit per employee at $1.6 million, more than Goldman Sachs at $1.24 million in 2007, and far more than Google at around $626,000.[4] Factory outsourcing, begun during the Yamauchi era, was essential to that estimate, as Nintendo tallied only 3,000 permanent full-time staff.

However, the Kyoto firm told the *FT* that the actual productivity level was likely even higher as some staff salaries were classified as R&D spending. Still, Nintendo's average salary came in at about $90,900, a level above industry peers in Japan, but still minimal compared to Goldman's $660,000 figure per employee in 2007, and far below some tech sector peers.

Along with better compensation, the new boss implemented a variety of Western management measures to the Japanese company, including performance-based raises and—with no mention of Hiroshi Yamauchi— a mandatory retirement age of 65. By the end of the decade, Iwata sat at the head of an eight-person executive board, including a lineup of officers that had all served Nintendo for more than 30 years, except himself with only about 10 years directly.

He said keeping an even keel personally and among staff was essential, including a sense that—as with the capricious share market—nothing should be taken for granted. "Part of my job description includes keeping our employees from getting delusional," he said.

"Mr. Yamauchi has a favorite saying—I hear he started saying it around when the original *Famicom* became a big hit: 'Keep your head on your shoulders and figure out where your strength ends and where dumb luck begins. Never forget that you were blessed by good fortune.'"[5]

Prediction that fortune would continue to shine on Nintendo and the video game industry abounded before the onset of the financial crisis. A June 2007 PricewaterhouseCoopers report predicted annual compound growth for the video game industry of 9.1 percent, with the market rising in size from $31.6 billion to nearly $49 billion by 2011.

The report said video game growth would be greatest in its largest market, the Asia-Pacific region, but over 10 percent in Europe, the Middle East, and Africa. To see that realized, further Nintendo expansion into China and North Asia would be essential.

However, the same report pegged U.S. sales growth at just 6.7 percent, the slowest major market, while the global financial crisis now had the potential to complicate the business strategy for the industry even further. For Nintendo, some unwinding of its tremendous success was to be expected.

NOTES

1. Andrew Pollack, "Seeking a Turnaround with Souped-Up Machines and a Few Name Games," *New York Times,* August 26, 1996; available online: www .nytimes.com/1996/08/26/business/seeking-a-turnaround-with-souped-up-machines-and-a-few-new-games.html?pagewanted=all; access date: August 25, 2010.
2. Bob Finnigan, "Notebook: Ichiro Gets to Share the Wealth," *Seattle Times,* February 28, 2005; available online: http://seattletimes.nwsource.com/html/sports/2002191928_marinotes28.html; access date: August 25, 2010.
3. "Japan's Richest: #1 Hiroshi Yamauchi," *Forbes,* May 7, 2008; available online: www.forbes.com/lists/2008/73/biz_japanrichest08_Hiroshi-Yamauchi_LZWJ.html; access date: August 27, 2010.
4. Robin Harding, "Nintendo Makes More Profit Per Employee Than Goldman," *Financial Times,* September 15, 2008; available online: www.neogaf.com/forum/showthread.php?t=335338; access date: August 28, 2010.
5. *Shukan Toyo Keizai,* July 24, 2006.

CHAPTER 11

Bouts of Ennu-Wii

B Y EARLY 2008, DS SALES HAD REACHED 70 MILLION UNITS, and Wii some 24 million, but signs of slowing handheld demand had emerged after four years on store shelves, while the TV-linked juggernaut had been hampered by occasional limited supply of new game titles and hardware, resulting mainly from voracious demand. Combined sales, however, had taken Nintendo to unknown peaks, but like the city of Kyoto itself, in which buildings must observe strict height and zoning rules to keep from upsetting a community balance, the company remained grounded in its aim for sustained growth and not merely a momentary view from the top.

Within a year, though, both consoles had begun to hit saturation points, almost exactly as the global financial crisis started to thin consumer spending. Nintendo tried to mitigate the slowdown with the launch of the handheld DSi and a raft of new Wii games, and for the most part, it was successful.

Its revenues in the business year ended in March 2009 approached ¥1.84 trillion, or over $16 billion, while almost a third of the total was operating profit: $5.6 billion, up a whopping 16 percent year on year. Even with two hard-fighting competitors, Nintendo owned a 55 percent market share with Wii, and more than 70 percent with the portable DS, while its software held the top four rankings in sales. Perhaps most humbling for Microsoft and Sony, neither the Xbox 360 nor the PlayStation 3 sold even half as many consoles as Wii, although combined PS3 and PS2 sales reached the mark.

Nonetheless, the Americas represented over 40 percent of Nintendo's revenues and Europe almost the same share, which put it in a vulnerable place if the adage that gaming was recession-proof proved untrue. Globally, video game software and hardware sales faced a tough environment in 2009, particularly in North America, as the economy weakened sharply in the financial crisis. According to industry-watcher NPD, U.S. video game software and hardware sales slumped more than 10 percent in March and April, and by May, turnover had fallen below the $1 billion threshold for the first time since August 2007.

Nintendo initially attributed the decline, in part, to the tremendous success of its "Super Smash Bros." and "Wii Fit" titles the previous year, rather than the raging global crisis that was battering carmakers and the U.S. housing industry in particular. The $250 Wii continued its near two-year run as the top-selling U.S. console, although the hardware saw double-digit year-on-year percentage sales declines. The DS—across its range of models—continued to hold its own, with about a 7-to-1 margin over Sony's PSP console.

However, Microsoft's Xbox 360 was the only console to see marginal year-on-year sales gains, taking the No. 2 title from Sony by mid-year. Nintendo continued to boast sales of at least 400,000 Wii consoles a month, more than two and a half years after the launch, but executives began to see signs that the worst global economy since the Great Depression was becoming its problem too.

UNHEALTHY DEMAND

In Japan, often at the forefront of consumer trends, President Satoru Iwata said the sales numbers had begun to show a mild consumer fatigue—an "ennu-Wii"—setting in. He said the company wanted to ensure that the early symptoms seen in Japan did not become a global ailment, although he downplayed the gravity of the numbers.

"Wii (demand) is not vigorous at the moment in Japan. In fact, it is the unhealthiest situation since its launch in Japan," he said in April 2009. "The speed at which information spreads is faster in Japan, and accordingly, the speed at which people get tired of any entertainment is faster here . . . From this year, we will introduce new titles and hope to energize the Wii market in Japan, as we did with the DS."

Nintendo even made an attempt through third-party developers to lure some PS3 and Xbox 360 players, with games such as High Voltage Software's first-person shooter (FPS) "The Conduit." Conduit, which was published by Sega for the Wii, was another attempt to offset an image of not making—or supporting—gun-action games, as well as concentrating too intently on non-gamers. Ultimately, the game saw extremely modest sales of about 150,000 for the launch quarter, while Sega Sammy Holdings announced losses of $109 million, not all from gaming.

The publisher was not alone as France's Ubisoft saw sales dive 51 percent in the quarter, which it blamed on a decline in sales of its DS casual games; it did not expect sales to improve in the next quarter, even with a number of new games coming to market.

Meanwhile, the latest installment of EA Sports' "Tiger Woods PGA Tour," a game developed for all three major consoles, earned critical applause for the perceived better putting feature of the Wii's MotionPlus controller, which also allowed spin on a virtual ping-pong serve or calibrations on trajectory for sports such as archery. Some asked why the original Wii kit did not have this functionality, thus requiring a peripheral at 40 percent of the console's cost itself, but Nintendo said the technology was not available at the time of the initial launch.

Third-Party Woes

Despite overtures to new game makers, Nintendo faced some criticism that its own titles had succeeded at the expense of third-party developers, as tougher financial conditions led some consumers to choose software created in-house over that from outside suppliers. Competitor Microsoft with its "Halo" and "Gears of War" series may have also contributed to this trend, which portended even greater shakeout for industry third-party players or even closer ties to the hardware giants.

Overall, publisher Activision's first-person shooter "Call of Duty: Modern Warfare 2" was the top seller globally in 2009, with nearly 12 million of the games flying off store shelves for developer Infinity Ward in a very abbreviated sales year. Wii titles—"Sports Resorts," "New Super Mario Bros.," and the two versions of "Fit"—followed. "Modern Warfare 2" entered the *Guinness Book of World Records* for the greatest first-day sales of any media property in history at $401.6 million, topping the $310 million record set by "Grand Theft Auto IV" in 2008 and the $170 million for "Halo 3" in 2007.

"Sports Resorts" went on sale in late July, and in the always-positive factoids on its retail feats, Cammie Dunaway, Nintendo's vice president of sales and marketing, offered a new jaw-dropper:

"We sold one copy of "Wii Sports Resorts" every 1.5 seconds continuously since it launched in the United States."[1]

The game sold about 13.6 million copies in the remainder of the year, trailed by "Super Mario Bros." and "Fit Plus" with over 10 million units each. Some other key titles included Capcom's "Resident Evil 5," for the Xbox 360 and PlayStation 3, while Nintendo continued to score with "Pokemon Platinum" and Square Enix's "Dragon Quest IX: Sentinels of the Starry Skies."

By May 2010, Nintendo bundled the new Motion Plus controller with its "Wii Sports" and "Sports Resort" games, along with its console—now available in black. Based on the still strong demand for "Sports Resort" alone, the move was seen as indicative of how seriously the company wanted to spur further Wii sales, even if it cannibalized other hit games.

On the downside, the video game industry saw tremendous restructuring in 2008 and 2009, which included major job cuts, studio closures, and ultimately lean game titles from major developers, as poor sales results continued. Midway Games, the maker of the popular "Mortal Kombat" series and once owned by media mogul Sumner Redstone, went bankrupt in February 2009, amid estimates that the chairman of CBS and

Viacom had pumped hundreds of millions of dollars into the Chicago-based firm over the years.

Redstone had sold his controlling stake in Midway to investor Mark Thomas in November 2008 for $100,000, as the company had reportedly not been profitable since the year 2000. Midway, founded in 1958, was best known for its "Space Invaders" game, a favorite of the youthful Iwata and other future game designers.

Other major game makers were also struggling.

After cutting 10 percent of its workforce from late 2008 in an effort to save $120 million, software giant Electronic Arts Inc. slashed another 1,500 jobs by November 2009. The California-based maker of the widely popular "Madden NFL" franchise also had to fend off market rumors that it was a takeover target. Company CEO John Riccitiello put some of the blame for EA's harder times on Nintendo.

"The Wii platform has been weaker than we had certainly anticipated, and there is no lack of frustration to be doing that at precisely the time where we have the strongest third-party share," Riccitiello said.

EA said it was "reaching out to Nintendo to find ways to partner to push third-party software harder."[2]

Numbers

Still, cumulative Wii sales passed 50 million consoles and the DS the 100 million mark by May 2009, with the third edition of the handheld finding a strong consumer reception. Overall, though, analysts saw global demand for Wii as becoming flat, at best, in the year ahead, while the DS was expected to show its first sales decline since its launch in late 2004.

"We find ourselves at an unprecedented stage where one in every six people domestically has a DS," Iwata said.

The DS marketing strategy, which had taken the console to ubiquity and beyond, now included the thinner DSi, a multifunction handheld with slightly larger LCD screens, two 0.3 megapixel cameras, music, Web browsing, a microphone, and enhanced audio. Debuting in Japan in late

2008 to mixed reviews, the console sold 435,000 units in its first week in the United States, and a million by the end of May 2009.

"We came to the realization last year that it became difficult to maintain market momentum used in existing market methodology. Therefore, we launched DSi . . . to revitalize the Nintendo DS market," Iwata said.[3] "Nintendo developed the DSi with an ultimate goal of one DS per person in a DS household."

The launch came amid growing speculation that the next application for handheld consoles would be telephony, using the sales metric of 300 million consoles purchased in 25 years, compared with 800 million cell phones annually. By August 2009, Nintendo had sold more than 1.7 million DSi units, and more people were asking when Nintendo would finally make a game phone, as industry observers saw the DSi as an attempt to approach Apple's realm of iPhone utility—without the phone.

As its profit picture worsened over 2009, Nintendo actually attributed some of the slowdown in DS sales to the success of the iPhone, a recognition that appeared to acknowledge a fourth major challenger. Nintendo's first-quarter profit fell 66 percent year on year to $426 million, while its share price had fallen more than 20 percent since the start of the year. The numbers would only become worse through 2010.

Going Mobile

Iwata and Nintendo of America (NoA) President Reggie Fils-Aime continued to deny telephony was an aim—at least until call fee structures changed.

"When we think about such possibilities [as telephony], we must ask if customers are willing to pay certain subscription fees, and what percentage would be willing to do so on a monthly basis," Iwata said. "If the day comes when customers do not need to pay additional cell phone subscription fees, then we can seriously consider it."[4]

Fils-Aime, in a separate comment, was even less optimistic, noting that the company saw value instead in offering constant Wi-Fi connectivity. "Telephony is not in our wheelhouse," he said.[5]

Nonetheless, some industry game makers, such as Japan's Capcom, increasingly planned new titles for the iPhone, a partial migration that analysts said Nintendo could not ignore. The motivation for game makers was obvious, as traditional sales channels had experienced double-digit percentage declines, while the number of consumers with smartphones in North America alone was seen rising from 60 million in 2008 to an estimated 240 million by 2013.

Skepticism about the play experience on smartphones remained rife, but Apple, in promoting its iPhone and iPod Touch, began to tout its portable gaming capabilities, as well as the App Store's more than 21,000 titles, while the company said games had become its most popular download. The iPhone screen, at about 3.25 inches, was about the same size as the original DS, a possible factor for Nintendo's decision to make the LCD view even larger in its later handheld models.

Some media reports said Nintendo and Iwata now considered Sony a conquered foe while Apple was the enemy of the future.[6]

APPLE

Prices for Apple games often were less than half Nintendo and Sony titles—occasionally even free—but the sheer abundance and still relatively low return for software makers kept developers' interest tame initially. Money was rolling in for Apple, but in early September 2009, at its "Rock n' Roll" conference, Steve Jobs and Phil Schiller called the smartphone the next level of "fun" in portable gaming, a word Nintendo had come close to copyrighting over the past three decades.

The executives showcased Apple's huge number of games, compared with an estimated library for the DS of some 3,700 titles, or a little more than 600 for the PlayStation Portable. Schiller said an estimated one in three iPhone users downloaded at least one game, equal to an installed base of over 16 million. Clearly, even if Nintendo would not enter Apple's phone space, Apple had unceremoniously tracked through Nintendo's Zen garden and was now doing a *bon odori* dance.

Nintendo had sold over 100 million DS consoles overall, but Apple's mobile platforms had reached 50 million sales in two years, with signs of demand growing further. KBC Securities game analyst Hiroshi Kamide told me that Apple's threat was not taken lightly by Nintendo or Sony.

"The success of the iPhone is something the gaming industry is looking at closely and the people who make consoles are very wary of," he said. "If you are a serious gamer, I don't think you will get that Apple [product], but you have to be aware of what they're doing. Social network players are seeing less successful companies also come with profit-sharing for their games."

Kamide had downgraded his rating on Nintendo's stock to a "sell" from a "hold" recommendation in October 2008, while other firms such as Goldman Sachs kept their "buy" calls, despite saying that each one-yen appreciation against the U.S. dollar would cost Nintendo $41 million, and each yen's rise against the euro about $62 million. From late 2008, the yen began a sharp climb, hitting a 15-year high against the greenback by August 2010 and flirting with a new record high. It also climbed more than 14 percent against the euro as concerns about Europe's debt and banks mounted.

Industry estimates put both Nintendo and Sony game gross profit margins at about 50 percent, compared to 30 percent or less for Apple games. From the perspective of a title developer, the per-game profit potential of DS or PSP software remained much more alluring than making titles for Apple. The greater volume of titles in the App Store also was less enticing to independent software makers because it reflected the greater competition to be found, and lower likely returns, until Apple's installed user base grew.

That was happening rapidly with Apple's latest product releases. Apple began the rollout of the iPhone in the home country of its Japanese game rivals and planned to enter China, the world's largest mobile market, in a deal with the mainland's No. 2 player, China Unicom. By October, Apple's profits and sales had streaked past analysts' estimates, while its share price hit a record high and continued a meteoric trajectory into 2010.

VIRAL GAMING

Meanwhile, video games, which had been closely linked in content or marketing with films for decades—usually blockbuster movies with complementary goods franchises, saw software makers create lower-budget titles as a viral marketing effort to popularize upcoming fare. Movie-linked games included "Fast & Furious" and "Harry Potter: Half Blood Prince," which developers would release shortly ahead of a film for free or at minimal cost as a promotional tool to fill theater seats. Instead of mega-games coming after major movies, these cheap or free titles would proliferate before a film, a sign the industry no longer had to apply high production values to blockbuster tie-ins.

However, as Facebook and other social networking sites began to flourish on the Internet, games also proliferated for the platform, such as Zynga's "FarmVille," "FishVille," and "Mafia Wars." These attracted some of the first-time players that Nintendo cherished, as Zynga's active monthly user base was estimated to exceed 230 million people, mirroring Facebook's numbers.

Annual revenues of the San Francisco–based Zynga were seen at about $300 million, with a market value estimated at over $1 billion. The game maker, founded in 2007 using Silicon Valley seed money, was one of the leading success stories of social-networking investment during the decade, but the major players were also looking at the business.

In a retooling mode, EA spent $680 million to buy mobile gaming leader Jamdat Mobile in 2005, which later allowed the parent firm to boast most of the top-selling games on Apple's platforms. EA also purchased Playfish Inc., maker of "Pet Society" and "Restaurant City," for an estimated $400 million, clearly comfortable with the financial returns of what was occasionally called "antisocial networking" because of the many unsolicited overtures to join in.

Nonetheless, social networking games alone were forecast to generate up to $2 billion in sales by 2012, according to market researchers at ThinkEquity LLC. Microsoft, which had invested $240 million in

Facebook in October 2007, was already in the mix with its MSN Games unit; the unit carried titles such as "Bejeweled," "Spades," and more than 1,000 other games, later partnering with Zynga for game distribution services using Facebook Connect and Windows Live Messenger.

The U.S. giant also pursued CrowdStar, maker of the "Happy Aquarium" game and the No. 3 developer of Facebook applications. Analysts saw this as another Microsoft attempt to expand more directly into social gaming across all platforms, but acquisition talks eventually broke off.

MICROSOFT'S MOVE

The industry overall might have been struggling, but Microsoft continued to advance. It solidified a No. 2 hardware position with sales of 30 million Xbox 360 consoles and gave a record growth forecast.

In May 2009, Microsoft estimated cumulative retail sales of $14.5 billion stemming from Xbox 360's hardware, software, and Live services since its launch, adding that consumers had downloaded one billion units of gaming and entertainment content from its Xbox Marketplace. The company was also targeting new relationships, such as pay-TV firms Canal Plus in France and BskyB in the United Kingdom, which would allow subscribers to watch movies and live sports broadcasts on the console.

Industry-watchers said the tie-ups allowed the Xbox to mimic cable TV, a development coming at the same time as studios began streaming their own content on Hulu.com, supported by advertising. Speculation grew that Microsoft wanted to dovetail its own potential monthly fee system by offering content such as Hulu, as it expanded the Live demographic to women, who were now one-third of Xbox users, as well as to adults with children under 18.

The company said its 2008 year-end sales had been the strongest ever in markets such as Europe, the Middle East, and Africa, besting the PS3 on the back of a price cut and "Halo 3" demand. Robbie Bach, president of Microsoft's Entertainment and Devices Division, said that although the preceding year had been its most successful, he anticipated some slowdown because of the global recession, which foreshadowed changes to come.

"My guess is the attach rate on games, when people buy consoles, probably is going to slow down, and we did see a little bit of that in the holiday season," he said. "People, last year, if they were buying five games when they bought a console, maybe this year they only bought four, and if they got two controllers when they bought a console, maybe they only got one extra controller this year."[7]

Most industry analysts said consumers were waiting for major console and game makers to blink and cut prices, and then would make purchases, while Nintendo had kept the Wii's price unchanged since its launch. The cycle for handheld consoles had shortened considerably, with multiple DS versions available, while reiterations of the larger TV-linked hardware had already been tried at Sony to revive demand.

PRICE PINCH

The Wii, at $250, was in a potentially vulnerable position, although Iwata and other officials maintained that Nintendo would not play the pricing game. "If our products are not much different from competitors, price cuts would generate significant fresh demand, but video games are just not that kind of product," Iwata said.[8]

For Nintendo, the fall in overall operating profit was blamed on a dearth of hit products, not the economy. The company still anticipated $5 billion in profit for 2009—the envy of many loss-making peers and coming in the same year as automakers, banks, and brokerages faced either bankruptcy or billions of dollars in red ink.

The Nintendo difference could also be seen in pay slips. Japanese employees on average saw their summer bonuses decline 16.6 percent, or over $1,500 from the preceding year, according to a *Nihon Keizai Shimbun* survey of some 700 major firms. For those working for Nintendo—now near the 4,000 mark—the summer bonus packet topped the national average of about $7,500, a position indicative of the company's overall better fortunes, and a top spot it kept in 2010.[9]

Yet the end of a string of earnings peaks for Nintendo appeared at hand. Its rivals slashed the prices of the PS3 and Xbox 360, so the company made a move it had vowed only months before to avoid: a Wii price cut. In late September, Nintendo dropped the console's price by 20 percent to just under $200, less than three years after its debut, talking about another 50 million potential gamers who could now see the entertainment as affordable fun.

Immediate sales reaction was noticeable in the United States, according to Fils-Aime. "There are literally millions of consumers out there who want a Wii and had been on the sidelines," he said. "They'd been waiting for that little nudge to go out and pick it up. . . . We believe it's what's pushing them over the edge."[10]

In the crucial holiday quarter, Nintendo sold 11.3 million Wii consoles, up 8 percent on the preceding year. A raft of new software further improved results.

SONY STRUGGLES

It was no consolation, but Nintendo's main Japanese rival was still aching, while finally caving in to its own cries to cut the PS3's near-$400 price tag. Sony forecast its second consecutive yearly loss, the first since listing its stock in 1958, while facing trouble on nearly every avenue of its consumer electronics business, with red ink of about $1.2 billion.

Sir Howard Stringer, with few left to blame as his tenure lengthened, reshuffled his management team in late February 2009, and the former media maestro added president to his existing titles of chairman and CEO, taking charge of the company's struggling core electronics unit. The 67-year-old chief said his new executive team, dubbed the "four musketeers," would be made up of digitally savvy executives who had worked outside Japan. Kazuo Hirai was in charge of network and gaming strategy. Hiroshi Yoshioka would serve as chief of the $50 billion consumer electronics division, Kunimasa Suzuki would act as Hirai's deputy, and Yoshihisa "Bob" Ishida would focus on Sony's TV business.

Ryoji Chubachi, now 61, who had come in with Stringer as the heralded answer to the "Sony Shock," became vice chairman, while the Welsh-born CEO had greater liberty to restructure without fear of favor, a direct contrast to the consensus-building approach that had left the former blue chip deep in a business morass. Stringer said the time for niceties had passed, adding a "chief transformational officer"— former IBM executive George Bailey—to bring a wonderful life to the embattled giant.

With the aplomb of a movie industry veteran, Stringer described the situation for Sony as similar to what faced the RMS *Titanic*.

"If the captain hits rough seas, he worries about his crew," he said. "When you hit an iceberg, you worry about the ship."[11]

Earlier, Stringer had announced plans to cut 16,000 jobs and close 6 of 57 factories across the globe. Those moves and other opportunities represented $3 billion in potential savings to Sony as its 185,000-strong workforce thinned; still, many analysts focused on questions such as where the company making "Made in Japan" famous would now produce its Bravia TVs, as its supplier firms would fall by over half to 1,200.

Stringer had spent the holiday season of 2008 in a Japanese hospital with stomach flu, but as a sign of his deeper commitment, he vowed to allot more time in Japan. He made this promise with no sign of flippancy or self-reproof, upping his presence in Sony's home country to two weeks each month. Of course, full-time residency had not particularly helped his predecessors, but it became less a promise and more a *sine qua non* for the executive. One report said as company fortunes became more pressured, Stringer remained in Japan for all but three weeks in the first quarter of 2009.

Once his health improved, Stringer often ended up in a hotel suite in a Tokyo neighborhood near Sony's Shinagawa headquarters, with his family back in England. Over the course of the next year, though, the time on the road began to find traction, as the company's recovery process started to see results.

Hirai in Charge

Kazuo Hirai had managed through Sony's highs and now at its lows. The dapper, bilingual Hirai, now 48, had tended the bleeding PS3 and its network business for two years in the wake of Ken Kutaragi's departure, inheriting his failed effort to link all of Sony's electronic division silos. His first task now was once again to put the game, TV, and movie units into a more cohesive sales and marketing team that could deliver content from the Internet in one fashion for any Sony-enhanced product.

The Bravia flat-panel TV line had not made a profit since its 2005 launch, losing an estimated $2.3 billion. Moreover, the PS3 entered the third year of its anticipated 10-year lifespan with few serious converts, although Sony said 20 million PS3 users had signed up to its network, with total sales by June 2009 at 22 million units.

Overall, Sony planned more than 360 games for its PS franchise, while some 30 percent of global titles in 2008 had been created for the former No. 1. The handheld PSP, meanwhile, had sold 50 million units, although Nintendo's DS, launched in 2004, had more than doubled that performance over roughly the same period.

Trying again to grab more market share from Nintendo's handheld line, Sony unveiled its PSP Go, priced about $250, and running on 16GB of flash memory. The smaller portable, while not an admission of failure with the PSP, offered download and storage capacity for games, music, movies, and pictures, as well as a wireless motion-sensor controller.

Hirai said the Go was designed for digital-media consumers, estimating storage of up to 10 games, while including new features, such as "Sense Me," in which the console compiles a song playlist based on a listener's moods and music library. The Go console was half the size of the PSP 3000 and weighed 40 percent less. Not intended to replace the existing PSP, sales began in North America in October, and spread around the globe by the end of 2009, with games downloaded from the PlayStation Store.

In an interview, Hirai said Sony's network had 24 million accounts making 450 million downloads, implying that PSP Go would be an attractive console for those who did not want to buy their games or content in retail stores.[12] He had earlier acknowledged, without mentioning Nintendo, that Sony needed to broaden its user base, creating games and content for casual users, but pledged that its console lifespan would be a decade, with core gamer satisfaction paramount.

However, broadsides from game makers and developers, tired of high production costs for slow-selling consoles and titles, had begun to emerge. It was clear the third-party suppliers had little memory of the riches Sony had once inspired.

Bobby Kotick, head of the largest U.S. game publisher, Activision Blizzard, said in an interview that his firm might cease making games for PS3, now the No. 3 console in the United States, as well as the PSP, because of high costs and poor sales.[13] Sony had cut the price of the Blu-Ray player-equipped PS3 in 2007, but Kotick said even at $399, the console was too expensive, while his firm found Sony games more difficult and costly to develop than those designed for rivals.

Industry analysts said consumers expected Sony to deliver a less expensive PS3, and were holding off on purchases until a price cut materialized. In April, Sony had trimmed the PS2 price to under $100, indirectly pushing the nine-year-old staple to outsell the PS3, while Microsoft had made its own cut in the Xbox 360 in 2008, with some console versions selling for as low as $200.

The Price Is Right

Sony executives, like Nintendo officials, said there was no hurry to cut prices again. However, industry watchers viewed the Activision comments as brinkmanship to expedite a Sony pre–holiday season announcement that would almost certainly slice at least $50 off of its console prices. By August 2009, Sony had sold 24 million PS3 consoles; the Xbox 360 had shipped 30 million, and the Wii about 52 million, meaning the No. 3 needed to energize its video game business dramatically or face another year at the bottom.

In response, Sony slashed $100 off a new, slimmer console, and sales immediately jumped; the PS3 and its 120GB hard drive saw 150,000 fly off Japan's shelves in just the first week. The console was a third smaller, using up to 30 percent less energy, while immediate industry predictions saw sales of the new PS3 and its supporting games jumping 20 percent.

By late September, Sony Computer Entertainment America CEO Jack Tretton said sales of the new model had soared over 300 percent to hit 1 million consoles, adding that such demand might leave retailers out of stock in the busy year-end season. At the Tokyo Game Show in October, Hirai told Reuters that every effort would be made to ensure holiday season supply, while saying he envisioned a return of the PS franchise to profit within two years.

At the industry event, Sony also announced a PSP price cut while unveiling the PSP Go in Japan, ahead of its autumn sales launch. However, as Hirai spoke at the industry show, an event that Nintendo usually did not participate in, Nintendo again moved to trump its Japanese rival, announcing a $50 cut in the Wii's price to near $200. Hirai later laughed about the timing of the Nintendo move, as we chatted at the Game Show, saying that a competitor's pricing would not dictate Sony's strategy.

The broad penetration Sony planned would rely more on online delivery, although Hirai said the firm had an understanding with its software retailers that the push was not an attempt to circumvent their businesses, and ultimately would bring more consumers to gaming. The PlayStation Network hit 50 million subscribers in 2010, and Sony aimed to sell $3.4 billion worth of movies and games over the service by March 2013, a result that would certainly keep some customers from leaving their living rooms.

Sony's Tretton, a 25-year veteran of the gaming business who had joined Sony Computer Entertainment at its inception in 1995, said online delivery would not end retail store buying, just influence it. "Clearly digital is here to stay. But I think at least in the gaming space, there's no period in the near future that I see it is going to completely replace physical media," Tretton added.[14]

One such digital tie-up for content provision came in late October, when Sony partnered with Netflix to offer rental movie access via the PS3 console; Microsoft already offered the service on the Xbox 360. Tretton, who oversaw strategic planning and business operations, was asked what he liked about Sony's main rivals and the elephant in the corner:

"I love [Microsoft's] money. They can afford to be more patient. We're very profit-driven. . . . Nintendo is almost the polar opposite. They know what they do well, and they stick to it," he said. "You certainly hear rumblings that Apple's now interested in gaming. It's a $25 billion business. Everyone should be interested in gaming."[15]

Ultimately, Sony lost some $1.4 billion in the last two years of the decade, but saw a return to the black coming, both in its bottom line and for its gaming business. By the first quarter of 2010, Sony had earned more than $700 million as the "transformation" began to take hold.

BACK TO THE FUTURE

The global financial crisis had pushed the Nikkei share average to its lowest level in over two decades as of March 2009, but slowly most Japanese stocks began to rebound, while Nintendo's ran in place. In sheer market capitalization, Nintendo had a value of about $36 billion, larger than electronics conglomerate Sony at $27 billion, but less than half of Apple and Microsoft, which each came in at over $100 billion.

Nintendo's price-to-earnings ratio was near 11, compared to Japanese software companies such as Square Enix with a level of over 40, or other industry firms at about 16, making it appear inexpensive. Meanwhile, Nintendo's Return-on-Equity (ROE) was over 20 percent, far above any Japanese game industry firm, while Sony's gaming business was still mired in losses.

Analysts said the global credit crunch had put a premium on what assets a company had on hand, if it was potentially liquidated. No one forecast such an end for Nintendo, but because it had farmed out potential overhead liabilities to third-party manufacturers and thus kept operations relatively small, the company's stock had actually been penalized by some investors, who ignored how much money a firm could make, instead looking at its break-apart value.

Also, to some degree, Nintendo was seen as both recession-proof and unlikely to benefit from an eventual global economic recovery. Credit Suisse Japan advised investors in May 2009 to remain underweight in Nintendo stock, but expected the company to outperform its own guidance, taking overall sales past 150 million consoles as it expanded further into emerging markets, as it had done already in South Korea.

However, Nintendo's quarterly profit more than halved to about $710 million, cutting its year-end profit forecast to about $4 billion. More tellingly, Nintendo slashed the Wii's sales forecast by almost 25 percent, while quickly introducing an even larger-screen DS to try to stimulate portable demand.

THE BEST FACE

At its November analyst briefing at the Imperial Hotel in Tokyo, which came a day after its results—and a subsequent sell-off in the Japanese stock market, Nintendo blamed the strong yen and Wii price cut for some of its numeric problems, while admitting its games were not driving console demand.

A significantly thinner Iwata sat next to Genyo Takeda and Shigeru Miyamoto, trying to put the best face on the worsening picture. Wii was losing a bit of its console market share to rivals but was not falling below a strong 40 percent perch, Iwata explained, while its software share had declined, although Nintendo continued to see a number of million-selling game titles.

Analysts said the big-screen DSi LL unveiled at the event was an interim sideshow ahead of next-generation products that would establish—or not—future growth prospects. Nonetheless, a three-year run of record profit was over. The company was still expecting billions of dollars in earnings that would be the pride of any other industry, but global investors, and consumers, wanted to know what was coming next from the former card maker. Competition in the 2009 year-end season looked like it was going to be tough.

Nonetheless, Nintendo predicted a strong U.S. holiday rush, based on hardware sales in October, when it sold more than 500,000 Wii consoles, while DSi and DS Lite turnover exceeded 450,000 units combined. Fils-Aime predicted a joyous *noel*, as well as a happy 2010 ahead, as weekly sales of the Wii had shot up 80 percent since its price cut.

The company's U.S. tracking numbers showed combined hardware sales of 1.5 million units during the key Thanksgiving week, which it extrapolated to sales of 150 consoles per minute. However, in some stores, notably the huge chain Walmart, a $50 gift voucher was included with Wii purchases, essentially taking the console's price down to $149, and meaning an even larger discounting had been undertaken to keep business firm.

With price incentives to stoke demand and speculation emerging about its next consoles, Nintendo found itself in a position similar to what it faced when the decade started—although now the industry No. 1. It was time again for Iwata and Miyamoto to lead the giant to even bluer oceans.

NOTES

1. Shigeru Iwata, Courtesy Foreign Correspondents' Club of Japan Archives, April 9, 2009.
2. Don Gallagher, "Weak Report, Job Cuts, Hit EA Shares," MarketWatch, November 10, 2009.
3. Iwata, Courtesy Foreign Correspondents' Club of Japan Archives, April 9, 2009.
4. Ibid.
5. Matt Richtel, "A Nintendo Phone? Not Our Thing, Executive Says," *New York Times*, May 26, 2009; available online: http://bits.blogs.nytimes.com/2009/05/26/a-nintendo-phone-not-our-thing-executive-says/; access date: August 27, 2010.
6. Leo Lewis, "Rivals Are Invading Its Patch, but Nintendo Is Ready to Go to War," *Times*, May 7, 2010; available online: http://business.timesonline.co.uk/tol/business/industry_sectors/technology/article7118570.ece; access date: August 27, 2010.
7. Benjamin J. Romano, "CES 2009: Microsoft's Mr. Xbox Looks Beyond Year of Record Results," *Seattle Times*, January 7, 2009; Available online:

http://seattletimes.nwsource.com/html/businesstechnology/2008601916_
webcesbachqa08.html; access date: August 27, 2010.

8. Iwata, Courtesy Foreign Correspondents' Club of Japan Archive, April 9, 2009.

9. "Japan Bonuses Plunge Record 16.6 percent," AFP, July 12, 2009.

10. Chris Nuttall, "Wii Sales Get Price Cut Boost," *Financial Times,* October 6, 2009; available online: http://blogs.ft.com/techblog/2009/10/wii-sales-get-price-cut-boost-nintendo-chief/; access date: August 27, 2010.

11. Richard Siklos, "Sony: Lost in Transformation," *Fortune,* June 26, 2009; available online: http://money.cnn.com/2009/06/24/technology/sony _digital_transformation.fortune/; access date: August 27, 2010.

12. Greg Howson, "Interview with PlayStation Boss Kaz Hirai," September 5, 2009; available online: www.guardian.co.uk/technology/gamesblog/2009/ jun/09/sony-games; access date: August 27, 2010.

13. Dan Sabbagh, "Sony Should Beware—Activision Chief Not Simply Playing Games," *Times,* June 19, 2009; available online: http://business.timesonline. co.uk/tol/business/industry_sectors/media/article6531367.ece; access date: August 27, 2010.

14. Quentin Hardy, "Sony's Game Plan," *Forbes,* October 8, 2009. Available online: www.forbes.com/2009/10/08/sony-videogames-playstation-intelligent-technology-tretton.html; access date: August 27, 2010.

15. Ibid.

CHAPTER **12**

3D and the Next Small Thing

THE THREE MAJOR VIDEO GAME MAKERS HAD ALL MODIFIED their consoles or cut prices, but anticipation was building about next-generation hardware, and what would, or could, make it new and compelling. Rumors abounded, but manufacturers themselves and obvious trends in the market raised the likelihood that gaming would move deeper into the third dimension from its 2D present.

Microsoft from June 2009 began public demonstrations of its Natal 3D games for the Xbox 360, which used special cameras to recognize body movements, offering a game experience in a virtual setting, without need of a controller. Natal purportedly took its name from Brazilian Alex Kipman, who developed the project at Microsoft, choosing an appellation from a city along the country's Atlantic coast, while the name also had Latin roots, meaning "born."

Natal games used an infrared projector and a monochrome sensor bar that read room dimensions and lighting, generating avatars for one or two players, while its face-, voice-, and motion-recognition systems put users inside buildings not yet built, or sporting arenas without actual walls. The hands-free technology potentially offered Microsoft a consumer must-have that would be backward-compatible with all Xbox 360 games, including the Halo franchise and its next edition, "Halo: Reach," released in 2010.

Nintendo had pioneered the cutting-edge concept of 3D game play with Shigeru Miyamoto's Nintendo 64 Mario game, but almost 15 years later its two main gaming rivals had become engrossed in updating the nearly 140-year-old technology of offering depth perspective and dovetailing it with other motion-sensitive plans and products. Microsoft's "Ricochet," a 3D breakout game in which players use their bodies as paddles inside a virtual site to ward off incoming balls, was one of the first titles previewed; it put the gamer inside the reverse-dodgeball game.

HANDS-FREE

In demonstrations at the 2009 Tokyo Game Show, Natal offered the same virtual workout potential as Nintendo's Wii, while a separate driving game required no car peripherals such as a wheel, brake, or accelerator, just hands and feet making the same motions as when on the highway. The car game was clearly still a work-in-progress at the event, but Microsoft later confirmed an intended autumn 2010 launch date for Natal, which would land in time for the year-end shopping season.

Microsoft's Phil Spencer, corporate vice president of its Game Studios, told me the company could have used Natal just to sell new games and peripherals, but decided to include existing Xbox 360 games and compatible software from the launch. Natal's recognition technology had utility beyond entertainment purposes, which included office use, such as hologram-like video conferencing, creating virtual PC surfaces, or research and development design done from within the creation itself.

Some compared Natal's virtual tool potential to those employed by John Anderton, Tom Cruise's character in the movie *Minority Report,* without need for a controller or special glove. Others called the project's technology derivative and less than a game-changer.

Robbie Bach, head of Microsoft's Entertainment & Devices Division, acknowledged the comparisons and paid tribute to Nintendo's Wii at the

Consumer Electronics Show in Las Vegas in January 2010, but said Natal would take gaming even further.

"Wii was an important innovation, it was a part step. Natal is a giant step," he said. "It's going to change the [gaming] experience in a pretty fundamental way."[1]

Microsoft contended that Natal was faster than Wii, required no controller, and provided a 3D experience for less processing power than a mobile phone. However, for all its novelty, Natal still seemed to be trying to find an identity based on comparisons to existing game experiences, although new content was on the way.

Along with Microsoft's current library, Bach said 70 percent of game makers were working on Natal-capable versions of titles. Early media reports said as many as 14 titles would be available at launch, which he predicted would redefine Microsoft's gaming history.

"This coming year will be Xbox's biggest 12 months since the beginning of the business," Bach continued, noting Xbox had sold 39 million consoles and over 500 million games since launching in 2001, equal to about $20 billion in retail sales.

Microsoft was relatively mum on Natal pricing, but some analysts said the technology could generate over $1 billion in related sales in the game's first year, if its price tag did not exceed $100. The software maker, which had tried for most of the decade to make its gaming unit profitable, came into the launch with a tailwind, reporting record overall third-quarter sales of $14.5 billion and net income of about $4 billion.

Shake-Up

Microsoft's entertainment division was only a fraction of its total business, but the Xbox 360 had seen strong 2009 year-end sales, while the industry overall slumped in early 2010, awaiting the next big (or small) development. That would come without Bach and fellow Microsoft Chief Experience Officer J Allard, who both left the company in a somewhat sudden announcement on May 25, 2010.

The division led by Bach was essentially dissolved in a larger restructuring at Microsoft, with the unit now coming directly under CEO Steve

Ballmer. Bach, the man who led Microsoft's Xbox charge over the last decade was retiring after 22 years with the company at age 48, while Allard would remain as a consultant.

In his note to staff about the changes, Ballmer praised Bach and said he was going out on a high note:

"This has been a phenomenal year for E&D overall, and with the coming launches of both Windows Phone 7 and "Project Natal," the rest of the year looks stupendous." He added, "Robbie has been an instrumental part of so many key moments in Microsoft history—from the evolution of Office, to the decision to create the first Xbox, to pushing the company hard in entertainment overall."[2]

Allard, who had once said it was his dream to frame Ken Kutaragi's resignation letter, said in his own note to staff that he would work on a couple of projects for the company. He did not mention the canceled "Courier" tablet plan, seen as a potential rival for Apple's iPad, but that was an issue that some company-watchers saw as among the catalysts for his decision to leave. Still, he left the door open to returning:

"If, at the next juncture, I decide to join a corporate tribe again, this place will definitely top my list."[3]

Neither man would be directly replaced.

With Bach's departure, Microsoft quickly abandoned its "Kin" social networking smartphone (in June, after less than two months on the market) amid weak sales and a critical bashing. Some analysts tied the departure of the two veterans to the division's poor mobile device performance. It had been unable to design an iPhone or iPad competitor, and earlier it had been responsible for the Zune, the digital music player launched in 2006 that never became a serious rival for the iPod. The men had led Microsoft's rise in the video game space to a No. 2 spot, but had been bested by Apple as parallel but crucial hardware platforms soared in popularity.

In June, Microsoft also announced a name change for "Project Natal" to "Kinect," planned for sales launch in November 2010 for $150, along with a new slimmer $299 Xbox 360. Some critics said even with the new motion-sensing interface and lack of a controller, Kinect games—expected to be a lineup of driving, dancing, pets, sports, and Disney—had yet to become a compelling reason to upgrade. Nonetheless, it would be a new generation of executives who would shepherd the products through.

Industry Avatar

Some of Microsoft's enthusiasm about the potential financial returns of Kinect and 3D technology was due to movie director James Cameron's monster-hit *Avatar*. The movie became a game for Xbox 360, PlayStation 3, and Wii, as well as for personal computers, and the spark for the industry to dream about bigger financial returns.

The 20th Century Fox film was estimated to have cost over $400 million to make and market, but quickly recouped those expenses on its way to topping Cameron's own *Titanic* as the largest-grossing movie ever. However, reviews of Ubisoft's "James Cameron's Avatar: The Game" were less than glowing, with one comment posted on GameSpot saying the title, priced from around $40, "transforms the magical into the mundane." It seemed to follow a line of recent games aimed at putting people in theaters, rather than staying at home and actually playing the movie-linked titles. Sales remained one-dimensional, and the film's producer, Jon Landau, blamed Fox for the lackluster revenues of the tie-in title, saying the company did not understand the needs of the software maker and the expectations of gamers.

"I wish it was coming together more. . . . 3D is the cheddar on the ice cream sundae. Down the road, everybody's going to expect it for every game."[4]

Nonetheless, with over $2.7 billion in worldwide sales by late April 2010 and the launch of feverish DVD buying, the effect of the larger film's success on the making of other 3D movies—and consumer electronic products such as consoles or home entertainment systems—was profound. Or at least the companies hoped it would be.

Analysts at Piper Jaffray predicted that overall 3D-related businesses, not just movies, would grow from $5.5 billion to $25 billion by 2012, while other 3D film and TV projects coming included Tim Burton's *Alice in Wonderland* and Stephen Spielberg's *TinTin*. Industry estimates had 20 of about 170 film releases planned for 2010 being made in 3D, twice the previous year's output, with some studios, such as Jeffrey Katzenberg's Dreamworks Animation, planning to make all future movies in 3D.

ESPN pledged to broadcast more sporting events in 3D, while the Discovery Channel said it would work with IMAX and Sony to develop more 3D TV channels. Sir Howard Stringer told me at a promotional event in Tokyo that Sony's hugely successful Michael Jackson film, *This Is It,* with revenues in the hundreds of millions of dollars, could find its way into the third dimension, if not seeing an actual sequel.

TWO DIMENSIONS OF 3D

Sony, still mired in restructuring and with the PS3 holding the same U.S. numeric console rank, needed another dimension for its own comeback story, and the technology appeared compelling. At Sony's 2009 year-end strategy briefing, Stringer, Kazuo Hirai, and a team of executives said the company intended to push 3D technology across the breadth of its consumer products and businesses, bringing in $11.4 billion in sales by 2013. PlayStation consoles, TVs and disc players, cameras, theaters, as well as more movies from Sony Pictures, would all become 3D-capable.

"Sony is the only company with end-to-end filming production, 3D conversion, home delivery and home display of 3D content," Stringer declared, eagerly changing the subject from an earlier plan to cut an additional 20,000 jobs and shutter 10 more factories.[5] He said the global recession had left Sony cautious, while Hirai said no supply issues were expected for the key holiday season. Later that day, credit agency Fitch cut Sony's rating and put it on negative outlook, citing the strong yen, weak sales, and earlier console price cuts.

Investors sold Sony's stock before and after its briefing, which became a full presentation of 3D's virtues, amazingly all in 2D. By mid-2010, Sony stock had fallen 40 percent during Stringer's tenure, and the company needed to find an audience for its 3D TVs and raft of new films and games, or the push would be seen historically as another backing of an imperfect technology at the wrong time.

Avatar director Cameron said in an interview that he had met Stringer shortly before Sony's major 3D announcement, trying to sell the Sony chief on his technology marketing plan.

"I had a closed-door, secret presentation to Howard Stringer of a new business venture, and I mapped out what I believed was going to be the future of 3D, and how many TV sets were going to be entering the home, and how there would initially be a dearth of 3D content."

"I basically mapped out an entire strategy that he promptly announced a week later at the Sony stockholders' meeting. His speech was pretty much culled verbatim from my presentation, so, thank you, Howard."[6]

Ultimately, Cameron expected *Avatar* to make more than $2 billion in total sales, which it did easily, seeing 3D as necessary for the film industry to give an audience a reason to venture to theaters, rather than only watch at home. Sony hoped that regardless of the location, implementation of 3D technology across its business lines would be lucrative and sustained, as its TV production remained in the red, and the company was now staring at its first consecutive annual losses in a half century.

Some analysts and investors said Stringer was looking through the wrong glasses, saying more expensive 3D equipment might not be a panacea in a spending-challenged market, regardless of whether the technology was exciting. Sony countered that its film production company had received orders for more than 11,000 3D projectors from movie theaters, while its first 3D Bravia TVs would begin sales in June.

Sony forecast 3D sales to make up as much as half of its TV turnover within four years. Consumers could continue to watch in 2D on the same TV sets, which was a needed failsafe in case the level of 3D programming content did not also take off as well. However, Stringer, in an admission of vulnerability, wasn't certain the strategy would work.

"We do have 3D cameras, and 3D video games, 3D content and Imageworks that does 3D for other studios. So, we have a lot of disparate assets, lots of beads on the necklace," he said. "The question is: 'Is the necklace going to add up to something concrete and profitable?' . . . We won't know for a little while."[7]

Rivals such as Panasonic and Samsung also produced 3D TVs requiring "active shutter" glasses, but some doubted whether the added dimension would become a must-have or even nice-to-have with still wallet-pinched consumers, some of whom had recently purchased high-definition TVs. Samsung, first to bring a 3D TV to market in February 2010, began selling its LCD unit for about $1,700, and also planned thin-ner models with more power-efficient LED screens.

The head of Samsung, Lee Kun-hee, held a closed-door meeting with Stringer in May 2010, when the two men supposedly discussed LCD panel shortages and a possible common standard for 3D technology as the business ramped up. The firms had run a joint LCD plant since 2004.

According to the Consumer Electronics Association, the industry would likely see total revenues of $165.3 billion in 2010, a slight increase from 2009, but coming amid further price cuts. One product not subject to a lower price was Toshiba's Cell TV, going for about $10,000, which promised to convert all broadcasts and library video into 3D in real time. Cell chips, developed with billions of dollars from Sony, Toshiba, and IBM, had originally been built into the PS3 before the consumer electronics giant sold off its production. The Cell-equipped TVs had more than 100 times the processing power of a standard model and 10 times that of a PC, but still required viewers to wear glasses to see 3D fare. As with many Cell developments over the years, though, Toshiba offered no predictions on sales.

On the games front, Sony's PS3 push would be linked to the launch of its Bravia 3D TV, and the console would be able to play 3D stereo-scopic titles or allow film-viewing through separate firmware upgrades. Sony made 3D software developer kits available from January, begin-ning demonstrations from April of its motion-control system "Move", equipped with a "PlayStation Eye" that could track player positions in games such as "EyePet," which allowed virtual interaction with animals in the "Nintendogs" vein.

The $100 Move motion-sensing platform for the PS3 would be sold as a bundled "Sports Champ" package from mid-September, with up to 20 game title available at launch and 40 by year-end. Other titles coming for the system, which was again being marketed as an upgrade for "core" gamers, included the latest EA "Tiger Woods" iteration, as well as versions of the popular car and gun fare, "Gran Turismo" and "Killzone."

Sony released its first stereoscopic 3D games in June using online downloads, with titles including "Wipeout HD," "Super Stardust HD," "Pain," and "MotorStorm Pacific Drift." By fall, the company planned to upgrade the PS3 to allow viewing of 3D Blu-ray discs, which would also be high-definition compatible.

The company's first quarterly results in which sales of its 3D onslaught would register showed a dramatic return to the black for Sony, despite a sharp appreciation of the yen against the dollar and euro. Now boasting a catchphrase of "make.believe," Sony hiked its full-year forecast 20 percent to near $2.1 billion, after a profit of $700 million in the quarter, while its share price surged in response.

Company officials, including Stringer, did not turn cartwheels in public, but they'd clearly had a first sign that the long nightmare was ending. "We still cannot wipe out uncertainties for the future, including the currency," said Chief Financial Officer Masaru Kato. "Still, the first-quarter results were much stronger than we had expected and we aim to maintain that momentum."[8]

Adding to doubt about demand were comments from Panasonic, which said the industry had badly overestimated potential sales of 3D TVs, and that Samsung was launching a price war that would quickly erase the returns from high-end products that the companies thought would be profit machines. Even Sony admitted that prices were falling faster than it had envisioned.

Samsung had cut the price of its 50-inch 3D plasma set to around $990, compared to a 3D Panasonic of the same size with higher resolution for about $2,500. Sony's 46-inch LCD model with 3D capability went for about $2,300.

GLASSES-FREE

In gaming, the 3D marketing blitz by Nintendo's rivals of their Kinect and Move products sparked some immediate comparisons to the Wii. President Satoru Iwata told the *Financial Times* in 2009 that Nintendo had tried the same technology used by the other companies for its hardware, but had rejected camera-based sensors for accelerometers.[9] However, Nintendo was not ignoring the 3D trend; a next-generation console, tentatively named "3DS" and debuting at the E3 show in 2010 (where it won the "Best In Show" award), was planned to arrive by year-end 2010 at the earliest, and most significantly would not require special glasses to use. The development amid billions of dollars in industry 3D investment was crucial, and a true Nintendo difference.

"I have doubts whether people will be wearing glasses to play games at home," Iwata said.[10]

The console was backward-compatible for DS games, and industry speculation grew that Nintendo would actually raise the new console's price—at least to the $250 level—because of the compelling technology. 3DS software prices, meanwhile, were also expected to see a 20 percent increase for games. Planned titles included "Nintendogs+Cats," a new "Mario Kart," as well as "Kid Icarus" and "Animal Crossing," but Nintendo held its pricing plans for 3DS close to its chest.

Nintendo's Hideki Konno was game platform producer for the 3DS, after helping to achieve success with earlier pet and racing games. He worked on the development of a Tag Mode or Bark Mode for the handheld, which would alert other users when players were nearby, as well as facilitate their trading game data. The 3DS would have a 3.53-inch top screen and a near 3-inch bottom touchscreen, use three cameras, including two that could take 3D pictures, as well as a motion sensor like the Wii.

Nintendo considered itself among the leading 3D pioneers, starting with its failed "Virtual Boy" console in 1995, which was unfortunately remembered more for producing migraines than sales. Legendary 3D software titles from Miyamoto for earlier consoles had not only changed perspectives for players within the game, but for the industry as a whole about gaming's potential.

Some analysts said because of the negative experience with Gunpei Yokoi's Virtual Boy console, Nintendo would be incredibly circumspect in trying a 3D console again, and thus must have absolute confidence that the new handheld would be a winner. Konno said that was the case, but elements of analog technology would continue.

"We have been waiting, going to tech shows and seeing the latest 3D technology, and the devices that support those features. We started to have more confidence that this might be a good time to bring 3D back to Nintendo," he said. "Not only myself, but Mr. Miyamoto was insisting that our next handheld had analog control . . . 3D is not the only feature that we are pushing toward with this hardware. . . . There is the possibility that both 3D and motion control could be used in the same software."[11]

THE NEXT GENERATION

By early 2010, Nintendo had sold 125 million DS consoles, and the potential for an upgrade was hoped to push that figure even higher, or at least maintain momentum until a new console line was launched. DS handheld sales had exceeded 10 million in 2009, while Wii continued to chug along, giving Iwata some confidence, after the financial crisis had hit consumer sentiment, Nintendo's earnings, and share price.

"It's now safe to say Wii has recovered from the slowdown," Iwata said in early 2010. "But I'm not sure it's prudent to use words like 'revival' or 'recovery' lightly before making absolutely certain that we can maintain this momentum."[12] Iwata said the DS had rewritten the textbook for console sales. "The DS was launched in 2004, and sales of the machine hit a record in 2009 in the United States. . . . That is totally different from the conventional sales pattern, in which game sales peak in the third year and take a downturn thereafter."

However, after the debut of the most recent DS, U.S. sales of the console actually fell over 40 percent in the quarter, as some potential consumers began to wait for the next 3D model. Sales of the Wii jumped by about 36 percent, as many looked to take advantage of Nintendo's recent price cut and had no indication about the possible launch plans of a new large console. Nintendo was well aware that telling the market a new model was coming was tantamount to signing off on your current hardware.

In the case of its portable console, Iwata explained that the 3DS was intended to replace the original handheld, with over six years of production involved.

"It's supposed to be the successor to the Nintendo DS. As soon as the development of the original Nintendo DS was over, we started working on the successor," he said."[13]

Miyamoto, meanwhile, said the intent with the 3DS was to create a platform that would not split up Nintendo's portable audience. "With the exception of the 'Virtual Boy,' all of the 3D experimentation that we've done in the past has always been based around the idea of a 3D-enabling peripheral or accessory. But whenever you do that, then you've segmented the market and you have consumers who may have the peripheral and can see the 3D, and then consumers who don't," he said. "With Nintendo DS, we've shown that we've been able to create something that can't be done on another device."[14]

Some company-watchers said that with new consoles such as the 3DS, as with the launch of the DS and Wii from 2004 to 2006, a Nintendo share climb could begin again. However, Nintendo's overall stock losses by mid-2010 had been far worse than those of its peers, with its valuation dropping about 20 percent. On the earnings side, Nintendo net profit fell 9 percent in the last quarter of 2009 to $2.1 billion, while the company now expected a full-year figure just under $3 billion.

The numbers for Nintendo continued to weaken, and by the end of the first quarter of 2010, Nintendo posted a quarterly loss of almost $290 million.

HIGH DEFINITION

Nintendo again found itself in need of a hit product or distinguishing technology or service, although this time without succession issues at hand. The 3DS, like the original DS in 2004, had to become a winner.

Meanwhile, making the Wii more user-friendly until the transition to the next-generation console was key.

In January, Nintendo announced plans to join its rivals and add Netflix's streaming video service for the Wii, offering some 17,000 films and TV titles in the hope of seeing purchases from some of its over 11 million subscribers, if they had not already committed to Xbox Live or PSN versions that launched earlier. The tie-in required a Wii software disc to deliver non high-definition video on demand, raising speculation that this would be among the first Wii upgrades, as well as 3D compatibility.

Even Miyamoto hinted that Nintendo was considering high-definition consoles after a near decade of pooh-poohing greater spending in the area, but with the caveat that the console would have to be fun. Some analysts said online software or console upgrades, such as the patches enabling 3D play, could extend console life, and because of prohibitive costs and low returns, hardware would likely not see the generational overhauls of the past three decades, meaning a lifespan possibly beyond the usual five years.

Nonetheless, competition had become just as fierce in 2010 as when Iwata took the Nintendo helm from Hiroshi Yamauchi at the start of the decade, while the internal challenges stemming from the company's success were just as serious as those generated by hardship. Nintendo, which had sold 3.3 billion video games and over 550 million consoles since 1983, had grown considerably larger to meet the needs of its global demand, adding about 300 employees in 2009 to near 4,400 overall, while continuing to outsource as it expanded.

Some software makers such as Square Enix predicted a "Wii 2" beta by 2011, and even Nintendo admitted it had been working on a Wii successor for some time. Still, Iwata said when and how it would debut were company secrets that executives themselves didn't know.

"The successor to Wii has already been under development and review since the completion of the Wii hardware design. It's quite another story as to exactly where or approximately when we will be able to make the next hardware announcement," Iwata said.[15]

Shigeru Miyamoto said some of the hit technology would live on, but possibly in an even smaller and less expensive console.

"My guess is that because we found this interface to be so interesting, I think it would be more likely that we would try to make that same functionality perhaps more compact and even more cost-efficient."[16]

Iwata said he saw life left in the Wii, while the now 50-year-old CEO remained generally upbeat in public as well as to staff through Nintendo's online "Iwata Asks" segment. Nonetheless, the Hokkaido native had begun to show a tougher veneer, as the breadth of competitors and product issues grew. Possibly, a lifetime in gaming had begun to take its toll.

In addition to Sony and Microsoft, analysts said Nintendo now had to consider Apple a rival, although Iwata, taking a page out of Yamauchi's book, would have none of it. When asked how he viewed Apple's iPad, which ultimately sold a million units in just 28 days, Iwata, a Macbook Pro user, responded with curtness that even the old curmudgeon would have appreciated: "It was a bigger iPod Touch. . . . There were no surprises for me."[17]

After a decade in which he had led Nintendo from the cusp of irrelevance to the summit of the industry again, the baton had truly been passed. Satoru Iwata no longer had to play nice anymore—he was the boss of the greatest video game company in the world. The only question that his predecessor would never have to face was: What could he do for an encore?

NOTES

1. Bill Rigby, "Microsoft's Natal Game in Stores in 2010," Reuters, January 7, 2010.
2. Dean Takahashi, "The Rise and Fall of Microsoft's Xbox Champions," GamesBeat, May 25, 2010; available online: http://games.venturebeat .com/2010/05/25/microsofts-longtime-entertainment-executives-robbie-bach-and-j-allard-resign/; access date: August 27, 2010.
3. Mary-Jo Foley, "J Allard's Goodbye Note," ZDNet, May 25, 2010; available online: www.zdnet.com/blog/microsoft/j-allards-goodbye-note-no-chairs-were-thrown/6334; access date: August 27, 2010.
4. Gus Mastrapa, "Hollywood Doesn't Get Games, *Avatar* Producer says," *Wired,* April 22, 2010; available online: www.wired.com/gamelife/2010/04/ jon-landau/; access date: August 20, 2010.

5. Mariko Yasu and Maki Shiraki, "Sony's Stringer Sees 3D as Next $10 Billion Business Update 2", Bloomberg, November 20, 2009; available online: www.bloomberg.com/apps/news?pid=newsarchive&sid=adp8a7FrDg.E; access date: August 27, 2010.,

6. Charlie Rose, "A Charlie Rose Q&A with James Cameron," *Business Week,* January 21, 2010; available online: www.businessweek.com/magazine/content/10_05/b4165054405494.htm; access date: August 28, 2010.

7. Mayumi Negishi and Franklin Paul, "TV Makers Bet Big on 3D, Payoff Uncertain," Reuters, January 7, 2010.

8. Mariko Yasu and Maki Shiraki, "Sony, Panasonic Withstand Strong Yen with Forecasts," Bloomberg, July 30, 2010; available online: www.bloomberg.com/news/2010-07-29/sony-panasonic-defy-european-crisis-stronger-yen-with-higher-forecasts.html; access date: August 28, 2010.

9. Robin Harding and Chris Nuttall, "Nintendo Rejected Rivals' Choice of Technology," June 4, 2009; available online: www.ft.com/cms/s/2/dfcdde86-513e-11de-84c3-00144feabdc0.html; access date: August 28, 2010.

10. Oliver J. Chiang, "The Future of 3D Video Games," *Forbes*, February 4, 2010; available online: www.forbes.com/2010/02/04/3d-avatar-television-technology-breakthoughs-videogames.html; access date: August 28, 2010.

11. Chris Kohler, "Nintendo 3DS Idea Man Pulls Back Curtain," *Wired,* July 12, 2010; available online: www.wired.com/gamelife/2010/07/hideki-konno/; access date: August 28, 2010.

12. Hiroshi Takenaka, "Nintendo Posts Record U.S. Sales in December," Reuters, January 5, 2010.

13. Evan Narcisse, "E3 2010: Techland Interviews Nintendo President Satoru Iwata," Techland, June 23, 2010; available online: http://techland.com/2010/06/23/e3-2010-techland-interviews-nintendo-president-satoru-iwata/; access date: August 28, 2010.

14. Craig Harris, "E3 2010: Shigeru Miyamoto likes Donkey Kong Country After All," IGN, June 17, 2010; available online: http://wii.ign.com/articles/110/1100039p1.html; access date: August 28, 2010.

15. Narcisse, "E3 2010: Techland Interviews Nintendo President Satoru Iwata."

16. Seth Porges, "Exclusive Interview with Nintendo Gaming Mastermind Shigeru Miyamoto," *Popular Mechanics,* December 18, 2009, available online: www.popularmechanics.com/technology/gadgets/video-games/4334387; access date: August 28, 2010.

17. Yuri Kageyama, "Nintendo Chief Unimpressed with Apple's iPad," Associated Press, January 31, 2010; available online: www.msnbc.msn.com/id/35172612/; access date: August 28, 2010.

EPILOGUE

T HE 2010 TOKYO GAME SHOW WAS A PERFECT TOUCHSTONE FOR the state of the industry going into the year-end season, with abundant new games and software makers, no major consoles to unveil, and Sony and Microsoft riding the last fumes of their respective four- and five-year-old hardware lines while pushing motion-sensitive kit that had debuted a year earlier. Meanwhile, Nintendo, regardless of the epic changes it had brought to the industry over the decade, as was its tradition, once again did not deign to participate—a decision evoking the era of Hiroshi Yamauchi.

The Kyoto giant had announced its first loss in two years in the April through June quarter. Demand for its handheld consoles had fallen off a cliff ahead of its new "3DS" portable, as consumer and corporate expectations soared for the "glasses-free" product. The console that would have been the belle of the game show ball, however, was nowhere to be found, with announcements of its exact launch date and price planned for a private event later in the month. As it had trumped its rivals at the Tokyo show in 2009 by cutting the Wii console's price, this year Nintendo upstaged the other companies by leaving the nagging question of when it would sell its 3D marvel unanswered.

As with past periods in the red, Nintendo attributed the approximate $289-million loss in part to the strength of the yen against the U.S. dollar and the euro, as the global giant now made 87 percent of its profits overseas. The company said a one-yen rise against the dollar hit sales by ¥6.3 billion, or about $74 million, while the same gain against the euro sliced returns by ¥3.6 billion. Nintendo was insulated by nearly $2.5 billion in previous full-year profit and a variety of currency hedges by which it expected to end the full year in the black. Meanwhile, Satoru

229

Iwata and his team pushed the themes that better times and products lay ahead, as rivals Sony and Microsoft also prepared for the year-end shopping season.

After changes in Japanese law on corporate salary disclosure, Nintendo had to report salaries or bonuses over ¥100 million, or about $1.18 million. CEO Iwata, who with game guru Shigeru Miyamoto had taken on industry rock star celebrity in his eight years' tenure, when Nintendo had sold over 73 million Wii and 132 million DS consoles (not to mention a combined 1.3 billion games), actually earned a relatively roadie-like salary compared to some peers. The now 50-something Iwata earned ¥68 million in base salary and a performance bonus of ¥187 million, approximately $3 million in total. Miyamoto, Genyo Takeda, and other board members received a combined total package of about ¥100 million apiece. (Their base salaries were not announced.)[1]

Compared with Sony's Sir Howard Stringer, who earned over $9.2 million, Sammy Sega Holdings CEO Osamu Satomi at $4.9 million, or even Square Enix CEO Yoichi Wada at $2.4 million, and Namco Bandai President Kazunori Ueno at $1.5 million, the Kyoto leadership seemed to be relatively underpaid for the multibillion-dollar successes achieved during the decade. However, salary discussion was not part of the Kyoto firm's corporate ethos and Miyamoto had long said it was the lifestyle and creative freedom that Nintendo afforded, rather than extra zeros on a monthly pay stub, that mattered most.

The topic did not become an "Iwata Asks" online session with staff, but at a mid-2010 shareholder meeting, investors threw some tough questions at the boss, including Nintendo's compensation and growth strategies. Iwata said with changes in the structure of corporate pay packages made five years earlier, offering stock options—often seen as boosting company performance or executive incentive—was not possible.

"Fixed compensation to each director, which is determined by the board of directors, basically reflects his duty position and the contribution he has made so far," he said. "Nintendo abolished the retirement benefit system for directors and auditors . . . and does not have non-cash compensation such as stock options."[2]

Hiroshi Yamauchi, whose billions of dollars in paper wealth as Nintendo's top shareholder had taken him to the pinnacle of Japan's wealthiest around 2007, continued to fall in global rankings as his shareholdings weakened further in value, coming in at No. 7 in Japan and No. 201 in the *Forbes'* world standings with a tolerable $4.2 billion nest egg in retirement.[3]

SHARING THE WEALTH

Considering the precipitous drop in Nintendo's share price from the ¥70,000 level, or about $580, only a few years earlier, Iwata said the Board was aware of its fiduciary responsibility to boost value and address the concerns of investors, but some developments such as the yen's appreciation and the European fiscal crisis were beyond company control.

"The announcement of Nintendo 3DS on March 23 drove [the share price] up and it reached ¥33,000 in early April. In May, however, the financial crisis in Greece led to a weak euro. Investors were afraid of Nintendo's future business with large sales in euros," he said. "If we can have our shareholders acknowledge in the mid- to long-run that pure luck alone could not have yielded the actual sales results of Nintendo DS and Wii, and that Nintendo . . . has the ability to sustain such performances, it will dispel the concerns about our future business and, as a result, lead to a high valuation."[4]

The first-quarter results had sent Nintendo's stock to a recent low, and by the end of July, shares had lost 23 percent since April 1, compared to only 14 percent for the Nikkei 225 benchmark index. By August, the stock stood near ¥23,500, as the yen's surge to 15-year highs continued to spook investors.

Yuuki Sakurai, CEO of Fukoku Asset Management, said Nintendo and Iwata had coped with the strong yen in 2007, which had trimmed up to $40 million in revenues with each yen appreciation, on the back of the sales success of the DS and Wii. Fukoku, which managed over

$8 billion in assets, expected the Kyoto firm to again weather the new *endaka* (strong yen period) with the release of new hardware.

The 3DS, like the original DS and Wii before it, was hoped to be a vehicle to carry Nintendo's share price to new heights and maintain its handheld dominance, although competition with its two main hardware rivals for motion-control and three-dimensional bragging rights was intensifying. Its ability to allow 3D play without special glasses again trumped competitors whose kit still required them, but the sales advantage was expected to be challenged soon and without patent infringement, as Toshiba said it had developed a 3D television that did not require the use of glasses, and other firms were certain to be in development.

Sony's motion-control "Move" games launched in September—for about $479 when completely bundled with a PlayStation 3 console, while Microsoft planned to release its no-hands "Kinect" system in early November for $300 when bundled with a low-memory, 4-gigabyte Xbox 360, or at a higher price for a more powerful console.

With the Wii selling for about $200, industry analysts did not expect substantial flight because of the new games alone. However, as in 2003 when Yamauchi said the upcoming DS console needed to become a hit, the 3DS had little latitude for failure. Overall, video game sales had begun to weaken, and according to industry-watcher NPD, retail revenues fell some 23 percent in the year to end-July. They reached about $25.8 billion—but that enormous sum was still a year-on-year contraction.[5]

In the first quarter of the new business year, DS sales fell over 40 percent, while Wii sales rose on the back of its "Super Mario Galaxy 2" hit, although down about 17 percent in the calendar year and facing a similar slump in software. Nintendo now expected to sell 18 million Wii consoles and 30 million of its DS consoles in the year, including the new 3D model once it was on store shelves.

Nonetheless, Iwata still touted the expansion of the gaming population, showing internal surveys in which the percentage of active users from 7 to 64 years of age in Japan had risen from 35 to 57 percent in the five years to the end of the decade, while non-users declined from around 30 percent to under 20 percent in major cities.[6]

In the United States, the expansion of the user population aged 6 to 74 showed the share of active players rising from 45 to 62 percent in the three years leading up to 2010. It more than doubled for the DS and Wii, although the non-user population still remained substantial.[7]

3DS

Iwata said the company would not use TV or traditional marketing avenues for 3DS, as its merits would be difficult to portray on 2D delivery platforms. Instead, many localized events with the three-camera hand-held would be planned, while Miyamoto said retooled favorites in 3D would have extra allure and the new console would be both backward-compatible and capable of showing movies.

"Trying to jump onto a tree in a Mario game is something that could have been difficult. With 3D visuals, you have such a clear sense of how far away objects are [that it's easy] . . . . With a game like 'Nintendogs,' the dogs really pop up out of that screen and you can see them," he said. "You're kind of looking and touching, and it feels like you're touching a real dog."[8]

Nintendo demonstrated versions of "Mario Kart" and "Kid Icarus Uprising," as well as Konami's "Metal Gear Solid: Snake Eater 3D" and other games in its public curtain-raisers for the 3DS, touting more than a dozen developers working on 3D games. However, in a diversion from Sony, it intimated that rather than an across-the-board console blitz, a 3D Wii was not in the works as the number of capable TV monitors was still minimal.

A full slate of "Iwata Asks" promotional videos on the new portable console were rolled out for the E3 industry summit, with Iwata and Miyamoto reminiscing about their 3D efforts over the last two decades and chatting happily about the new console's attractions, such as its "3D analog slider" allowing players to set their own degrees of multidimensionality.

"This project did not start with the concept of 3D viewing with the naked eye. . . . Discussing what kind of hardware can do more than the DS was the actual starting point," Iwata said.[9]

Amid a flood of "e-reader" products hitting global markets, the Nintendo president hinted that the 3DS might have some similar information download capabilities, based on its Wi-Fi and 3G connectivity to media sources. That helped to fuel speculation that the firm would join the electronic book fray, which already included Apple, Sony, Amazon, and a growing list of other firms, which all quickly slashed their prices in an effort to become more competitive.

Nintendo's growing direct, or indirect, competition with Apple, even without telephony services for its DS, made any suggestion that the Japanese firm would enter the e-book space come across as escalating a budding rivalry. It attracted attention even though Sony and Microsoft had been just as aggressive in taking on Apple's more-than-dabbling in video games and applications.

After long saying Apple was not a rival, Iwata also ruled out any cooperative efforts on the software front with the U.S. firm or other hardware makers.

"The other companies' devices often have characteristics that Nintendo will never adopt. It is not a question of which company is right or wrong, but rather that they have different philosophies," he said. "At this point we do not have any intent to supply software for the other companies' hardware."[10]

In a separate interview, Iwata again downplayed the idea that Nintendo's agenda was being set by Apple.

"When the functions of mobile phones became advanced, enabling users to play games on them, many experts said the Game Boy Advance would be overwhelmed by handsets, but that did not happen,"[11] he said. "One of our reasons for being is to keep presenting customers with new games that cannot be offered by mobile phones."

"The last thing we want to do is follow what somebody else is doing."

WII 2

Nintendo was still making new games for its Wii, including the long-awaited Zelda title, "Skyward Sword," but its next major hurdle would be the console dubbed the "Wii 2" by analysts and the media. The company admitted that it would not be unprepared when the moment was appropriate to launch, but it offered no insights on what console capabilities would make migration worthwhile for the tens of millions of current Wii owners, except to say it would surprise gamers.

NoA chief Reggie Fils-Aime hinted in early 2010 that the Wii successor was not on the horizon anytime soon, but whether that meant one or two years—a possible debut at the 2011 E3 Summit—was uncertain.

"The next step for Nintendo in home consoles will not be to simply make it HD but to add more and more capability,"[12] he told CNBC. "We'll do that when we totally tap out all the experiences for the existing Wii, and we are nowhere near doing that yet."

At the Tokyo Game Show, Microsoft and Sony pushed their new games, such as "Halo Reach" and "Call of Duty: Black Ops," as well as a wealth of titles utilizing their respective Kinect and Move technologies. Nintendo, which had noted the 25th anniversary of its "Super Mario Bros." launch earlier in the week without an event or victory lap for the game that sold 40 million copies and launched a series, was back in Kyoto with as little pomp and circumstance as it could muster.

Microsoft Game Studio Vice President Phil Spencer said sales of the "Halo" prequel had hit an astounding $200 million in its first day, certain to have a knock-on impact on consoles, including an Xbox 360 special edition with the game bundled inside. The launch of the $60 title topped any game or movie in 2010 until that point, and was expected to eclipse "Halo 3" sales.

"What 'Halo: Reach' numbers tell me is gamers are there. They are willing to buy the great experiences when they come out. The fact we are exceeding 'Halo 3' numbers out of the gate tells me that the industry is in a healthy state," he told me, in an interview near Microsoft's Kinect demonstration area.

Despite analysts' doubts that "Halo" users would also be interested in its motion-sensitive Kinect games, Microsoft offered 15 titles, budgeting hundreds of millions of dollars for the November launch, with 30,000 retailers expected to sell 3 million units in two months.

The former No. 3, which had seen its Xbox 360 lead the Wii and PS3 in console sales for three consecutive months, had begun to develop a swagger, even with changes at the top of its games unit that brought in new Interactive Entertainment boss Don Mattrick to follow Robbie Bach. Mattrick, who reported to CEO Steve Ballmer, had led the Xbox Live team since 2007, which now had 23 million members and was seen as the main factor behind an estimated $850 million profit in the first nine months of the business year. Mattrick, who came over from Electronic Arts Worldwide Studios, would not miss a beat in transition, Spencer said.

"With his background at EA, with his background in creating his own entertainment studio, building his own products, he really understands this industry and this consumer."

The Xbox 360 was 3D-capable and Microsoft was spending on new games, but Spencer told me he was not convinced the technology was finding its proper niche.

"There's a lot of investment in 3D right now. I really think 3D has to move along as a creative medium. Right now, it's more of a shock medium and it kind of wears out."

For Sony Computer Entertainment chief Kazuo Hirai, shock and awe were needed from the predicted 3D boom, while he said PS3 sales were likely to meet the full-year sales target of 15 million consoles. With the retail debut of its Move earlier in the week, Sony separately ruled out 3D play on its PSP handheld.

"We want the consumer to enjoy 3D in the best possible environment," he said.[13] "At this stage, this is only possible on the big screen, with glasses."

Hirai, who almost a decade earlier had prematurely declared the end of the console wars, had to cede ground to a rival that was not even in the Tokyo Game Show building, but whose 3DS would push the industry toward the next stage of its long battle. However, some video game veterans said that with the breadth of delivery platforms and services, trying to encapsulate the competition now as just hardware-based or driven by a single technology was a simplification no longer appropriate for the era.

Nintendo, launched in the 19th century and driven by one family and later a legendary cast of game and console design wizards over three decades, might well agree. That is, it might agree if the still-proud Kyoto firm would admit to having rivals—or even peers—in the multibillion-dollar industry, or at some day in the future would be willing to be in the same building.

NOTES

1. Alexander Sliwinski, "Nintendo Ceo Iwata Doesn't Earn As Much As You'd Think," Joystiq, June 29, 2010; available online: www.joystiq.com/2010/06/29/nintendo-ceo-iwata-doesnt-earn-as-much-as-youd-think/; access date: August 21, 2010.
2. Nintendo, "The 70th Annual General Meeting of Shareholders Q&A," June 29, 2010; Available online: www.nintendo.co.jp/ir/en/library/meeting/100629qa/index.html; access date: August 21, 2010.
3. "The World's Billionaires," Forbes, March 10, 2010; available online: www.forbes.com/lists/2010/10/billionaires-2010_The-Worlds-Billionaires_CountryOfPrmRes_13.html; access date: August 23, 2010.
4. Nintendo, "The 70th Annual General Meeting of Shareholders Q&A."
5. Matt Matthews, "NPD: Behind the Numbers, July 2010," p. 1, Gamasutra, August 16, 2010; available online: www.gamasutra.com/view/feature/6027/npd_behind_the_numbers_july_2010.php; access date: August 22, 2010.
6. Nintendo, "The 70th Annual General Meeting of Shareholders Q&A," June 29, 2010, p. 4: "Transition of the Japan Gaming Population"; Available online: www.nintendo.co.jp/ir/en/library/meeting/100629qa/04.html; access date: August 22, 2010.
7. Nintendo, "The 70th Annual General Meeting of Shareholders Q&A," p.4.
8. Chris Buffa, "Interview: Nintendo's Shigeru Miyamoto on 3DS, Retro, Zelda and Pikmin 3," Joystiq:Beta, June 16, 2010; available online: www.joystiq.com/2010/06/16/interview-nintendos-shigeru-miyamoto-on-3ds-retro-zelda-and/; access date: August 22, 2010.
9. "Iwata Asks: Nintendo 3DS Shigeru Miyamoto," n.d.; available online: http://e3.nintendo.com/iwata-asks/#/?v=iwataasks_miyamoto_3DS; access date: August 23, 2010.
10. Nintendo: "The 70th Annual General Meeting of Shareholders Q&A."
11. "3D Handheld Device to Catch On Quickly: Nintendo Chief," Nihon Keizai Shimbun, June 30, 2010 (available on Factiva).

12. Reggie Fils-Aime, "Wii at the Movies with Netflix," CNBC, January 13, 2010; available online: www.cnbc.com/id/15840232?video=1384701517& play=1; access date: September 7, 2010.

13. Isabel Reynolds, "Sony Says Likely to Meet Annual PS3 Sales Target", Reuters, September 16, 2010; available online: http://ca.reuters.com/article/techno logyNews/idCATRE68F1TL20100916; access date: September 17, 2010.

INDEX

239